Buying or Leasing a Car
TOP TIPS TO REMEMBER
When Buying a New Car from a Dealer

1. If you don't like the way you're treated, politely tell the salesperson that you are displeased, and why you're displeased. If nothing changes, leave and don't return.

2. Be honest. Not telling the truth just increases the stress of car shopping and can work against your best interests.

3. Be prepared to disclose certain personal information such as your Social Security number, income sources, work history, number of dependents, and other debts and obligations on the credit application.

4. When you find a car you like, make an appointment to test drive a demonstrator with equipment that closely matches the car you're interested in.

5. Ask all the questions you can think of to get the answers you need to make an informed decision.

6. If the salesperson asks you, *How much do you want to pay?* respond with this: *I think you should tell me the lowest price you'll accept for this vehicle. You tell me what you want and I'll decide whether I want to pay that price – after I check with a few more dealers. And just as I haven't told you what other dealers are asking for this car, I won't tell them what you want either.*

7. Stick firmly to your budget, which you should have determined at home, and insist on being told the vehicle's true selling price, not the monthly payments.

8. Sit behind the wheel in the model you like. Examine the control layouts and assess the blind spots. Check the seating position and the fit of the safety belts and head restraints. Make sure the seats are comfortable.

9. If this is a return visit to the dealership, find the salesperson you dealt with on your first visit and do business with that individual.

10. Take the vehicle for a test-drive. Then back in your own car, make some notes on the strong points and weaknesses of the model you just drove.

STEPS FOR BUYING A NEW CAR OR TRUCK

Step 1 Make a list of three to five models to review.

Model 1 _____   Model 4 _____

Model 2 _____   Model 5 _____

Model 3 _____

Step 2 Visit dealers and rate vehicles using a 1 to 10 scale (10 being the best).

	Model 1	Model 2	Model 3	Model 4	Model 5
Front-seat comfort	_____	_____	_____	_____	_____
Rear-seat comfort	_____	_____	_____	_____	_____
Front-seat room	_____	_____	_____	_____	_____
Rear-seat room	_____	_____	_____	_____	_____
Seat belt fit	_____	_____	_____	_____	_____
Vision	_____	_____	_____	_____	_____
Control layout	_____	_____	_____	_____	_____
Head restraint adjustments	_____	_____	_____	_____	_____
Cargo Capacity	_____	_____	_____	_____	_____
Entry/exit ease	_____	_____	_____	_____	_____
EPA ratings for fuel efficiency	_____	_____	_____	_____	_____
Appeal of Design	_____	_____	_____	_____	_____

Step 3 Concentrate on the two most promising vehicles. Obtain pricing reports.

Step 4 Drive these two vehicles. Rate (using 1 to 10 scale).

	Model	Model
Handling	_____	_____
Acceleration	_____	_____
Braking	_____	_____
Maneuvering ease	_____	_____
Steering effort/feel	_____	_____
Visibility/dash reflections in windshield	_____	_____
Ride qualities	_____	_____
Body integrity	_____	_____
Heating/air conditioning	_____	_____
Instrument legibility	_____	_____
Headlight performance (at night)	_____	_____
Control layout and function	_____	_____
Noise levels	_____	_____

Step 5 Record your additional written comments on the performance of each vehicle.

Step 6 Determine your used car's approximate value.

NADA price _____   Other price guide _____

Offer dealer one _____   Offer dealer two _____

Offer dealer three _____

Price range of comparable models in paper: from _____ to _____

Step 7 Review financing options.

	Source 1	Source 2
Amount to borrow	_____	_____
Interest rate	_____	_____
Repayment period	_____	_____
Total interest expense	_____	_____
Prepayment penalty?	_____	_____

Step 8 Note any rebates or incentives and their expiration date.

Step 9 Obtain prices from dealers on favorite model.

Step 10 Obtain insurance quotes on favorite model.

Step 11 Check dealership's reputation.

Step 12 Review all notes and findings.

Step 13 Make purchase and enjoy the vehicle.

AAA Auto Guide

BUYING

OR

LEASING
A CAR

with
Jim MacPherson

AAA PUBLISHING

President & CEO	**Robert Darbelnet**
Executive Vice President, Publishing & Administration	**Rick Rinner**
Managing Director, Travel Information	**Bob Hopkins**
Director, Product Development	**Bill Wood**
Director, Sales & Marketing	**John Coerper**
Director, Purchasing & Corporate Services	**Becky Barrett**
Director, Business Development	**Gary Sisco**
Director, Tourism Information Development	**Michael Petrone**
Director, Travel Information	**Jeff Zimmerman**
Director, Publishing Operations	**Susan Sears**
Director, GIS/Cartography	**Jan Coyne**
Director, Publishing/ GIS Systems & Development	**Ramin Kalhor**
Product Manager	**Lisa Spence**
Managing Editor, Product Development	**Margaret Cavanaugh**
AAA Travel Store & E-Store Manager	**Sharon Edwards**
Print Buyer	**Laura Cox**
Manager, Product Support	**Linda Indolfi**
Manager, Electronic Media Design	**Mike McCrary**
Manager, Pre-Press & Quality Services	**Tim Johnson**
Manager, Graphic Communication Services	**Yvonne Macklin**
Project Coordinator	**Sandy Tate**
Art Director	**Barbra Natali**
Paginator	**Scott Richards**
Copy Editor	**G.K. Sharman**
Cover Design	**Dunn+Associates Design**

Published by AAA Publishing
1000 AAA Drive, Heathrow, Florida 32746

Copyright © 2001 AAA Publishing. All rights reserved.

ISBN 1-56251-577-2
Stock Number: 537501

ABOUT THE AUTHOR

Jim MacPherson

Author Jim MacPherson writes more than 100 automotive columns each year for the readers of *The Hartford Courant*. Since 1987, he also has helped thousands of listeners of his radio program with his advice on buying, servicing and repairing vehicles. For several years, he managed financial services for AAA's Automobile Club of Hartford, where he was responsible for making thousands of loans for people buying new or used vehicles and conducting seminars about how to buy a car. Jim also managed the AAA club's driver education and traffic safety programs.

Table of Contents

Introduction 11

Chapter 1 Research and Homework 15
   Step 1: Assess Your Needs 16
   Step 2: Develop a List of Vehicles to Consider 19
   Step 3: Visit Some Dealers 23
   Step 4: Drive the Cars 25

Chapter 2 Strategies for Success 27
   Ways to Save 28
   Keeping Costs Under Control 32
   Compare Insurance Costs 34
   You'll Have to Fill 'er Up 35
   Rules to Remember 35

Chapter 3 Vehicle Safety 47
   A Good Fit 48
   To Be Safe You Must Be Able to See 49
   Air Bag Safety 50
   Safety Demands Good Handling 51
   Crash Performance 53
   The Three Major Crash Tests 55
   Center of Gravity 58
   Carrying Loads 58
   Children in the Car 60
   Be as Safe as Possible 60

Chapter 4 Leasing 65
   What a Lease Is 66
   Advantages 66
   Leasing Has Advantages for Manufacturers 67

Why We Don't All Lease **68**

Where to Go for a Lease **70**

The Anatomy of a Lease **71**

Now Things Get Complicated **73**

The 'Money' Factor **73**

Take It or Leave It **73**

Other Fees **74**

When the Lease Ends **75**

Open or Closed **76**

The Trouble with a Valuable Trade-In **77**

Reduced Incentives **77**

The Verdict **77**

Leasing Checklist **78**

Checklist for Leasing a New Car **79**

Chapter 5 Buying a Used Car **85**

The Disadvantages **87**

Selecting a Model **89**

Research the Car **90**

Where to Buy **91**

Finding the Good, Rejecting the Bad **93**

Do-It-Yourself Evaluations **94**

The Test Drive **100**

Certification Programs **103**

The Case of the Missing Title **104**

Used-Vehicle Checklist **106**

Sample Dealer Sticker **116**

Chapter 6 Selecting a Vehicle for a Beginning Driver **117**

What Not to Buy **122**

More Safety Suggestions **123**

Draw Up a Contract **124**

Vehicle Use and Operation Agreement **126**

Chapter 7 Using the Internet **129**

Visit a Manufacturer's Website **130**

Visit a Dealer's Website **132**

Visit Third-Party Sites **132**

You Can Solicit Offers **133**

What You Can't Do **134**

What Dealers Think **135**

Sites You Should Know About **136**

Chapter 8 Financing the Purchase **141**

How Expensive a Car Should You Buy? **142**

Paying Cash **146**

Before You Apply for a Loan **147**

Taking a Loan **151**

Rebates **153**

Subsidized Loans **154**

Other Sources for Money **155**

Financing a Used Car **156**

Refinancing **159**

Get a Loan Before You Find a Vehicle **159**

Read Before You Sign **159**

AAA Financial Services **160**

Chapter 9 Selecting a Dealer **161**

How to Find a Good Dealer **162**

The Dealer's Report Card **166**

Chapter 10 Techniques of the Dealer **169**

What You and the Dealer Owe Each Other **171**

The Sales Process **172**

Question No. 1: 'Can I Help You?' **172**

What to Expect on the Way to the Car **173**

Question No. 2: 'Are You Planning on
Buying a Car Today?' **174**
Question No. 3: 'What Would I Have to do to
Get You to Buy Today?' **175**
Question No. 4: 'Will There be a Trade-In?' **175**
Question No. 5: 'Will There be Someone Else
Involved in the Purchase Decision?' **175**
Question No. 6: 'How Much Do You Want to Pay?' **176**
Question No. 7: 'How Much a Month Do
You Want to Spend?' **177**
Controlling the Purchasing Process **177**

Chapter 11 Options **179**
Safety Options **180**
Comfort and Convenience Items **183**
Appearance Packages **186**
Engines and Transmissions **187**
Suspensions, Wheels and Tires **187**

Chapter 12 The Pricing Game **189**
Determining the 'Right' Price **191**
The Pricing Waltz **192**
Try This Approach **193**
A Different Experience **197**
One-Price Dealers – Version One **198**
One-Price Dealers – Version Two **198**
How to Handle the Trade-In **199**
Rebates and Incentives **200**
Holdbacks **200**
Invoice vs. Dealer Cost **201**
Association Surcharges **202**
When to Buy **202**
Get It in Writing **204**

Chapter 13 Buying Services and Other Options **207**

Auto Brokers **208**

The Bird Dog **211**

Group Referral Programs **211**

Other Options **213**

Chapter 14 Staying on the Right Track **215**

Are You Vulnerable? **216**

Before You Sign on the Dotted Line **217**

Misleading Advertising **217**

Contract Confusion **220**

Failure to Disclose **223**

Liquidated Damages **223**

Warranty Questions **224**

Also Consider the Swap **225**

Title Problems **225**

Prolonged Negotiations **226**

Conveyance Fees **226**

Trade-In Evaluations **227**

Price Hikes After You Take Delivery **228**

Problem Loans **229**

Problems with Service **229**

Service Schedules **233**

When a Problem Turns Really Ugly **234**

Chapter 15 Handling the Financing and Insurance **235**

Financing **237**

Dealer Packages **238**

Insurance Products **239**

Extended Service Contracts **239**

Chapter 16 Taking Delivery **243**

In Conclusion **247**

Index **249**

Introduction

Buying a new car or truck should be simple. You want to make the purchase. The dealer wants to make the sale. But what seems so straightforward in theory can be surprisingly complex in practice.

In the chapters that follow, AAA will take you through the entire car-buying process. Whether you're interested in a new vehicle or a used one or plan to buy from a dealer or an individual, you'll find information to help you every step of the way. We'll outline how to select a vehicle, what to look for when you arrange financing, how to evaluate leases and the best way to use rebates. We'll also clue you in on the techniques that dealers use to sell you a new car or truck.

If you're like most people, the real work of buying a new vehicle takes place before you ever set foot in a showroom. First you need to set a realistic budget, choose the type of car or truck that fits your needs rather than the one that's in vogue at the moment, and do some basic research that can minimize the time spent shopping and test driving.

In today's rapidly changing automotive marketplace, the complications don't stop there. For instance, in addition to the traditional range of body styles and classifications – sedans, station wagons, pickup trucks, sport-utility vehicles, minivans, coupes and convertibles – you'll find vehicles that blur those distinctions. These vehicles, called hybrids, include models that look like SUVs but are more like passenger cars than trucks when you look under the sheet metal. As a result, they may not be able to tackle the really rough off-road terrain that truck-based SUVs handle with ease. On the other hand, hybrids can deliver superior ride and handling on paved surfaces – and go farther on a gallon of gasoline.

You'll also have to decide whether you want to embrace new technology. Another type of hybrid combines a gasoline engine with a battery-powered electric motor to deliver better fuel economy. The batteries never need to be plugged into a wall outlet for recharging; spare power from the gasoline engine and regenerative braking take care of that task.

Then there's the array of new high-tech electronic accessories, such as navigation and roadside assistance systems that can locate your vehicle using global positioning satellites.

In all, some 1,000 different models vie for your attention. Granted, some of the apparent variety is the result of applying various levels of trim to one basic body. Yet even simple changes in trim level – and the subtle changes in suspension calibrations, wheels and tires that often go with them – can have a significant effect on how the vehicle rides, how it handles and how comfortable it is for day-to-day use.

Add a wide choice of options, new drivetrain technologies and vehicles that aren't what they seem to be and is it any wonder that car shoppers throw up their hands in bewilderment?

If, on top of everything else, the mere thought of negotiating the price stresses you out, you're not alone. Few new or used vehicles sell for the initial asking price. Most are discounted, but some sell for more than the manufacturer's suggested retail price. Negotiation is expected.

In this respect, buying a car is more like buying real estate than loading a cart at the grocery store. The purchase of a new car or a new home is similar in another way: money. While the average home is still about six times more expensive than the average new vehicle, a car or truck often is your second most expensive purchase. Over time, it's not unusual for transportation expenses to surpass housing costs for many families. In some households, car payments are higher than the mortgage payment.

Now, add concerns over safety and reliability and the question of whether to buy new or used and it's easy to see why many consumers wish they could avoid car shopping entirely. If you're one of them, this book is designed to help. Even if you don't think vehicle shopping is an ordeal, you can glean a tip or two from these pages.

This car-buying information is just a small part of AAA's continuing effort to serve the needs of all motorists, including 43 million AAA members. If you're a member, you already appreciate the emergency assistance and up-to-date travel information available by phone, over the Internet or at one of the more than 1,000 AAA offices throughout North America. Yet these are just two of AAA's many services.

In fact, some of the AAA employees who regularly assist car-buying members have contributed tips to this book in an effort to help you. You'll find their suggestions and insights, based on the experiences of countless AAA members, in every chapter. In addition, many AAA offices also offer pricing information, low-cost auto loans and the expanded insurance coverage you'll need after you bring your new set of wheels home. AAA also can help members when they shop for a new or used vehicle.

When you read this book you'll discover that you have a great deal of power in the car-buying process. Use it correctly and you'll end up with the car or truck you need, at a price you can afford, delivered by a dealer who will give you good service.

It doesn't require super-human effort or exceptional skill to succeed on the car lot. All you really need is the ability to be honest with yourself and others, the nerve to ask questions if you don't know what's going on and the understanding that you'll probably make a small mistake or two along the way – as will most of the dealers, incidentally.

A good car at a fair price awaits you.

CHAPTER

1

Research and Homework

In This Chapter
• • • • • • • • • • • •

- Determining what you need in your next car or truck
- Which models best suit your needs
- How to develop a list of vehicles to consider
- What to do when you visit a dealer

Step 1: Assess Your Needs

The process of buying a new car or truck starts with research. Before you cross a showroom's threshold or talk to a salesperson, you have to do your homework. For many people, the most difficult aspect is the most important: an honest self-appraisal that keeps needs and wants separate.

To do this self-appraisal, it helps to keep a log of all your trips during a typical month. In other words, don't start the log during vacation week.

Record the distances and reasons for your trips, the number of passengers, the cargoes you haul and any problems or shortcomings you encounter in your current car or truck, such as inadequate space for a passenger, a rough ride over a stretch of broken pavement or steep hills that leave your vehicle gasping.

The log is important for several reasons, but mainly because people are forgetful. Just as dietitians make their clients write down everything they eat so they can see just how many chips and cookies they're consuming, so too should we record in this log what we do every time we get behind the wheel.

Sometimes when we go shopping for a new car, we dream of long cross-country travel and start looking at models that would be ideal for this use. Or we dwell on a difficult experience for which the vehicle we owned turned out to be woefully inadequate, and vow that our next car or truck will be able to handle this situation with ease.

If the reality is that you use your car to commute to and from work, drop the kids off at school activities and go to the grocery store, dry cleaner and home center, buying for the worst-case scenario can be a big mistake. Consider the case of one AAA member who turned to his local AAA office for advice on buying a new, full-size passenger van.

Full-size vans, it should be noted, are not minivans. They are large, truck-based vehicles that, when set up for passenger use, often serve as airport shuttles or as commuter vans. They ride firmly, handle sluggishly and consume significant amounts of fuel. However, when you have to move nine to 15 people, they're hard to beat.

In this case, the buyer would use the van mostly to commute to and from work, which turned out to be an exceptionally long 120-mile round trip. The

AAA adviser, who immediately assumed that the man carpooled with other people, was surprised to learn that he made this trip alone each day.

The adviser asked him why he felt he needed a 12-passenger van. The man said that several family members came from Europe each year to visit and he needed a vehicle this large to tour the area. This man was buying a vehicle to meet his worst-case need, despite the fact that it was ill suited for 51 weeks of the year!

The AAA adviser suggested he consider a midsize sedan for the commute instead. By choosing the sedan instead of the van, he was able to lower the purchase price, nearly double his fuel economy, reduce his insurance costs and end up with a more comfortable, better handling vehicle for the 30,000 miles a year of commuting that he did. Fuel savings alone came to $1,600 a year – more than enough to finance the $450 rental of a full-size passenger van for the week when his family visited.

Other people buy full-size pickup trucks for an occasional trip to the home center, despite the fact that many of these centers will deliver bulky purchases at a very reasonable price or offer rental trucks for do-it-yourself transport. Other occasional hauling chores often can be handled by handyman services. Still other buyers opt for four-wheel drive systems – a $1,000 to $3,000 expense – just to handle one or two snowy days a year. Think carefully about your real needs before you buy your next vehicle.

> **Did You Know?**
>
> If you intend to keep a vehicle for many years, which makes sense if you want to keep transportation costs low, plan ahead. Your 12-year-old, for example, who fits so nicely in the back seat of a compact sedan now, may turn out to be a star basketball center by the time he or she turns 16. Where, in that new compact you're considering, will the kid sit in four years?
>
> *Tip Provided by AAA Arizona*

That said, be aware that you likely will keep your car or truck for a long time – which is almost always the most economical strategy – if you genuinely like the vehicle. Therefore, even if all your needs are met by a model that you just know, deep in your heart, will never make you happy, you should definitely consider something else. There is nothing wrong with buying a sportier, safer, more prestigious or better looking vehicle if it makes you happy. Just be sure that it won't become a financial burden you'll regret later.

Here are some suggestions for vehicle types that might meet your actual needs:

Major Use	Model to Consider
Single person or young couple	Subcompact or compact sedan
Single person or young couple with small cargoes	Subcompact or compact sedan
Family of four to six with luggage, supplies, recreational equipment, etc.	Station wagon or minivan
Business use, carrying clients	Midsize or large sedan or wagon
Traveling slippery or snow-covered roads with one passenger and/or light loads	All-wheel drive compact sedan or wagon
Traveling slippery or snow-covered roads with several passengers and/or significant loads	All-wheel drive midsize sedan wagon or minivan, hybrid SUV with all-wheel drive
Towing a small boat or trailer	Any sedan, wagon or minivan rated by the manufacturer as suited for the weight and task
Towing a larger boat or trailer	Compact or larger SUV or pickup truck
Recreational uses, camping, cycling, etc. some dirtroad use but no rugged off-roading	Minivan, station wagon or hybrid SUV
Recreational uses, major off-road operation expected in rugged conditions	Four-wheel drive SUV, four-wheel drive or compact crew cab pickup truck

Many buyers find that a subcompact or compact sedan meets all their needs. For those who require more room, a small wagon or minivan should do nicely.

However, for many motorists, the thought of buying such mundane vehicles is abhorrent. The reason, as auto and truck manufacturers have long known, is that vehicles are as much about fashion as transportation.

That some vehicles are fashionable or popular while others are not undoubtedly will influence you when you buy your next car or truck. There is nothing inherently wrong with this, as long as you recognize that your decision is based on how you think you'll look in the vehicle, or what others will think of it, as opposed to what you need the vehicle to do.

Step 2: Develop a List of Vehicles to Consider

Now that you have thought about what you need, it is time to make a list of vehicles that you think would be good choices and fit in your budget. To make sure you consider as wide a range of cars or trucks as possible, try to include at least three – preferably five – different vehicles.

To draw up a list of vehicles to meet your needs, consult one of the many buying guides you can find on newsstands, in bookstores or at the library. A good example is the *AAA Auto Guide: New Cars and Trucks*, which is published annually. It reviews approximately 200 different vehicle platforms that form the basis for nearly 700 different makes, models and trim lines. It provides numerical scores for each vehicle in 20 different performance categories, including ride, handling, acceleration, comfort and room. It also rates interior and exterior workmanship and value. In addition, it outlines the strengths and weaknesses of each vehicle it tests and gives pricing information.

Did You Know? Need a pickup truck? Don't forget that the load box is usually open to the weather and that items in the back are easily stolen when you park the truck. That means whatever you cannot fit in the passenger compartment will be exposed to the weather, including your luggage, groceries and valuable items.

Tip Provided by AAA East Penn

To use this guide, outline your requirements for your next car or truck in writing. For example, let's say that you need a car primarily for commuting to and from work. Since you also have a minivan, the ability to carry your two teen children in the back seat is not that important, although it would be a nice extra. Finally, note your budget.

As you look through the reviews, you quickly discover that some cars stand out while others seem to offer less potential. Some you can reject immediately because they're too expensive. Incidentally, never reject a car or truck because it costs too little. If, for example, you have a $35,000 budget, you might be very surprised at how well some $25,000 vehicles would do if you gave them a chance. There's nothing that says you have to spend every penny you budgeted.

You should then check the cars on your list against the latest list of so-called "twins" in AAA's annual *New Cars and Trucks* guide. Make sure you're comparing truly different cars or trucks in your initial selection. Twins are cars and trucks that are built on the same platform and are, therefore, nearly identical in performance and features. This is true despite the fact that they are sold under different brand names by different dealers. Examples include the Chevrolet Cavalier and Pontiac Sunfire, which are nearly the same car, and the Ford Taurus and Mercury Sable. However, some twins are so different that they deserve separate evaluations, such as the Lincoln LS and the Jaguar S-type or, to a lesser degree, the Chrysler Sebring and the Dodge Stratus.

Sometimes twins cross over from one manufacturer to another, such as the Ford Ranger and Mazda B-Series compact pickups, the Honda Passport and Isuzu Rodeo and the Chevrolet Prizm and Toyota Corolla compact sedans. Nearly 100 different cars and trucks have a twin.

Here's a listing of twins – which may turn out to be triplets, quadruplets or quintuplets:

Subcompacts, Compacts and Sporty Cars

Chevrolet Camaro, Pontiac Firebird

Chevrolet Cavalier, Pontiac Sunfire

Chevrolet Prizm, Toyota Corolla

Chrysler Sebring coupe, Dodge Stratus coupe, Mitsubishi Eclipse, Mitsubishi Galant

Volkswagen Golf, Volkswagen Jetta, Volkswagen New Beetle

Midsize Sedans and Coupes

Acura CL/TL, Honda Accord V-6

Chrysler Sebring sedan, Sebring convertible, Dodge Stratus sedan

Chevrolet Impala, Chevrolet Monte Carlo

Ford Taurus, Mercury Sable

Infiniti I30, Nissan Maxima

Lincoln LS, Jaguar S-Type, Ford Thunderbird

Pontiac Grand Am, Oldsmobile Alero

Toyota Camry, Lexus ES 300

Large Cars

Buick Century, Buick Regal, Pontiac Grand Prix, Oldsmobile Intrigue

Cadillac Seville, Buick Park Avenue, Oldsmobile Aurora

Chrysler Concorde, Chrysler LHS, Chrysler 300M, Dodge Intrepid

Ford Crown Victoria, Mercury Grand Marquis

Pontiac Bonneville, Buick LeSabre

Minivans

Chevrolet Venture, Pontiac Montana, Oldsmobile Silhouette

Dodge Caravan, Chrysler Town & Country, Chrysler Voyager

Nissan Quest, Mercury Villager

Pontiac Aztek, Buick Rendezvous

Trucks and SUVs

Chevrolet Astro, GMC Safari

Chevrolet Trail Blazer, GMC Envoy, Olds Bravada

Chevrolet Express, GMC Savana

Chevrolet Silverado, GMC Sierra

Chevrolet S-10, GMC Sonoma

Chevrolet Suburban, GMC Yukon XL

Chevrolet Tahoe, GMC Yukon, GMC Denali, Cadillac Escalade

Chevrolet Tracker, Suzuki Vitara

Ford Explorer, Mercury Mountaineer

Ford Ranger, Mazda B-Series Pickups

Ford Expedition, Lincoln Navigator

Ford SuperCrew, Lincoln Blackwood

Honda Passport, Isuzu Rodeo

Nissan Pathfinder, Infiniti QX4

Toyota Highlander, Lexus RX300

Toyota Land Cruiser, Lexus RX470

Here's how to use this list at the beginning of your search. Let's assume that you decided to buy a midsize sedan. After looking through a buying guide, you conclude that based on price, the following models deserve to be considered: Toyota Camry, Ford Taurus, Nissan Maxima, Mercury Sable, Chrysler Sebring and Dodge Stratus. Checking the list for twins, you discover that the Sebring and the Stratus are related. So are the Taurus and the Sable. Therefore, in your initial search, you need to look at only one of each set. Of course, if you find one of the twins unacceptable, you might want to try the other just to make sure that neither version works for you, since not all twins are identical.

If you plan to buy a used car or truck rather than a new model, your new-vehicle buying guide can still be useful. Manufacturers make and sell most vehicles for four or more years before undertaking a redesign – some vehicles have lingered in production for more than a decade – so the description in a new-vehicle guide can help you determine which used cars to consider. Exceptions are models that the buying guide proclaims are "new" this year or last. Also, if the guide lists a feature – side-impact air bags, for example – on the newest model, understand that it may not have been included on older models.

If you're sure about buying a used vehicle, you probably should consult one of the many used-car buying guides available. We outline the steps for buying a used car in Chapter 5.

In addition to buying guides, you'll also find many current automobiles covered extensively in magazines devoted to cars and driving. Bear in mind, however, that many of these magazines – sometimes called "buff books" – target auto enthusiasts. As a result, they often emphasize performance, acceleration and high-speed handling, both in their written copy and in their selection of vehicles to test. In cars and trucks that offer two or more engines as options, the magazines will probably report on the models with the most powerful motor.

Car buffs also opt for more aggressive suspension systems that often deliver a stiffer, busier ride in the hopes of improving handling. They are enthusiasts, which they have every right to be, but their criteria for judging a car or truck may not be your criteria.

General consumer magazines and auto-buying guides such as AAA's focus more closely on what the majority of buyers look for in a new car or truck. Their findings reflect the typical balance of safety, good handling, comfort, roominess and value that most people seek when they shop for a vehicle.

Step 3: Visit Some Dealers

On your initial visits to a dealer, simply look at the vehicles on your list and sit in them. Usually you can try only one vehicle on your list at each dealer, but some dealers offer more than one brand and you may be able to take advantage of this dual franchise setup. When you sit in the car, make sure the seat is comfortable. Spend a few minutes behind the steering wheel, both to get used to the driving position and to be sure that you have enough room. Also make sure that you can reach the controls, that you can see well

Did You Know? Don't have the time or energy to traipse from dealer to dealer to sit in the cars on your list? That is one reason for visiting a new car show. Most urban areas feature one new car show each year. In some areas, such as Detroit, Los Angeles, Chicago and New York, auto shows are major events that generate worldwide notice. Others are decidedly lower key affairs. But all car shows give consumers an opportunity to sit in the driver's seat, try out the back seat, poke around the trunk and under the hood and pick up literature that should make the shopping process easier. Admission is usually less than $10 per person, and attending one of these shows can save you many hours of comparison shopping. You might even find an interesting vehicle that did not make your initial list.

Tip Provided by AAA Auto Club South

in all directions and that the inside or outside mirrors don't block your view. Adjust the seat and buckle the seat belt. It should fit easily and comfortably across your hips and cross your shoulder without touching your neck.

Assuming that the car passes this first test of fit and comfort, sit in the front passenger seat. Surprisingly, front passenger seat room and adjustment range don't always mirror that of the driver's seat. In some models, leg room also may be reduced by the design of the vehicle. Some manufacturers, for example, raise the floor a few inches on the passenger side to make room for the catalytic converter, which is part of the exhaust system underneath the car. That can affect the comfort of a taller passenger.

If back-seat comfort is important, try sitting there, too. Be sure the front seats are positioned the way they likely will be when you sit in the rear. As you get in, take note of the size of the rear door openings. Some models with smaller openings may make entry and exit difficult. If you have to mount child-safety seats in the back, take a seat with you to see how it fits. If you have more than one child seat to use, take them both to be sure the car can handle your needs. In two-door vehicles, see just how easy or hard it is to get into the back seat.

You also should try out the third row of seats that are often available in sport utility vehicles, station wagons and minivans. Access to these seats generally is awkward and the room and comfort they offer is limited. If you find an otherwise attractive vehicle that simply isn't comfortable for you, don't buy it. No set of features can overcome the prospect of thousands of miles in discomfort.

Finally, take a look at the trunk or cargo area. Remember that a big trunk compartment may not be particularly useful if the trunk lid opening is small. One salesman, who bought a luxury car with a trunk that easily looked big enough to hold his sample cases, was distressed to discover that several of his samples were too large to fit through the trunk opening.

Some trunk hinges also can intrude significantly on luggage space and crush anything that gets in their way when you go to close the lid. Other hinges have no effect on luggage capacity. Check this out if luggage room is important to you.

Step 4: Drive the Cars

Approach a salesperson at a dealership that handles the model you're interested in and ask to take one out for a drive. The salesperson probably will try to determine where you are in the car-buying process before making the arrangements, which is completely understandable. Simply say that this car is one of several you're considering and that you still have others to look at. That should be sufficient.

You'll probably be asked to show your driver's license and the salesperson may photocopy it. Although it does give the dealer the means to contact you later, either by phone or through the mail, there is a perfectly legitimate reason for doing this: safety. It is not unheard of for a customer on a test drive to try to steal a vehicle, to assault the accompanying salesperson or to be involved in an accident. That the dealership does some screening before letting a complete stranger drive one of its vehicles is entirely proper.

On the test drive, you want to pick a route that duplicates the type of driving you normally do. In other words, if you drive on the highway a great deal, a quick drive around a city block will not be enough. You have to go on the highway. If the log you kept points out a stretch of broken pavement that makes your current car ride uncomfortably, try this same patch of road in the demonstrator, if possible. Also tackle any hills that your current car finds a challenge.

If you typically drive with a heavy load consisting of either cargo or passengers, that will be harder to replicate on your initial test drive. Do remember, however, that weight often will affect ride, handling, acceleration and braking. If a model turns out to be promising after your first drive, you may want to return for a second test drive with two or three friends or family members. You can ask them what the rear seat feels like while you analyze what adding their weight does to the vehicle's performance.

In some cases, dealers or automakers allow a potential buyer to take a car or truck for a day, sometimes two. This is a great opportunity to see what a vehicle is really like over a longer period of time.

Another way to try a vehicle for a longer period is to rent one. This can be valuable even if you don't need a rental – but if you rent one on a business trip or vacation, so much the better.

After your test drive, make written notes of your impressions. Record what you liked and what you didn't care for so you can compare accurately after you drive all the vehicles on your list.

By driving many different cars, you might find that one or two models stand out. That means you can now concentrate on those vehicles. Or you could come to the conclusion that any model will do. This is better news yet, because it gives you many more choices and the opportunity to look for the very best deal offered by the different manufacturers and dealers.

If, however, you really like only one or two models, take a look at the list of twins to see which other vehicles might be similar. Drive these cars or trucks too. Again, you might find one version preferable to the other, or you might discover that you could be happy with either, which again expands your options when it comes to looking for your best deal.

CHAPTER

2

Strategies for Success

In This Chapter
• • • • • • • • • • •

- How to reduce your cost of transportation
- What not to say at the dealership
- Two rules to keep you in the driver's seat during negotiations
- Three transactions that make up the purchase and why you should keep them separate

Ways to Save

Whether you're buying groceries or transportation, you don't want to pay more than the going price. Getting the best buy takes work.

When grocery shopping, you compare prices and quality. But when you're contemplating a new car or truck, your cost-benefit analysis should include more than just initial price and vehicle quality. You must also think about how you'll use this vehicle, how long you plan to own it, what the likely cost of maintenance and repairs will be and how much it will cost you to insure it.

Concentrate on squeezing every last nickel from the dealer's margin and you may well lose sight of the real costs of vehicle ownership. Each year, AAA and Runzheimer International, a management consulting firm based in Rochester, Wis., research what it really costs to own and operate a new car or truck. Though primarily focused on compact, midsize and full-size sedans, the report also includes compact SUVs and minivans.

The report assumes that you buy the vehicle, not lease it; that you'll drive 15,000 miles a year; and that you'll own it for four years. The result: the average cost per mile is 51 cents. Since the study avoids expensive luxury cars, big trucks and sporty models, it is safe to assume that many vehicles actually cost their owners much more to drive.

In the 2001 edition of *Your Driving Costs*, AAA and Runzheimer International looked at the prices for running a compact four-cylinder Chevrolet Cavalier, a midsize six-cylinder Ford Taurus, a full-size eight-cylinder Mercury Grand Marquis, a six-cylinder two-wheel-drive Chevrolet Blazer sport-utility vehicle and a six-cylinder Dodge Caravan minivan. Driven 15,000

While many manufacturers proudly note that their costly luxury models depreciate more slowly than average, they almost always cite the advantage in percentages. But you pay for the depreciation in dollars. That means that a more expensive car with lower than average depreciation, as measured in percentage, will almost always end up costing much more than a lower priced car that has a higher percentage rate of depreciation. Before you buy a luxury car believing it will depreciate no more than a lower priced car, and perhaps even less, translate the expected depreciation from percentages into dollars.

Tip Provided by Automobile Club of Pioneer Valley

miles a year, the cost per mile for these vehicles ranged from 44.3 cents for the Cavalier to 59.2 cents for the Mercury Grand Marquis.

The study found depreciation – the difference between what you paid for your vehicle and what you could get for it if you had to sell it right now – to be the largest single cost of ownership. The adage is true: you don't know how much a vehicle has really cost you until you sell it. Any buyer who wants to get the most for his or her transportation dollar knows that depreciation is a critical consideration.

Here are some strategies to help you reduce the cost of depreciation:

- Keep the vehicle for at least six years, preferably longer. Depreciation takes its biggest bites during the first three years of ownership. It is not unusual for a new vehicle to depreciate $3,000 or more the very minute it's driven off the dealer's lot. Many vehicles lose 25 percent of their value during the first year of ownership, another 15 percent the second year and 10 percent more by the end of the third year.

- A vehicle can lose half of its value in just three years. Fortunately, after that point, the slide in value stays at about 10 percent per year for the next two or three years. The effect that length of ownership can have on the cost per mile for depreciation can be seen in the following chart.

Year of Ownership	Depreciation Cost per Mile: Single Year Only	Cumulative Depreciation Cost Per Mile
1	41.7 cents	41.7 cents over 15,000 miles
2	25.0 cents	33.3 cents over 30,000 miles
3	16.7 cents	27.8 cents over 45,000 miles
4	16.7 cents	25.0 cents over 60,000 miles
5	16.7 cents	23.0 cents over 75,000 miles
6	10.0 cents	21.0 cents over 90,000 miles

Assumptions: $25,000 purchase price, depreciation at 25 percent the first year, 15 percent the second year, 10 percent during the third, fourth and fifth years and 6 percent the sixth year. Average of 15,000 miles each year.

As you can see, the longer you keep your vehicle the less you pay for depreciation for each mile you drive. As the car gets older and depreciation becomes less meaningful, maintenance and repair costs will become a far larger consideration.

There are some additional points to remember when you think about depreciation.

- While a vehicle subjected to average use may lose about half its value in the first three years, it only covers 45,000 miles during this time. Since many vehicles today can easily go 160,000 to 200,000 miles with proper maintenance, this means that a 3-year-old car still has 72 percent or more of its useful life remaining, as measured on the odometer. For that reason, a used car can be the most cost-effective transportation option. That's why we devote Chapter 5 to buying a used vehicle.

- Not all vehicles depreciate at the same rate. Some cars and trucks lose 60 percent of their value in three years, others only 40 percent. If you plan to keep your vehicle for only three or four years, by all means pick a model that historically retains more of its value rather than a model with higher than average depreciation.

Did You Know?

A vehicle's depreciation history doesn't guarantee what its value will be after you buy it. Collective shifts in buyers' tastes or sudden changes in the market can have a tremendous effect on vehicle values. For example, if sport-utility vehicles should suddenly fall out of fashion, you can expect their values will slump. The past probably indicates the future, and is worth examining. But what the future will hold, nobody knows.

Tip Provided by AAA Southern Pennsylvania

- In theory, buyers who plan to keep their next new vehicle "forever" need not consider depreciation at all. After all, when you've completely used up this car or truck, its value will be determined by the price it brings as scrap, a market in which differences among makes and models mean little.

- In jurisdictions where registration fees or annual taxes are based on a vehicle's market value, there's even a case to be made for choosing a model that depreciates faster than average. The faster it depreciates, the less you pay in taxes or registration fees as the years pass.

- However, despite our best thinking now, we may not be able to predict our needs tomorrow. If you have to sell your vehicle earlier than planned and you picked a model that depreciates more than average, you'll pay a price for that decision when you sell. You'll also get a smaller settlement check from an insurance company if the vehicle is stolen and never recovered or declared a total loss after a crash.

- Another way to minimize the cost of depreciation is to choose a less costly car or truck. Almost always, these vehicles will depreciate less.

Did You Know? For low-mileage buyers who finally buy the luxury car they've always wanted, depreciation can have a dramatic effect on their transportation costs. Combine their reduced annual mileage with the higher dollar amounts of depreciation on most luxury vehicles and it is not unheard of for these buyers to pay almost $1 per mile for depreciation. But remember, this cost is finalized only when the car is sold or traded in.

- You can reduce your depreciation expenses by avoiding optional equipment. Never select and pay for an accessory that you don't really want in hopes that it will increase the vehicle's value when you sell it. Even options considered essential will not add as much to the value of a late-model trade-in as they cost when new. For example, if you bought a four-cylinder Dodge Stratus sedan in 1998, the automatic transmission would have been a $1,050 option. Two years later, it would only add $500 to the value of the car. If you want the automatic, by all means buy it. But don't buy it, or any other option, assuming you'll get your money back when you sell the car. You won't.

As your car or truck ages, the value of optional equipment erodes further. As the *N.A.D.A. Official Used Car Guide*® notes, "[The] editors

PITFALLS For buyers planning to sell after only two or three years, a closed-end lease often makes sense. At least it will free the lessee (that's the person to whom a lease is granted) from having to worry about how the manufacturers' actions will affect resale. In recent years, we have seen heavy incentives on new cars and trucks knock the legs out from under the value of used examples of the same models. A $3,000 incentive package on a new model can often lower the value of a late model specimen of the same vehicle by nearly $3,000. If you need to sell at that moment, you can expect your depreciation costs to move sharply higher. A sudden $3,000 reduction in value on a car with just 30,000 miles on the odometer can add 10 cents per mile to the cost of ownership.

believe that most optional equipment has little or no value on older vehicles. This is especially true of options which cost relatively little to begin with and which deteriorate with age or use."

When notorious bank robber Willie Sutton was asked why he robbed banks, he replied, "That's where the money is." Car buyers who want to lower their transportation costs should recognize that, in most cases, depreciation is where much of your money will go when you buy a new car or truck. If you handle depreciation properly by choosing a vehicle wisely and keeping it a long time, you can end up thousands of dollars ahead in the game of vehicle ownership.

> **PITFALLS** If your stockbroker suggested an investment that was guaranteed to lose half of its value in inflation-adjusted dollars in three years and never recover, no matter how long you owned it, you'd probably look for a new broker. Since that is what cars generally do, thinking of them as an investment seems wrong. They are an expense. So forget about "your automotive investment." Instead, think in terms of how to minimize your automotive expenses.
>
> ***Tip Provided by CAA British Columbia***

Keeping Costs Under Control

Something interesting has been happening recently that should be good news for car buyers. By all reports, new vehicles, whether from an American or foreign manufacturer, have become much more dependable. This is not to suggest that all vehicles are created equal when it comes to reliability and repairs. Some are better than others. Unfortunately, there is no way to determine just how good the particular vehicle you're considering will be. Not even historical data on rates of repair or owner satisfaction levels can tell you how the vehicle you're planning to buy will do for you.

Fortunately, you can get an idea of the cost of repairs by asking the cost of an extended repair agreement, one that offers bumper-to-bumper coverage. These policies are also known as extended warranties or mechanical breakdown insurance. Since these policies are sold by companies that keep very close tabs on models which require extensive repairs and which don't, the cost of a policy for a particular vehicle can give you some valuable information, even if you don't buy the coverage. Be sure to use the same source or provider though, since profit margins vary widely by seller.

An additional source of information is J.D. Power and Associates, which surveys new-car buyers to determine problems during the first 90 days of ownership and vehicle performance at the two-year mark. While the information is gathered primarily for the auto industry, and the company does not release data on vehicles that turn in below-average performance, it still can give you an indication of differences in quality among the various makes and models you're considering.

The likelihood of a car needing a repair, however, is really only half the story. These surveys don't report the cost of repairs. It's possible for vehicles that are somewhat less dependable to boast repair costs that are quite reasonable. For example, one vehicle may have an ignition module that, should it fail, costs $40 to replace. The ignition module in another car could cost $300 or more. That's why some cars that have a less than sterling reputation for avoiding repairs often can be less costly to own than models with better repair records. It is up to you to consider the relative importance of convenience and dependability.

Maintenance is another area in which there can be significant differences in the costs of ownership. Before you buy, ask what the service department at the dealership charges for the required maintenance that the vehicle will need while you own it. Mostly, you'll need oil changes and basic inspections, which are usually suggested at intervals of 5,000 or 7,500 miles.

Without a doubt, it costs more to maintain and repair a luxury car than a standard, mass-appeal midsize sedan. However, it may cost you, the first buyer, less. The most important reason is that more and more manufacturers of luxury cars cover the cost of maintenance during the warranty period – and warranty periods on luxury vehicles tend to be longer than on lower priced vehicles.

Even oil change costs can be more reasonable. A handful of luxury cars have systems to assess the condition of the oil in the crankcase and tell the driver to get it changed only when it really needs to be done. As a result, some cars are going 10,000 miles or more between normal service. One luxury automaker's representative noted with amazement that the car's monitoring system let a salesman rack up 17,000 highway miles before calling for an oil and filter change.

Tip Provided by Connecticut Motor Club

Some cars also require more costly services at 15,000-mile increments. Others call for even more thorough procedures every 30,000, 60,000 or 100,000 miles. The trend among luxury models is to include all service during the original warranty period in the purchase price. Take all of these factors into consideration. Make sure the service department gives you reasonably good estimates for the total cost, including parts, labor, environmental disposal fees and any other surcharges you may have to pay, of each service you're likely to need.

While these estimates are no guarantee of what you'll really pay three or four years from now, they can give you an idea of the relative costs today. Just remember that the cost of parts and labor will change.

You don't have to have maintenance done by the dealer to keep the warranty in effect. You must, however, complete the work called for by the manufacturer and keep the receipts, which should show that the appropriate lubricants were used and that the services were performed in a timely manner.

Compare Insurance Costs

An expense that can vary markedly from vehicle to vehicle is the cost of insurance. Before you sign any purchase contract, be sure to take the list of new cars or trucks that you are considering to your insurance agent and ask about the price of coverage on each one. Consumers are often surprised at what they learn by doing this. Seemingly close competitors can have significantly different insurance premiums. In some cases, differences among vehicles vary according to your age, driving record, how you use your vehicle or where you live.

If you are going to lease or finance the vehicle, be sure to include the appropriate charges for collision and comprehensive coverage in your

PITFALLS

Always call your insurance agent before you buy any new or used vehicle. Ask what your premium for coverage will be if you make the purchase. This phone call could prevent a very unpleasant surprise, especially if you are looking at a sportier model.

Tip Provided by
AAA Western Pennsylvania/
West Virginia/South Central Ohio Inc.

comparisons. Both will be required by either the leasing company or the financial institution that makes your loan.

Some automakers have affinity programs with insurance companies that can lower the cost of insurance if you buy that brand of car. In addition, you may want to get quotes for different insurance companies if a model you really like seems to be exceptionally expensive to cover with your current company. AAA offices may be able to offer affinity insurance programs for members with good driving records.

You'll Have to Fill 'er Up

While gasoline remains surprisingly reasonable in cost, especially after adjustments for inflation are made, it can still add significantly to the cost of vehicle ownership. Say that gas costs $1.50 a gallon. Driving 15,000 miles a year in a 36-mpg compact rather than a 17-mpg truck can save you $700 per year.

Rules to Remember

As you contemplate your first visit to a dealership, there are three rules to keep in mind:

- Never fall for a vehicle before you strike a deal.
- If you don't like the way you are being treated, shop elsewhere.
- When it comes time to make the purchase, keep the separate elements of the transaction separate.

Never Fall for a Vehicle Before You Strike a Deal

Because you have choices when you go car shopping, you have power. There is no reason why you have to deal with a boorish or high-pressure salesperson, accept a car you really do not want or tolerate being taken for granted. When you decide that only one make or model will do, however, you give up much of your power. The fact is, there are probably at least four or five different vehicles that would meet your needs. Keep this in mind and you'll find the entire car-buying process much easier.

To do this, you must be a little coy. Be friendly, be honest – after all, that's what you expect the dealer to be – but don't tell the salesperson everything you're thinking as the discussions progress. You never want to commit yourself in your mind to buying any vehicle until just a second or two before you sign the contract. If you do, you lose almost all of your power.

Consider what this eager customer told a salesman on the showroom floor. "That's the car I want. I can't believe you've got one just the way I want it! And you have it in black with the sport package. Do you know, I've been to seven dealers and none of them had a black one, which I really want, much less a black one with the sport package. This is perfect!"

Did You Know?

In one way, buying a vehicle is the same as leasing a vehicle. You must start by negotiating the purchase price. In a lease, it's known as the capitalized cost, or cap cost. Both the cap cost and purchase price are subject to negotiation. Don't allow the language to confuse you.

If at any time during the purchase process you don't understand something, ask questions. If you're still confused after you hear the explanations, collect your belongings and politely excuse yourself to call back another day after you have found satisfactory answers to your questions.

Shopping for a new car can be exciting. However, don't let yourself get caught up in emotion in the presence of the salesperson. Comments such as "this is the one" may reduce your ability to negotiate a fair deal.

Tip Provided by
AAA Mid-Atlantic

Do you think the dealership is going to be nearly as flexible with this customer as they would be with someone who says, "I'm interested in this car, but you know, I've also looked at two competing models that are pretty nice. Actually, I heard that one of the other cars has more passenger room."

The customer continues, "You're right, black does seem to be a rare color, but I've heard it's hard to keep clean. Does it also come in silver? That might be better for me. But, I'll tell you what, let's work out a price on this one so I can think it over."

It is important to remember that you cannot just say you are willing to buy any number of different models, you actually have to be willing to do so. If you are not, accept the fact that you have given up much of the strength you would otherwise enjoy in this transaction.

The good news is that there are so many excellent cars and trucks available today, and so many places to buy, that you really can purchase any number of different makes and models and still end up with a safe, reliable, comfortable vehicle that meets your needs. Take advantage of that rich selection and you'll find shopping easier and the ultimate deal you strike, better.

You Deserve Good Treatment

Not being treated the way you would like when you go shopping for a vehicle? Mention it to the salesperson and a manager. If nothing changes, leave. Nothing sends a louder, clearer message than walking out. Remember that you have many options. Not only is the dealer unlikely to be the only source in your area for the make and model you like, you have several other makes you can and should consider.

In all fairness to the auto retailing industry, it should be noted that customer complaints about poor service and inept treatment have dropped markedly in recent years. Most people find car shopping to be a surprisingly easy and friendly experience. If you have not been shopping in a new vehicle showroom in the past four or more years, you might be pleasantly surprised by what you find.

Still, some dealers don't seem to have gotten the word that good customer service is important. Interestingly, most recent complaints are about not getting attention at a dealership rather than dealing with a rude or poorly trained salesperson. In some cases, salespeople for popular models adopt an "If you don't want to buy it, somebody else will," attitude. Customers also complain about a salesperson's lack of product knowledge. Rude or abrasive treatment, the fear of many infrequent car shoppers, seems to have disappeared almost completely.

Part of the reason for this newfound interest in good customer treatment has to do with competition. The other part is that dealers realize that you have more information and power than ever before. Not only do you understand that you have several good alternatives to any model on the showroom floor, the dealer knows it, too.

Manufacturers also have become more concerned with how well their dealers treat you. They now offer better training for dealership personnel and have established premium certification programs that recognize their best dealers. Then, to keep track of what is going on, the automaker surveys you after the sale to make sure that you were treated well. Dealers who perform well on these surveys often receive additional incentives that either add to their profit or give them a chance to be even more competitive.

Dealers take these surveys so seriously that one customer received a little speech right after signing a contract. The salesperson pulled out a copy of the survey and said, "You'll be getting this from the manufacturer in a few weeks. It covers your experiences at this dealership. If there are any questions for which you would not feel comfortable saying we did an excellent job, please let me know now so we can rectify any problem." You really do have power. Use it.

Keep Transactions Separate

As you approach the purchase of a new or used car or truck, recognize that you most likely will be involved in a minimum of three separate transactions. The first is the selection and purchase of the vehicle itself. The second is the disposal of your old car, unless you plan to add to your family's fleet or you're buying your first vehicle. Finally, you have to finance your vehicle purchase.

Each separate part of the deal represents a profit center for some business somewhere. Obviously, the dealership would like to keep each component of the sale for itself, and often you'll find that the dealer is competitive in each arena. But you won't know that unless you keep each part of the deal separate.

Perhaps the most difficult step in the process is determining what your used car is worth. You also want to determine your best financing option. Because financing is such a complex and expensive process, it's handled separately in Chapter 8.

It's entirely up to you how you want to split the components of this transaction. When all is said and done, you may find that your interests are best served when you arrange your own financing or sell your used car independently. Then again, you may not.

Undeniably, it is tempting to allow the dealer to handle the entire transaction. What could be more convenient than simply driving your old car into the dealership at the appointed hour to pick up your new car? The salesperson and service personnel treat you royally as you hand over the keys to your old vehicle. The salesperson then pulls out a file folder containing all the paperwork – completely filled out, of course – for you to sign. When it comes to financing, the dealer already has the check. All you have to do is endorse it. The entire transaction takes just minutes, barely enough time for the service personnel to switch the contents of your glove compartment and license plates from your old car to the new.

That's certainly an easy way to complete the sale, but it might be the expensive way to do it. Consider these possibilities, any one of which will cost you money:

- While the purchase price for the new vehicle is good, the allowance for your trade-in is not. That could cost you several hundred dollars.

- The financing rate is actually 1 percent higher than you could have gotten elsewhere. While 1 percent may not sound important, it will add more than $1,000 to your total payment.

- The low financing rate so prominently displayed on the showroom window is not available on the model you want.

- Unfortunately, the credit agency report does not qualify you for that 0.9 percent financing that's so heavily advertised by the manufacturer. But you're in luck: The dealership has managed to place you with a lender offering 10.9 percent financing.

- The financing contract computes interest using a formula that penalizes you for paying the loan early, as you plan to do. Incidentally, you have plenty of company when you do this. The majority of car loans are paid early. Unfortunately, in this case you pay more for being early.

As you can see, you may pay a price for the convenience of one-stop shopping. However, by insisting on keeping the financing and trade-in appraisal separate from the purchase negotiations, and by doing your homework, you can usually lower the total price you pay.

Keeping the purchase of your new car, the sale of your old car and the financing separate also lets you keep much better track of the deal as it progresses. Once you choose your next vehicle, the transaction really becomes little more than a numbers game. The numbers, in this case, are your dollars, of course, and this is home turf for the salesperson and managers. They do this drill dozens of times a day in a busy dealership – not always with success, incidentally.

You, on the other hand, may do it a dozen times in your life. You know who has more practice. That said, there is nothing sinister about this state of affairs. You expect these people to know what they are doing. If they didn't, the dealership would go out of business.

Because they are so familiar with the entire pricing process – and you're not – the staff may be tempted to take shortcuts when laying out the numbers for you. These shortcuts, in turn, may cloud your understanding of just what's going on.

It's also possible that the salesperson thinks that he or she – more women are selling cars these days – has explained everything satisfactorily. After all, the salesperson understands precisely what is going on.

In some dealerships, customers who ask questions may be put off by a phrase such as, "You're really only interested in the bottom line, right? That's what you're going to pay."

That phrase has a great deal of appeal. Do you really care if the new car you are buying suddenly becomes $1,000 more expensive if an equal amount is added to your trade in?

"Hey," the salesperson might ask, "you're really only paying the difference between the two either way, right?" And what does it really matter what interest rate is on the contract when you can see that your monthly payment is just as promised? It's right there in black and white for all to see.

Some salespeople shift effortlessly from quoting the total price of the vehicle to using only monthly payments. "If you add the power windows, power locks and power mirrors," this salesperson says, "your payment would only go from $349 a month to $369. Doesn't that seem reasonable?" Indeed, who would even consider cranking windows up and down when for only $20 this same feat can be accomplished at the push of a button?

Of course, you should be thinking that this is $20 a month. And just how long is that finance contract anyway? Better yet, you should be saying that to the salesperson who's leaving you in the dust. While not all salespeople or dealerships do this, hit the brakes if you run into one that does.

"I realize that you do this all the time," you might say. "But this is new to me. You're going to have to slow down so that I can understand it, which I need to do so I can feel comfortable buying this car from you." If that doesn't stop the high-speed flow of numbers based on list prices, discounted prices and payment schedules, leave the dealership. There are plenty of dealers who want your business and who are willing to earn it. Find one and you'll be much happier.

Keeping the Trade-In Separate

To strike your best deal, you have to learn your car's current value. This is the computer and information age, so determining what your trade-in is worth should be a snap. Unfortunately, it's not. There are simply too many factors that go into determining the market value of the car or truck you want to sell to make the process fast and easy. Still, you need to have a reasonable idea what you should expect from a dealer when you go to trade in your current vehicle. Here is how you can find out about your car's current value.

In many parts of the country you can start the process at your local AAA office, your bank or library, or by logging onto the Internet. Your AAA office, bank or library probably has a current used-car price guide that covers the year, make and model of the vehicle you intend to trade. The most commonly used guides are the *National Automobile Dealers Association Official Used Car Guide*® and the *Kelley Blue Book*™ (where the term "blue book" for all used-car price guides comes from − and yes, the book is blue).

Remember that the prices in these guides do not constitute an actual appraisal of your car or truck. For that, you should have your car examined by a skilled, experienced person who knows the used-car market in your area. Instead, the numbers in the price guides represent an estimate of what a car like yours, in saleable condition, is worth.

Be aware that there are often significant differences among the various used-car price guides. Before checking any guide, make sure it is for your region of the country because geography affects vehicle values. A convertible in New England tends to drop in value with the onset of winter. In Southern states, that doesn't happen. Similarly, optional four-wheel drive may have limited value on a sport utility vehicle in Florida − but in the Rocky Mountains, it can add $1,000 or more to the asking price.

Since many dealers use it, we will refer to the *N.A.D.A. Official Used Car Guide*® to illustrate how to estimate the value of the vehicle you plan to trade. The guide provides three different prices for each make and model listed – the trade-in value, the loan value and the expected retail price. In addition, the guide gives additional information on how the presence or absence of certain options might affect the value of the vehicle.

For this example, let's say that you own a 1996 Toyota Camry. The first thing you have to do is find the model you own. Is it a two-door coupe, a sedan or a station wagon? Is it a DX, the least expensive trim line, or an XLE, the most expensive version? Does it have a four-cylinder engine or the V6?

If you want to develop accurate figures and you are not sure which trim level, engine or basic equipment you have on your car, don't guess. Go out and look at the vehicle. Many people have to do this when asking for a blue-book value from a bank or at a local AAA office.

Continuing our example, you determine that your car is the Camry four-door in LE trim with the V6 engine. You can verify this conclusion by looking at characters four through eight in your car's VIN (vehicle identification number, the 17-character ID visible through the windshield on the driver's side) against the *N.A.D.A Official Used Car Guide.*® For your Camry, those numbers and letters should be "BF12K." If they aren't, you've made a mistake. For example, the characters "BG12K" would indicate that your car really was equipped with the four-cylinder engine. Don't be embarrassed if you're not sure or have made a mistake. You have a lot of company.

In this case, however, the car is equipped just as you thought it was. Therefore, the guide reports that this model should be worth $12,850 as a trade-in, that a bank would likely loan no more than $11,575 to its next buyer and that the dealer would charge a retail customer $15,025 for it.

The next step is to review the optional equipment section. Your car has a factory-installed sunroof and alloy wheels, both of which are listed in the options section. The sunroof adds $450 to the trade-in value, the loan amount and the retail price. The alloy wheels add another $150 to each of these prices. Notice that there is no profit margin for the dealer on optional equipment. The dealer who pays you trade-in value for your car and then sells it at the retail price will make the same profit on a loaded or stripped model. At least that is the theory.

In some cases, what's an option in some trim levels will be standard equipment on others. If your car happens to have an accessory listed as standard ("Std" in the N.A.D.A guide), you cannot add it to the trade-in, loan and retail prices. For example, if your car had a power seat, it would add $125 to the value of the vehicle. However, if you had a Camry XLE, the top trim level, the power seat would be standard equipment and as such already would have been included in the trade-in, loan and retail prices. The guide will explain which options are standard equipment in each trim level.

As you look at the car guide, you'll also note that it calls for deducting specified amounts of money for vehicles without certain accessories. In the case of your Camry, for example, models without power windows will have $125 subtracted from their trade-in, loan and retail prices. Since your car has this feature and is equipped with each of the other accessories that are in the "deduct without" section of the price guide, you have no subtraction to do. Simply do the following math:

	Trade-In	Loan	Retail
1996 Toyota Camry LE V6	$12,850	$11,575	$15,025
Add for Sunroof	450	450	450
Add for Alloy Wheels	150	150	150
Totals	$13,450	$12,175	$15,625

Now you have to consider the mileage and condition of your vehicle. At the beginning of the Toyota listings in the N.A.D.A book, you'll see that the Camry is considered a Class II vehicle. Checking the mileage charts, which deduct for higher than expected mileage while adding value for lower than expected odometer readings, you are pleased to note that your car falls in the "average" category. Generally, the price guides assume average mileage to be 12,000 to 15,000 miles a year. If your vehicle is above or below that range, the guide directs you to make the necessary adjustments.

Finally, take an honest look at your car. Condition counts on the used-car lot and if your vehicle has any mechanical or cosmetic shortcomings, the dealer will deduct reconditioning costs from the amount he or she offers you.

For example, those tires with thin tread will cost you, as will that parking lot scrape on the rear fender and the small hole in the upholstery that happened when you forgot about the screwdriver in your back pocket. Faults you've learned to ignore could easily knock $1,000 or more off a dealer's estimate of your car's value.

You also might find your car worth less if there are a lot of comparable models available on used-car lots in your area. This can happen when a manufacturer's captive leasing company auctions off a large number of models similar to yours just as you want to sell. If that occurs, you could lose several thousand dollars more on a late-model vehicle.

So, what is your car is really worth? The answer is simple: It's worth as much as you can get for it. No more, no less. If you find that upsetting, stay out of the used-car business. However, since you do have a used car that you want to sell, you should now open your newspaper to the classified section and see what other owners with cars similar to yours are asking. Also, look at ads from dealers who may have a carbon copy of your car for sale.

You may even want to stop by a used-car lot or two to see what they'd be willing to offer you for your car. You can choose lots associated with a new-car dealership or independent operators; just be sure to pick a lot that sells cars like yours. If the price seems significantly out of line with your expectations, ask the dealer why. He or she may see something wrong with your car that you have overlooked. Or the dealer may think you are desperate and will take any offer. Most people are shocked by how little most dealers want to pay, but you never know until you ask.

Of course, you can also sell your car on your own. Do not, however, think that you will be able to get the guidebook's retail price for it. Retail prices usually go to reputable dealers who offer warranty coverage (in some states this is a legal requirement for dealers selling certain cars and trucks) and who have checked and reconditioned the vehicle. You can't offer these services, nor should you. For clean cars in good to excellent condition, most casual sales, which are transactions between private parties, occur at a price between the retail listing in the price guides and the wholesale or trade-in value.

There is a significant exception to this rule. As cars age, they become less and less attractive to new-car dealers wanting to stock their used-car lots.

Offers for your older vehicle will reflect that. In many cases dealers who take your older car in trade immediately wholesale it for a sum close to the minimal amount they offered you for it.

However, serviceable cars that are able to pass state-mandated inspections often have a street value far greater than this wholesale value. One AAA member in the Northeast reported being offered $500 for her aging Toyota when she went to trade it in for a new Honda. The car ran well but the paint was dull, the interior was a little dirty and the odometer had passed the 120,000-mile mark.

So just before she was to pick up her new car, she spent a day washing, scrubbing, vacuuming and waxing the Toyota. An ad in the newspaper attracted a buyer and she ended up selling it for $2,000.

For states with a sales tax on new cars, however, there may be a trap awaiting the unwary owner who sells a more valuable car on his or her own. Some states allow the dealer to calculate the sales tax on a new car after the trade-in allowance has been deducted from the selling price. This amounts to a tax break for buyers who sell their used cars through a dealer. Here is how it works:

If you own a car that the dealer is willing to pay you $20,000 for and you're buying a $30,000 vehicle, you'll pay sales tax only on $10,000 if you trade in this vehicle, which is the cash component of the deal. If you sell your vehicle yourself, you'll pay sales tax on the full $30,000 cost of the new car. In a state with a 7 percent sales tax, that means another $1,400 in sales tax if you sold the car yourself. In other words, you'd have to sell your car privately for $21,400 just to equal your dealer's offer.

CHAPTER

3

Vehicle Safety

In This Chapter

- Why manufacturers ignore half of the safety picture
- How the simplest items can affect your safety
- How to live with air bags
- What the crash tests really tell you
- What you need in a car if you have children
- Which options can enhance your safety

For many buyers, safety is more important than styling, riding comfort, value or fuel economy. And the industry is responding. While government regulations require many of the safety features on today's cars and trucks, they don't require the enthusiastic marketing of them that we often see. Crash-test footage that would have made both industry execs and the public squirm in 1956 is commonly used in today's TV ads. Safety now sells.

That fact also is reflected in the many safety devices that automakers offer, in some cases ahead of – or even in the absence of – government mandates. Side-impact air bags, for example, first introduced by Volvo in 1996, are now common. They're not required by any federal standard and there are no regulations governing their performance. They do, however, help manufacturers meet mandated side-impact safety standards in some vehicles.

Unfortunately, all those film clips showing cars crashing into immovable barriers or other vehicles can give people a distorted perspective on automotive safety. Today, more and more people define a "safe car" as one that will protect them in a crash. Perhaps equally important, however, is how various models help a driver avoid the crash in the first place.

A Good Fit

How you fit in a vehicle and how comfortable you are driving it are the first components of the safety equation. If, while car shopping, you come across a vehicle that's uncomfortable, your safety will be compromised if you buy it. If you're concentrating on how to relieve your aching back, you probably won't be paying close enough attention to what's going on around you on the road.

Similarly, cars and trucks can hasten the onset of driver fatigue and compromise your safety. High noise levels, poor glare control on bright days, weak ventilation and uneven temperature control ultimately will make you tired faster when you're driving.

One often overlooked aspect of proper seating, for both fit and comfort, is the position of the head restraint. It isn't really a headrest, even though many people call it that. Its job is to lessen your likelihood of suffering whiplash and painful neck injuries in a rear-end collision.

For head restraints to protect you, they must be positioned properly. The center of the head restraint should reach the ears of the person in the seat. The top should reach between the person's ears and the top of his or her head. It also should be no more than 2 inches from the back of the head. If you have to raise the head restraint to get it in the proper position, you should be able to lock it there. If it doesn't have a locking mechanism, it likely will collapse in a crash. This increases your chance for injury.

Unfortunately, some consumers may not appreciate a properly designed head restraint. The 2-inch distance requirement means that either their hair or hat comes in contact with it on a regular basis. Unfortunately, trying to save your hairdo or headgear can make the head restraint less effective in protecting you in the event of a rear-end collision.

To Be Safe You Must Be Able to See

Being safe means you should be able to see as much as possible around your car or truck. But vehicles vary widely in the levels of visibility they offer drivers. Roof pillars and other parts of the vehicle can significantly limit your view of the road.

A blind spot is anyplace outside the vehicle that you can't see because of the structure of the vehicle. Every car and truck has blind spots, some of which can cover a surprising amount of territory. Just ask someone who has backed over a child's bicycle in the driveway.

Even vehicles that seem to let you see the road immediately in front of the bumper actually restrict your vision of the pavement ahead by at least 15 to 20 feet. Similar blind spots occur to the right of the vehicle. To the left, it is not unusual to have the door panel obscure your view of 6 feet of pavement. It's to the rear, however, that the problem of restricted vision can be the most severe. It's not unusual for the trunk or tailgate assembly to obscure up to 40 feet of pavement immediately behind the car. Depending on your height, you may find that the inside or outside rearview mirrors also create blind spots.

Roof pillars are another major contributor to obstructed vision. In some cars, those around the windshields can hide a pedestrian crossing the street until the very last second. The right rear pillar often blocks the driver's view when backing out of a parking space or when entering traffic at an angle.

Control placement also contributes to good vision. Your ability to reach the lights and wipers and other controls, as well as the intuitive nature of their operation, are safety factors to consider. The less time you spend with your eyes off the road, the better.

SAFETY

For years, many automakers offered only black instrument panel tops. When buyers complained about the lack of color coordination, manufacturers responded with instrument panel top pads that matched the rest of the interior. Now buyers say they're distracted by reflections on a bright, sunny day. The reflections worsen as windshields approach a 60-degree angle, which they often do for enhanced aerodynamics. So before you buy any vehicle, drive it on a sunny day and see if the reflections distract you or limit your ability to see. You can reduce windshield reflections with a dark dash cover. Intended to reduce damage to plastic instrument panels caused by long exposure to the sun, these covers also cut reflections. Mail-order houses sell them for most makes and models.

Tip Provided by AAA Hoosier Motor Club

Before you buy any car, make sure you can see outside in all directions. Then be sure the seat is comfortable and the car is quiet enough for you to resist fatigue on long trips. It really is a matter of safety. You can react to what goes on around you only if you can see it and if you are alert enough to take appropriate action. No crash test film addresses these safety factors.

Air Bag Safety

The addition of air bags makes choosing a car that fits you properly even more important. A driver should sit 10 to 12 inches away from the air bag. A front-seat passenger should move the seat as far back from the dash as possible.

To determine whether a car allows you to get far enough away from the air bag while you're in the driver's seat, measure the distance from your sternum to the steering wheel hub. If you don't come up with at least 10 inches of space, try readjusting the seat. If, after experimenting with different seating positions, it's still not possible to establish the space you need, look for another car.

Shorter drivers may find that adjustable foot pedals are a way to get the distance from the wheel that they need. These pedals are beginning to show up either as options or standard equipment on some models. An alternative: consider installing a brake or accelerator pedal extender.

Safety Demands Good Handling

In addition to giving you a comfortable, proper fit and a relatively unfettered view of the world, a vehicle must respond predictably and appropriately when you operate the accelerator, brake and steering systems. The way a vehicle responds to the driver's control while traveling at highway cruising is called "handling." When many people say "handling," however, they mean maneuverability. The ease of getting in and out of a parking space and the effort required to turn sharply at low speeds are important considerations for many car shoppers. However, these factors are but a small part of what determines a vehicle's handling capability or its safety.

A research tool such as the *AAA Auto Guide: New Cars and Trucks* can help you find cars and trucks that handle well and are therefore better at collision-avoidance maneuvers — rapid acceleration, responsive steering maneuvers and short stopping distances at higher speeds, for instance. Guides often include the distance each vehicle will cover in a stop from 60 or 70 mph, comments on the higher-speed handling characteristics and a gauge of the vehicle's ultimate steering ability. They also comment on how easy the vehicle is to control in quick, high-speed turns and whether it has a tendency to surprise a driver with unexpected responses. This is important to know before you have to test your new car's maneuverability in a sudden, crash-avoiding lane change.

These dynamic handling capabilities are referred to as a vehicle's active safety component. They are difficult to assess and the ratings are often subjective. They also do not lend themselves to the one- to five-star rating system that the National Highway Traffice Safety Administration uses to quantify a vehicle's crash-test performance. As a result, few manufacturers try to sell this aspect of safety with anywhere near the level of enthusiasm that they reserve for publicizing favorable crash-test results. Yet active safety capabilities are vitally important when you are on the road.

How cars maneuver and handle is one of 20 performance categories rated in the *AAA Auto Guide: New Cars and Trucks*. Using a scale of 1 to 10, with 1 being worst and 10 ideal, vehicles tested in recent years have earned scores ranging from 3 to 10 for their handling capabilities. The majority earned scores of 6 to 8, with 7 suggesting an average performance. All things being equal, it makes sense for you to select a vehicle with a higher handling score.

Braking is also a critical component of a vehicle's active safety. In the *AAA Auto Guide: New Cars and Trucks*, both the braking distance required for a 60-mph stop and a numerical rating of the braking performance on a 1-to-10 scale are provided. The braking distance ignores your reaction time, which can add significantly to total stopping distance, of course. Instead, it gives you an idea of how much distance you will need to bring the car to a stop once you have your foot on the brake. A skilled driver conducts the tests on dry pavement.

Obviously, the shorter the stopping distance the better the braking performance. In the most recent guide, stopping distances from 60 mph ranged from an excellent 99 feet to an uninspiring 164 feet.

Other factors also have to be considered in assessing braking performance, including ease of maintaining control during an emergency stop, feedback that the driver receives through the brake pedal, stability of the vehicle on a variety of surfaces and the ability of the car or truck to make repeated stops without losing much of its braking power to fade.

Fade occurs as the brakes become hot, as they will after repeated stops or a long downhill stretch that requires constant application of the brakes to keep speed under control. Some brakes are hardly affected by this heat. Others lose much of their stopping power. To give you an idea of how hot they can get, consider that it's not unusual to see brake rotors glow a dull red in some nighttime races. Hard braking can generate that much heat.

Cars or trucks with ABS generally do much better in helping a driver maintain control during difficult stops than do vehicles without it. In addition, the issue of pedal feedback – important in keeping the brakes of a non-ABS equipped vehicle just on the verge of locking without actually allowing them to stop the wheels from turning and thus prompting a skid – is not a major factor with ABS.

Acceleration is another key component of active safety. The ability to speed up is sometimes very important in avoiding a crash, though it plays a lesser role than the vehicle's steering and braking capabilities. In addition, while a lively response to the accelerator is undeniably pleasant – "throttle therapy" is how some people describe it – it usually comes at the price of poorer fuel economy. Finding the right balance of acceleration and power on one side and fuel efficiency on the other can be a challenge. Generally, cars with faster acceleration are also more costly to buy and insure.

Be sure to read any description of a vehicle's handling that you can find. It can give you valuable insight into how the car or truck will respond during emergency maneuvers. It would be neither wise nor legal to determine these capabilities for yourself while driving on a public road, so an appropriate buying guide is a must for anyone looking for a new car or truck.

Crash Performance

Unfortunately, even with a good view of the road and a superbly responsive vehicle, it's not always possible to avoid a crash. When a crash happens, the active safety components that were so important in collision avoidance suddenly mean little to our safety. The vehicle's passive safety characteristics now come into play.

First and foremost, you and every passenger in your vehicle must wear a seat belt. Seat belts are classified as an active system since you must engage them – by buckling up – to provide protection. Seat belts enhance the protection provided by passive systems such as air bags. Air bags are considered passive devices because they require no action on your part to provide protection. Many passive safety features that can protect you in a crash are either rendered meaningless or severely compromised when you do not buckle up. Seat belts prevent crashes also by keeping the driver behind the wheel during emergency maneuvers or after a minor crash that does not stop the vehicle.

Did You Know? While weight is not an advantage in a crash with an immovable barrier, it is in a collision with another vehicle. The occupants of the heavier vehicle almost always come out with fewer injuries than those in the smaller, lighter vehicle. Comparing frontal crash test results for different cars and trucks is valid only if all of the vehicles are in the same weight class.

The combination lap belt and shoulder harness is your first line of defense in a crash. When you shop for a new vehicle, make sure that the lap belt fits snugly around your hips, not your abdomen or stomach, and that the shoulder strap goes across your collar bone about half way between your shoulder and your neck. The belt should exert slight but comfortable pressure on your body.

To accommodate the wide variety of driver shapes and sizes, most models now have height-adjustable shoulder belt mounting points for the driver and front-seat passenger. A few models also offer this feature for the outboard seating positions in the rear. If you cannot get a proper fit once your have the seat adjusted properly, check to see that the belt mounting height over your shoulder is adjusted correctly. If it is, and you still can't get a proper and comfortable fit, shop for another model.

If you find a seat belt that's too small to fit properly on a model you otherwise might want to buy, ask about seat belt extensions or longer replacement belts. You can talk to the dealer or directly to the manufacturer.

Once you are properly seated and buckled up, the combination of vehicle structure and restraint systems are all that stand between you and serious injury in a crash. The sides of the vehicle are made as rigid as possible to protect passengers in event of a side impact. Meanwhile, the metal in front of and behind the passenger compartment is designed to crumple in a controlled manner in a crash. In other words, the engine compartment and the cargo area or trunk will give way, softening the blow for passengers who are properly restrained by seat belts. In minor crashes, there may not be much deformation of either the front or rear. In more serious accidents, the degree of deformation increases. The goal of the safety engineers is to build a body structure that will allow the ends of the car to collapse in a controlled manner while keeping the passenger compartment intact.

Unfortunately, this doesn't always happen. In some frontal collisions, for example, the crumpling doesn't stop where the passenger compartment begins. Deformation continues, intruding into the passenger compartment. In severe frontal collisions, the instrument panel, steering wheel or passenger floor area may be pushed toward the occupants, increasing their likelihood of significant injuries. How a vehicle performs in a crash is determined in actual crash tests.

The Three Major Crash Tests

Three widely publicized crash tests are done by two separate organizations in the United States. The National Highway Traffic Safety Administration carries out both full-barrier frontal and side-impact testing. The Insurance Institute for Highway Safety performs an offset-barrier frontal test and is experimenting with developing its own side-impact testing procedures. The two frontal crash tests measure different aspects of a vehicle's performance.

Unfortunately, there are no guarantees. Even if you select a model that is highly rated in these tests, you could still be seriously injured or even killed in a crash. Fortunately, models with higher ratings do seem to have lower levels of deaths and injuries in real-world crashes. However, there are so many variables in a real-life crash that it's impossible to predict what will happen based solely on test results.

NHTSA New Car Assessment Program

They say that back in 1914, John Dodge took the first two cars to carry his name off the assembly line and drove them into a brick wall at nearly 20 mph. When a startled employee asked why he did it, he reportedly said, "I might as well, because someone else is going to do it when these cars get on the road."

Today's crash testing is far more scientific. In the most widely recognized test, the federal government's National Highway Traffic Safety Administration assesses how well a vehicle protects its two front-seat occupants when it hits a barrier at 35 mph. The vehicle is driven into an unyielding wall at a 90-degree angle so that the crash involves the entire front of the car or truck.

Scientists then analyze the stresses to which the test dummies − one in the driver's seat, the other in the front passenger's position − were exposed.

Did You Know?

In NHTSA frontal crash tests, the number of stars represents the possibility that you'll sustain a serious injury, one that's life-threatening and requires immediate hospitalization. Even in a five-star vehicle, you stand a 10 percent chance of being hurt. Here's what the other stars mean:

4 stars = 11 percent to 20 percent chance of serious injury
3 stars = 21 percent to 35 percent chance
2 stars = 36 percent to 45 percent chance
1 star = 46 percent or greater chance

Tip Provided by Automobile Club of New York

By measuring the force on the dummies' head, chest and femurs, or thigh-bones, the agency can assign a safety score of 1 to 5 stars. One star is the worst rating, 5 is the best.

This crash really tests the car's restraint system, which consists of the seat belts and air bags. To some extent it also tests the structure of the vehicle, though meaningful intrusion or shortening of the passenger compartment is rare. For the latest crash test results, visit their website at www.nhtsa.gov.

IIHS Crash Tests

If the NHTSA frontal-tests emphasize the performance of the restraint system, the IIHS testing examines how well the structure of a vehicle holds up in offset barrier crashes. A frontal offset test focuses all of the energy generated by the collision onto a small portion of the vehicle's front body structure – unlike the NHTSA test, which propels a vehicle into a fixed barrier at a 90-degree angle and lets the entire front dissipate the crash forces. The offset test more closely approximates what happens when a car hits a tree or when a driver drifts over the center line and clips a car coming in the other direction. In this type of crash it would be unlikely for the two cars to hit squarely, front bumper to front bumper. Instead, only about half of the left front of the first vehicle is likely to strike a comparable portion of the oncoming car.

The IIHS replicates this situation by driving a car at 40 mph into a barrier so that only 40 percent of the front structure bears the entire brunt of the crash. The test is extremely rigorous, exceeding the forces generated in 98 percent of all offset frontal collisions. The demanding nature of the test is obvious: windshield pillars are sometimes forced up and back as the driver's side of the passenger compartment is shortened. More than a foot of passenger compartment space may be lost as the floor, instrument panel or steering wheel are pushed back.

Based on the results, IIHS rates the vehicle's structure, the control that the restraint systems exert on the test dummy in the driver's seat and the severity of injuries that an actual driver might sustain to the head, neck, chest, legs and feet.

Measuring the potential for foot and leg injuries may seem unimportant to many car shoppers. On the contrary. Recent improvements in seat belt use, the addition of air bags and stronger vehicle body structures mean that people who might have died in frontal crashes are now surviving – only to be disabled by painful foot and lower leg injuries that are slow to heal.

Despite the higher speed in the IIHS trial, head and chest injury scores are often lower than in the NHTSA tests. That's because the front structure crumples more in the offset barrier test, which involves only a portion of the vehicle.

In addition to these measurements, IIHS also evaluates head restraint design and bumper performance. Bumper evaluation often has more to do with insurance claims than vehicle safety, although previous tests have revealed that minor bumps, typical of what might be sustained in a parking lot, can affect vehicle lighting systems or cause tailgates to pop open. For the latest crash test results from the IIHS, visit the www.iihs.org website.

Side-Impact Testing

Many safety experts believe that side crashes are the most difficult for auto engineers to handle and for passengers to survive. While the front and rear of most auto bodies can be significantly compacted without affecting the passenger compartment, there is almost no crush space in the doors. That should highlight the importance of the decision of the National Highway Traffic Safety Administration to institute a side-impact crash-testing program for new cars and light trucks.

That light trucks, which ride higher than passenger cars, have become more and more popular complicates side-impact crash testing. In the NHTSA tests, the moveable crash barrier simulates the front of a typical passenger car. It is driven into the side of the stationary test vehicle to re-create the type of crash that might take place in an intersection.

Since the crash sled is based on the dimensions of the front end of a typical passenger car – the hood, grille and front bumper – it strikes the test vehicle lower in the driver's doors than a truck, van or sport utility vehicle would. A taller crash sled built to resemble the front of a truck could make it more difficult to protect the dummies in the test vehicle from injury.

The NHTSA side-impact test is further limited by the fact that it does not measure head or neck injury potential. The side-impact dummies, called SIDs, are designed to determine the risk of injury to the thorax – specifically, the ribs, spine and internal organs – by measuring the acceleration and compression of the thorax during the crash. The SIDs are placed in the driver's seat and on the left side of the back seat. Vehicle performance is rated on the 1- to 5-star scale.

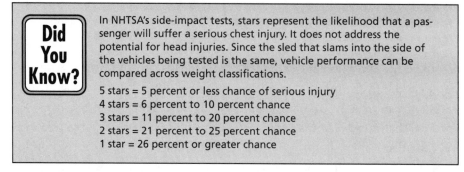

Did You Know?

In NHTSA's side-impact tests, stars represent the likelihood that a passenger will suffer a serious chest injury. It does not address the potential for head injuries. Since the sled that slams into the side of the vehicles being tested is the same, vehicle performance can be compared across weight classifications.

5 stars = 5 percent or less chance of serious injury
4 stars = 6 percent to 10 percent chance
3 stars = 11 percent to 20 percent chance
2 stars = 21 percent to 25 percent chance
1 star = 26 percent or greater chance

Center of Gravity

As vehicles become taller, or as their owners place loads higher in the cargo area or on the roof, the center of gravity rises. With a higher center of gravity comes the greater likelihood that the vehicle will roll over in a crash or during a skid.

To determine the probability of a rollover, the National Highway Traffic Safety Administration has chosen to use a mathematical formula rather than a dynamic test. It uses the traditional 1- to 5-star rating system, with 5-star vehicles being the least likely to roll.

Occupants of compact and smaller SUVs and compact pickup trucks suffer a higher percentage of fatalities in rollover accidents than do the occupants of passenger cars. Buyers considering a small SUV or pickup should consider their needs and the additional risk associated with this type of vehicle.

Carrying Loads

Many buyers believe that once they have their minivan, pickup truck or SUV, they can carry anything. Unfortunately, the truth is this: the fact that a cargo fits does not mean that you can or should carry it. Granted, these vehicles are flexible when it comes to carrying all kinds of cargo, but they also have definite limits on how much weight they can handle or how big a trailer they can tow.

It may not be easy to determine just how much weight your vehicle can carry. While manufacturers are willing to list the GVWRs, or gross vehicle weight ratings, they are not as eager to spell out how much weight you really can add, in either passengers or luggage.

They're reluctant because the GVWR figure includes the weight of the vehicle and its cargo. And that's the problem. The more the vehicle weighs, the less cargo it can carry. Making a blanket recommendation, therefore, is difficult because options can change the weight of the vehicle. Rather than weigh each car or truck as it comes off the assembly line and subtracting its poundage from the GVWR to determine the maximum payload, most manufacturers just provide the GVWR and leave the fine points up to the owner.

Many owners ignore the details of cargo capacity and simply assume that their rugged SUV is more than capable of carrying a heavy load. Unfortunately, some SUVs are decidedly weak when it comes to coping with cargo. Among the new class of smaller SUVs, none can carry 1,000 pounds. One, the 2001 Toyota RAV4, can carry less than 800 pounds. Put four 200-pound passengers in the vehicle and it's overloaded, even before adding a single suitcase.

Other SUVs, minivans and pickup trucks may suffer similar overloading without their owners ever being aware of the problem. Overloading not only shortens the life expectancy of chassis components, it also adversely affects handling and braking. Overloading has been implicated in tire failures and, over time, can doom wheel or axle bearings, weaken springs and strain engines and transmissions.

For buyers interested in carrying maximum payloads, specifying four-wheel drive on trucks could be a mistake. This often lowers the vehicle's carrying capacity, as the added weight of the four-wheel-drive components increases the weight of the vehicle without changing the chassis' GVWR. The more the truck weighs, the less it can carry or tow. If you intend to carry a significant amount of cargo, make sure the vehicle you buy is rated for the load. For most vehicles, the capacity is less than 1,000 pounds. Some compact SUVs would be overloaded with just half a ton of cargo or passengers.

Children in the Car

As any parent who has struggled with a child safety seat can tell you, it is not easy to carry a child safely. The major difficulty has been the need to use safety belts designed to protect adults to secure a child's safety seat instead.

With spot checks showing that more than 80 percent of parents install a child's safety seat incorrectly, there was an obvious need for improvement. As of September 1999, the federal government required manufacturers to install anchorage points for child seats with top tethers in many vehicles. In 2000, the requirement was expanded to cover light trucks and multipurpose passenger vehicles.

Also, as of September 2000, vehicle manufacturers had to install a new child-seat mounting system in some of their passenger cars and light trucks. Effective September 2002, all vehicles built for sale in the United States will be required to have the new system, called LATCH or ISOFIX.

These anchorages for top tethers and the lower mounting bars are designed to let parents mount child seats easily, securely and – most importantly – correctly. To take advantage of this new child-seat mounting system, parents will also have to buy a child safety seat that can lock onto the vehicle's lower mounting bars and be tethered at the top. Parents and parents-to-be should look for these child-seat mounts when shopping for a vehicle.

Some manufacturers offer built-in safety seats for young children as options in some vehicles. These are almost always extremely easy to use. However, before basing your decision on the availability of such seats, make sure your child fits the requirements for height and weight spelled out in the owner's manual. Also make sure that your child is comfortable in the seat.

Be as Safe as Possible

While all cars and trucks seem to have an ample assortment of safety features as standard equipment, reading the fine print in the sales brochures and carefully checking your new-car buying guide can be time well spent. You'll quickly discover significant differences in the safety features of various makes and models. Here are some points to consider.

Safety Belts – The vehicle should have a combination lap and shoulder belt for the driver and each passenger. While all cars with a back seat have had combination lap and shoulder belts seat for more than a decade, not all cars offer three lap and shoulder belts in the back. Often the lap and shoulder belts are limited to the two outboard positions, while the center seat has only a lap belt. In most crashes, a lap belt – though better than nothing – does not give the same level of protection as a lap belt and shoulder harness. If you plan to carry three people in the rear seat, select a car with three combination lap and shoulder belts.

Some safety belts offer additional, worthwhile features. The first is a pretensioner. This device, usually triggered at about the same time as the air bags in a crash, reels in any slack that may exist in the seat belt. Tightening the fit lets the belt provide far more protection to the wearer. Look for pretensioners in the vehicles you're considering.

Many vehicles also offer seat belts with force limiters, which reduce the pressure on the chest during a severe collision. As a result, you're less likely to suffer severe injuries.

Dual Stage Air Bags – These are front air bags that compute the force of the crash, determine a passenger's seating position and know whether the seat belt is buckled when a crash occurs. They then choose whether to deploy at partial or full force, giving you a higher level of protection than single-stage air bags. If there's no one in the passenger seat, some air bags won't deploy on that side, which reduces your repair costs.

Side Air Bags – Increasingly popular, there are three types of side air bags. One is mounted in the door or seat and is designed to protect your midsection. Another is a door- or seat-mounted unit with a dual-chamber design that protects both the thorax and the head. The third type is mounted above the door and deploys as a curtain or tube for head protection. Side curtain designs can protect outboard passengers in the rear seat as well as the driver or front-seat passenger. Though they're a worthwhile feature, side air bags

---

SAFETY

If your new car has seat-mounted side air bags, you can forget about using seat covers of any kind, including those popular sheepskin throw covers. They interfere with air-bag deployment. Interference limits the bags' effectiveness and can injure passengers.

Tip Provided by
AAA Minneapolis

may complicate travels with children, who sometimes fall asleep in positions that can reduce the bag's effectiveness or even add to the risk of injury. In some cars, door-mounted side air bags in the rear seat are optional.

Passenger-Side Air Bag On/Off Switch – Rear-facing child-safety seats should go in the back seat of a vehicle. But what if you have a sports car or pickup that doesn't have a back seat? Then you need a way to turn off the air bag on the passenger side. If you're looking at a two-seater but need to carry an infant in a rear-facing seat, make sure the vehicle includes an on/off switch. Not all do. Some vehicles without a manual switch offer an automatic system that disables the passenger-side air bag when an appropriate child-safety seat is used. The key word is appropriate – you can't use just any seat, you have to buy the one that works with the system.

Antilock Brakes – A worthwhile option, even at prices approaching $1,000. While ABS won't necessarily shorten stopping distances or repeal the laws of physics, it will help you maintain control and steering ability during emergency stops, regardless of the condition of the road surface.

Traction Control – Using the ABS computer, traction control senses when a wheel begins to spin on a slippery surface and reduces power so it can regain traction. If that doesn't work, some systems also apply the brake to the wheel in trouble. Vehicles with traction control display a surprising amount of go-power on slippery surfaces. Some approach, but do not equal, the capabilities of four-wheel-drive vehicles. Some systems can be switched off, allowing the driver to spin the tires when needed. In soft, fresh, fluffy snow, for instance, a spinning tire can sometimes dig down to pavement for a better bite.

If you are in the market for a used car, note that some earlier traction control systems worked only at lower speeds, usually at 25 mph or less. Newer systems function at all speeds.

Stability Enhancement Systems – While these are marketed under a variety of names, including Electronic Stability Program or ESP, AdvanceTrac and Stabilitrak, their purpose is the same. They are designed to help a driver control a skid, often reacting and saving the day before the driver is even aware of a problem. At first confined to luxury cars and trucks, stability control systems are now working their way onto the option lists of less expensive vehicles. They are worth buying.

Brake Assist – Research shows that most drivers don't apply their brakes as firmly as they should in an emergency. Brake assist is designed to tell an emergency stop from a regular one, then take over and hit the brakes with full force. Used in concert with ABS systems, brake assist should not provoke a skid. If the driver backs off the brake, brake assist immediately bows out of the picture. In an emergency, brake assist can considerably reduce stopping distances and the likelihood of crashing.

Electronic Tire Pressure Monitors – There are two types now available. One is a computer-based system that uses the ABS sensors to determine wheel speed. When it senses one wheel turning faster than the others, taking into account cornering and normal differences in tire wear, it alerts the driver to check the tire pressure. The problem with this system is that if all four tires are evenly under inflated, the computer will not pick up the problem. Newer systems use transponders inside the wheel to sense pressure levels. Neither system should be used as a substitute for regular maintenance. Sensors are standard equipment with tires designed to run on zero pressure in an emergency.

Rear Wiper and Washer – If this isn't standard equipment on the minivan, hatchback or SUV you want, get it if it's offered as an option. Light drizzle can block your rear visibility in seconds. A rear wiper and washer system really is a necessity.

Sport Suspension Upgrades – These systems can enhance handling. However, better handling often comes at the expense of riding comfort on rough pavement. Surprisingly, however, some of these suspension system upgrades actually improve both handling and riding comfort. Try out the system you are considering before you buy, just to be sure.

Xenon Headlights – The white, even blanket of light that these factory-installed, high-intensity headlights provide on low beam must be seen to be appreciated. They're an expensive option, but frequent night drives make them worthwhile. Barring a collision, the bulbs should last for the life of the car. Take a night test drive on a dark road and you won't want to pass on this option.

Cargo Compartment Net – If you buy a wagon or an SUV, understand that you won't have a trunk to carry cargo. Some odds and ends may end up permanently stored in the back. Unfortunately, if you're ever in a wreck, these items could go flying around and cause damage. A strong net or a solid screen separating the cargo area from the passenger compartment can keep stuff from smacking you in the back of the head.

Navigation Systems – Factory-installed units can tell you audibly where you should turn to reach your destination. Never having to take your eyes off the road to read directions can make you a safer driver. However, the systems are expensive and the dash displays may be distracting and confusing. Programming also can be difficult and time consuming and should never be attempted while driving.

Active Anti-Whiplash Systems – To protect you in a crash, the head restraint should be about 2 inches from the back of your head. Since many people think that's too close for comfort, some automakers offer an active head-restraint system. In a rear-end collision, this anti-whiplash technology harnesses the force of your body against the seat back to move the head restraint into a more protective position. Other systems allow the front seats to move down and back a little to cradle the occupant.

Electronically Dimming Mirrors – While many cars and trucks offer interior rearview mirrors that dim electronically, only a few extend the dimming action to the driver's outside rearview mirror. This feature reduces glare, which can make night driving more comfortable.

Electric Defrosters – Almost all cars and trucks have an electric defroster for the rear window, either as standard equipment or an option. Not all convertibles or pickups offer it, though it's a feature worth having in all climates. Also valuable are electric defrosters for the outside mirrors and, in colder climates, electric heaters for windshield washer nozzles.

Remote Entry and Central Locking – This is more than a convenience. By letting you enter your car quickly and lock the doors behind you, it's also a safety feature.

Leasing

In This Chapter

• • • • • • • • • • •

- What a lease is
- Does leasing really save you money?
- Advantages and disadvantages
- How to handle a lease's complexities
- What you can negotiate

Go shopping for a new car or truck and you will quickly discover why leasing is so popular. While the prices of new vehicles have stabilized in recent years, numbers on the sticker are still going up. The average customer now pays more than $24,000 for a new vehicle.

If you put 20 percent down on this car vehicle and finance the remainder at 7 percent interest for 36 months, your monthly payment will be $593. Few families want to make a financial commitment that large. In fact, most people can't. Extending the loan to 48 or 60 months, which would lower the payment to $460 or $380 respectively, quickly loses its appeal when you calculate how much more interest expense you'll incur. Finance for three years and the total interest is $2,142. That increases to $2,869 for a four-year loan and $3,611 for a five-year loan.

Enter leasing. With manufacturers promoting it actively as an antidote to higher prices, leasing has grown from less than 10 percent of the market a decade ago to about 33 percent today. Automakers have done more than just advertise, they've used financial subsidies to promote leases. The tactic has been extremely successful.

What a Lease Is

A lease is a long-term rental agreement. It usually lasts 24 to 36 months, although it can be for shorter or longer periods of time. The lessee – that's you – agrees to take the vehicle and use it for a given time and a specified number of miles. You promise to return the car in good condition to the lessor – that's the leasing company – or the lessor's agent.

Advantages

Leasing has many advantages. Buy the vehicle and you will pay for the entire car. Lease the car for three years and you only pay to "own" it for that period. After you return it, the lessor can resell this valuable asset on the open market. Your monthly payment – $593 to buy the vehicle in our example above – could drop to just $349 a month in a typical subsidized lease. A car payment of $349 beats $593 every time.

Leasing, therefore, appeals to many consumers. It can be ideal for people who know how much they'll drive during the lease period, like to get a new car every two or three years, take good care of their vehicles and have the necessary credit to qualify for the transaction. "Buy assets that will appreciate in value, rent or lease depreciating assets," leasing advocates say.

Since most leases are short, lessees always have a relatively new vehicle and few repair expenses. Not only do new cars rarely break down, the warranty almost always covers the repair costs when they do.

Leasing a new car every two or three years also lets the lessee take advantage of the latest safety technologies almost as soon as they appear. Few buyers who hold onto their cars have been able to benefit from electronic stability control systems, dual-stage air bags or the latest in side air-bag technology. Lessees can enjoy these advances within three years, and may already have a car with these features.

People who trade every two or three years find leasing offers other advantages, too. Perhaps most importantly, you eliminate the potentially messy process of haggling over the value of your trade-in. In a closed-end lease, trade-in value is established on the day the lease is signed. If the estimate turns out to be too high, it's the leasing company that suffers the loss. If the resale estimate is low, many leasing contracts allow the lessee to get back some – and occasionally all – of the money.

For businesses, the self-employed or people whose work requires a lot of driving, leasing may offer certain tax advantages. An accountant or tax specialist can determine what a lease could mean on your next tax return.

Leasing Has Advantages for Manufacturers

Automakers have reason to like leasing, too. People who lease are almost twice as likely to get another of the same brand when the lease is over as people who buy. Lease returns also give automakers a steady supply of late-model, usually clean used cars that are very profitable for dealers to resell.

As a result, manufacturers began to shift their marketing incentive dollars – the old "buy a car, get a check" promotions – from buyers to lessees about 15 years ago.

Subsidized leases – "subvented" is the industry term for them – ruled the market throughout the 1990s. Manufacturers could bolster sales of any model instantly just by promoting an attractive, cut-rate lease. It moved the metal in a way few other promotions could.

Why We Don't All Lease

Leasing is not perfect. If it were, we'd all be taking delivery of a new car every three years.

The first and perhaps most important problem is that leasing forces a customer into an expensive "ownership" pattern: short-term possession of a new vehicle. New cars and trucks depreciate rapidly during their first two or three years. After that, the rates drop significantly. Lease a car for two or three years and you'll pay for depreciation, just as you would if you bought the vehicle. If you faithfully follow the leasing scenario, you will return the car when the contract is over and lease another new vehicle for another two or three years. At that point, you instantly return yourself to the top of the depreciation slope, where you once again pay for the most expensive years in a vehicle's life.

Buy a car instead and you decide how long you'll keep it. If it works well, as most do, you can hang onto it for six years or longer. Every year you own it, you pay less for depreciation and effectively lower your cost per mile.

Many leasing advocates suggest that leasing is really just another form of financing a purchase. It's an argument with some validity. What they say is this: Lease a car for two years and if you like it, you can turn around and buy it by taking out a two-year loan when the lease is over. You'll be in roughly the same position as the person who bought the car using a four-year loan. In theory, that's true. But in the case of many subvented leases, it's not that simple, as you'll soon see.

Do you drive a lot? If so, you can still lease a vehicle. Just be sure to have the real mileage you need written into the contract instead of the standard 12,000 or 15,000 miles a year. "Buying" the miles up front costs about half of what you'd be charged at the end if you went over the limit.

Tip Provided by AAA Central Penn Automobile Club

Something else to consider: The contract can limit where you use the vehicle and how many miles you can drive it. As the Association of Consumer Vehicle Lessors notes, some regional leasing companies may require that the car stay within a given geographical area. Get transferred to an office across the country and you might not be able to take the car with you.

The leasing contract might even limit where you can drive on vacation. Read the details to see if jaunts to Canada or Mexico are allowed under the terms of the agreement.

> If you decide to buy your leased vehicle at the end of the contract, you won't have to pay for wear and tear or excess mileage. Of course, if your car has gone many miles over the limit or is in poor shape, the price you pay – which was spelled out at the beginning of the deal – will undoubtedly be more than the vehicle is worth. In extreme cases of high mileage or abuse, however, paying this price may be your best bet.

Then there is the issue of mileage limits. You might think you know how many miles you'll drive over the next three years, but circumstances can and do change. Take a new job requiring a longer commute and that 10,000-mile-per-year lease may suddenly become unlivable. Granted, you can always exceed the mileage limit, but a provision in the contract spells out how much each extra mile will cost you. Usually it's about 15 cents, which works out to $1,500 for every 10,000 miles over the limit. CNW Marketing Research, a company that follows the leasing market, notes that more than half of all lessees with a 10,000-mile-per-year limit end up paying for extra miles. Average bill for this joyriding: $2,000.

Leasing contracts also call for the customer to keep the car in good condition. That means having all the factory-required maintenance done on time and avoiding those little cosmetic assaults such as parking lot dings, scratches, nicks and chips that can add up to excess wear and tear. CNW Market Research notes that more than one lessee in three ends up paying for excess wear and tear at the end of the lease. Average charge: $1,850.

Excess wear and tear is a touchy issue. One person's "normal use" is another person's definition of abuse. Generally, excess wear and tear is applied to lessees who return cars with tires that have less than one-eighth-inch of tread. These consumers also will pay for broken or missing accessories or equipment; stains that cannot be removed from upholstery or carpeting; larger scratches, nicks and dents; a cracked, broken or starred windshield; and any damage to lighting system lenses.

Many dealers offer free inspections for lessees who'll be returning a vehicle within 90 days. The dealer can give an idea of what needs to be repaired and how much the leasing company is likely to charge to do the work. You can arrange repairs on your own, of course, but be warned: Poorly – that is, cheaply – done repairs count as excess wear and tear.

Some companies spell out the definition of excess wear and tear in the lease. State regulations limit what others can claim is excessive. Some manufacturers try to resolve misunderstandings with a few simple rules. For example, one captive leasing company (a lessor totally owned by an automaker) says that any scratch, nick or dimple dent on metal that can be covered by something the size of a credit card is considered normal wear and tear. Another developed a plastic disk. If the scratch or nick fits within the inner circle, there's no charge. Anything larger, however, and you can expect that nick in the paint to put a nick in your wallet.

Leasing also presents problems for people who absolutely, positively have to cancel the contract before it expires. Penalties can be severe, even if the termination is involuntary, as it would be if the car were stolen and never recovered or declared a total loss after a crash.

Where to Go for a Lease

There are an estimated 10,000 leasing companies in the United States. Some are regional players while others are national in scope. In addition, almost every automaker has a wholly owned leasing subsidiary. Often it is part of the company's wholly owned financial services company that specializes in financing for customers who prefer to buy.

Most consumers end up dealing with the leasing company owned by the automaker simply because it's the only source for a subvented lease, one with cash incentives than can significantly lower your monthly payment.

In the absence of factory subvention, however, you can get a competitive lease just about anywhere. Open the phone book to the automotive leasing section and you might be surprised by the number of options you have.

The Anatomy of a Lease

While many customers look only at the monthly payments when comparing leases, other factors also deserve careful consideration. For a better understanding of what they are, let's simplify the leasing process.

Let's assume that the lessor starts with a **capitalized cost** for the vehicle. This is the amount that you agree is the price of the new car or truck. From this capitalized cost, we deduct any down payments, known as the **capitalized cost reduction**. Similar to a down payment when you buy a car, this capitalized cost reduction can include cash you pay before taking delivery of the vehicle and the value of your trade-in, if it is applied to the lease. Manufacturer rebates also can be used for capitalized cost reduction. Subtract the capitalized cost reduction from the capitalized cost and you get the **adjusted capitalized cost**.

> The best time to sign a lease is early in the model year. Most leasing companies increase their monthly payments four to six times as the model year progresses. Why? Depreciation, of course. In addition, many automakers impose small price increases as the year goes on. Lease late and you'll not only pay a higher manufacturer's price, but more for depreciation as well.

Next, the lessor estimates what the vehicle will be worth at the end of the contract. This is the vehicle's **residual value**.

Now the lessor subtracts the residual value from the adjusted capitalized cost and divides this amount by the number of months in the lease. This becomes one part of your monthly payment.

The other significant portion is made up of what's called the **rent charge**. This is the cost of the money that the lessor has spent to obtain the car or truck. It also includes profit that the lessor has to make to pay overhead and stay in business. Add the rent charge to the monthly depreciation – the difference between the adjusted capitalized cost and the residual value, divided by the number of months in the lease – and you get the base amount you have to pay each month. Now simply add taxes and in our simplified version, you know what your lease will cost you. Let's look at an example:

Capitalized Cost of Your New Vehicle	$24,000
Less Capitalized Cost Reduction	
Cash Down	(4,000)
Trade-In Allowance:	(3,500)
Adjusted Capitalized Cost	16,500
Less Residual Value	(12,000)
Total of Base Monthly Payments (Depreciation)	$ 4,500

Rent Charge (Profit Plus Overhead)	$ 4,320
Total of Base Monthly Payments	4,500
Grand Total	$ 8,820

Number of Months in Lease	36
Grand Total Divided by Number of Months in Lease	$245.00
Plus 6 Percent Tax	$ 14.70
Monthly Payment	$259.70

As a means of comparison, had you borrowed the $16,500 for three years at 7 percent interest to buy the car, your monthly payment would be $509.47. Of course, at the end of three years, you'd own the car, which should be worth $12,000. With a lease, all you have at the end of three years are memories – plus the $8,991.72 that you didn't spend on monthly payments.

Incidentally, had you leased and then paid yourself the difference between the loan payment and the lease payment – $249.77 – each month and earned 6.5 percent on the balance, you'd have $9,871.26 in cash when the lease was over. To end up with $12,000 in cash – that is, the value of the car – at the end of the lease, you'd have to earn 20.75 percent interest on your money.

Now Things Get Complicated

Most leasing transactions end up being more complicated than the example given above. A manufacturer may offer a "zero down" promotion, in which many of the costs associated with the beginning of a lease are added to the capitalized cost – also called "cap cost" – and spread over the length of the lease. Or the customer may owe more on the trade-in than it's worth. In other cases, excess mileage or wear and tear charges on a previous vehicle are added to the cap cost of the new lease.

Even when there's no capitalized cost reduction, you may have to make a payment to take possession of a new leased vehicle. Common charges include a security deposit (refundable, if you keep the car in good condition), a lease inception fee, title fees, taxes, registration fees and the first month's payment. Costs such as extra insurance coverage are added to the cap costs as well.

The 'Money' Factor

For many years, the leasing industry called this component the money factor which is similar to interest paid on a loan, and many dealers still refer to it by this name. However, the Federal Reserve Board's Regulation M, which governs leasing agreements, doesn't recognize this charge as interest, even though it varies with loan interest rates. Therefore, the lease calls this sum "rent."

Take It or Leave It

Many consumers just accept the conditions spelled out by the lessor. Customers who would bargain to buy a new vehicle just accept the first offer on a lease. Generally you can bargain when leasing. The cap cost is as subject to negotiation as the purchase price of a new car. In fact, it's not a bad idea to shop around for the best purchase price first. If leasing then seems the better option, plug that price into the cap cost section of the lease. The lower the cap cost, the lower your monthly payments will be. By the way, cap cost discounts should not affect residual value since it's referenced against the manufacturer's suggested retail price.

Residual value usually isn't negotiable. A leasing company uses its experience or an outside authority to set it. In addition, the lessor may buy insurance to cover any potential loss when the lease is over. This loss would occur if the residual value estimate turns out to be too high. In this case, the insurer also has a say in the figure.

While terms are generally negotiable, some special leasing promotions from the manufacturer may not be. These can include generous discounts on the capitalized cost and participation by both the dealer and manufacturer in subsidizing the lease.

Tip Provided by
AAA East Tennessee

However, different leasing companies often come to different conclusions on residual values. Sometimes the differences can be significant. You can always shop around for a better – that is, higher – residual value.

You also can compare the charges for rent. This interest substitute is based on the price of money when you go shopping and, to a degree, on your credit history. Shop around.

If a company offers a lower rent charge but also a lower residual value, calculate what effect this will have on the total cost of the lease. Fortunately, this should be easy enough to compare based on industry disclosure requirements.

Often, a dealer will move you from one leasing company to another – dealers often work with several different companies – depending on which one can offer you the best overall deal. If you review the lease for one vehicle and then decide to lease another model, don't assume that the new contract has the same provisions as the first one. It may be from an entirely different company.

Other Fees

Look carefully at the inception and disposition fees. These often amount to several hundred dollars and significantly increase your costs.

You also want to determine whether the lease comes with gap protection. **The gap is the difference between what you'd receive from your insurance company if the car were totaled in a crash and what you'd owe** under the involuntary termination clause of the leasing contract. Some leases include this coverage, others don't. Read the contract carefully and be sure you understand the early termination clause.

When the Lease Ends

Most lease agreements let you buy the car at the end of the lease. It may not be a good idea to do so, however, even if you like the car and want to keep it. It all depends on the price specified in the contract and how that compares to the vehicle's true value. Leasing companies can be overly optimistic when they establish residual value at the beginning of the lease. The Association of Consumer Vehicle Lessors reported recently that, for the average leasing company, vehicles sold at auction brought about $2,600 below residual value.

Since the purchase price at the end of the lease is usually the residual value, it doesn't make sense to pay more for your leased vehicle than it's worth on the open market. If you still want to buy the car, you might not be able to finance it without making a substantial down payment.

This has led many lessees to try to buy the vehicle at its fair market value. Leasing companies, apparently fearing collusion between customer and dealer, usually refuse to allow this type of sale. The philosophy seems to be "If you want to buy the car, you'll do it for the agreed price. Otherwise, the car goes to auction." Nothing more graphically demonstrates that you are not leasing the car from the dealer. You are doing business with a leasing company, which bought the car from the dealer.

Some contracts now specify that you can buy the car for a price listed in a named used-car guide at the end of the lease. That, in theory, should allow you to pay a price closer to market value when the lessor guessed too high on the residual value. If the residual price estimate turns out to be too low, however, this provision could eliminate any equity you have in the vehicle.

You develop equity in a leased vehicle when the contract allows you to buy it for less than it's worth. Under those circumstances you can recapture the amount that, in effect, you overpaid for depreciation by buying the car and then selling it. For example, let's say that the lessor set the vehicle's residual value at $14,000. You discover that you could easily get $16,000 for it as a trade-in. If your buyout price is $14,000, go for it.

Often, however, you don't even have to buy the car to tap this equity. You can assign your right to purchase it for $14,000 to the dealer, who then takes the $2,000 in equity and applies it to your next lease or purchase.

Open or Closed

Sometimes you hear the terms "closed-end" and "open-end" to describe a lease. As a general rule, consider only closed-end leases, which mean that you're not responsible for market conditions that might reduce the value of your leased car and cause it to be worth less than the residual price. A closed-end lease is also called a "walk-away" lease because that's exactly what you can do: walk away.

Several factors can make your vehicle worth less than its residual value at the end of the lease. Perhaps the lessor simply guessed wrong. Or maybe the manufacturer, suffering from slow sales and a glut of new versions of the model you are about to return, decides that the way to move the new ones is to offer a $3,000 rebate. While this tactic improves sales, it also depresses the value of similar late-model vehicles on the used market. If this happens just as you return your vehicle, and you have a closed-end lease, it's the leasing company that takes the hit.

An open-end lease, by contrast, makes the lessee – that's you – responsible for market conditions. Open-end leases often look good because the monthly charges are lower. And while there are limits to your liability, you're better off avoiding open-end agreements.

Most leases are closed-end. However, at least one company has offered a closed-end lease that should have been considered an open-end contract under some circumstances. Lessees had the option to buy the vehicle at the end of the lease, but they had to declare their intentions when they signed. For those who refused to buy, the lease remained a closed-end instrument. For those who took the purchase option, the contract became, in effect, an open-end lease. The lessee immediately became responsible for the trade-in value. One of the beauties of leasing, under most contracts, is that you can decide to buy at the end of the lease when you know the value of the vehicle and can compare it to the buyout price.

The Trouble with a Valuable Trade-In

If you are about to sign your first lease, many dealers will try to get you to take cash back for your trade-in rather than use it to reduce the cap cost. There are two reasons for this.

First, the higher the cap cost, the higher the rent charge can be – which increases the leasing company's profit potential. Second, with leasing generating such high levels of customer loyalty, the dealer doesn't want to lose you next time around. Like the chess player who thinks several moves ahead, the dealer knows that a large down payment will give you an unusually low monthly payment. When you come back for lease number two, however, you'll have little or no equity to use to reduce the cap cost. A high cap cost can significantly raise your monthly payment and, the dealer fears, scare you away from a second lease.

By encouraging you to take the value of your car back in cash and invest it elsewhere, the dealer gets you used to paying a typical leasing charge. Three years down the road, the dealer figures, you won't object to the payments for leased vehicle number two.

Reduced Incentives

Manufacturers recently have suffered significant losses on leases because they guessed wrong on the vehicles' resale values. As a result, they are beginning to appreciate customers who buy and have reduced the generous leasing incentives common in the past.

Leasing companies are also adopting more realistic residual values, which in turn increase the monthly payments or require a larger down payment or cap cost reduction. Consequently, you may find leasing less attractive than it once was.

The Verdict

Leasing is neither good nor bad. It is, rather, just another option to consider. Whether it makes sense for you depends on many factors, including the level of subsidy from the manufacturer and whether you have a high-yield investment option for the money you save on monthly payments.

If you keep a car for a long time, tend to drive many miles, abuse your car, have pride of ownership, don't care about driving a new vehicle or have weaker credit (leasing companies often demand a more creditworthy customer than do lending companies), leasing probably is not for you. And if subvention isn't available, leasing can be the more expensive option.

Still, leasing has its place and you might find it ideal. Just be sure to look before you plunge into the agreement.

Leasing Checklist

	Yes	No
1. Can you be sure you won't drive more than 45,000 miles over the next three years?	❑	❑
2. Do you take very good care of your vehicle's appearance?	❑	❑
3. Do you take very good care of your vehicle's mechanical systems?	❑	❑
4. Do you buy a new car every three or four years?	❑	❑
5. Do you finance your new car purchases?	❑	❑
6. Do you have good credit?	❑	❑
7. Is *not* owning a car unimportant to you?	❑	❑
8. Is driving a new car important to you?	❑	❑
9. You aren't concerned that you will always have car payments.	❑	❑
10. Can you get collision and comprehensive insurance economically?	❑	❑

Add up your score. Give yourself two points if you answered yes to question No. 1 and one point for each additional question you answered yes.

Total score:	8 to 11 points	Leasing is probably for you.
	6 or 7 points	Leasing might be OK for you.
	5 points or less	Buy your next vehicle.

Checklist for Leasing a New Car

This is not a lease contract, an agreement or a legal document. If you're considering leasing a new car, read and use this form carefully, and read the leasing agreement carefully as well. You may have to negotiate the following amounts with the leasing company.

1. Manufacturer's suggested retail price $_____
    (the sticker price)

2. Dealer-installed options you want on the car and
    their costs

    Option A_____ Cost $_____

    Option B_____ Cost $_____

    Option C_____ Cost $_____

    Option D_____ Cost $_____

    Total cost of dealer-installed options $_____

3. Total cost of vehicle (add items 1 and 2) $_____

4. Cost of taxes, title and license $_____

5. Lease acquisition fee (if you buy the vehicle, you $_____
    don't pay this amount)

6. Amount of refundable security deposit $_____

7.   Optional insurance or warranty items

You aren't required to buy these items. Your lessor should be able to provide you with a detailed explanation of what these products and services are and their benefits to you. These items will increase your monthly lease payments unless the lessor provides them free of charge. Consider your need for each item carefully to decide if you can afford these extra costs. If you still want these items, you may be able to buy them from independent suppliers at a lower cost than what the dealer or leasing company will charge you.

Credit life insurance and disability	$_____
Extended warranty	$_____
Vehicle maintenance agreement	$_____
GAP coverage (often included in the lease)	$_____

Total cost of insurance or warranty items $_____

8.   Total capitalized cost of the lease $_____
(add items 3, 4, 5, 7)

9.   Initial payment

Your initial payment – whether as cash or a trade-in or both – can be used to reduce the capitalized cost of the lease, thereby reducing your monthly payment. All or part of this amount may also be used to pay for costs not included in the total capitalized cost.

Amount of your cash payment $_____

Amount for your trade-in $_____

(This may be a negative number
if you owe more than the vehicle
is worth.)

Total initial payment $_____

Of this total, the amount being used to reduce the $_____
capitalized cost

Of this total, the amount being used to pay the following amounts, which are not included in the capitalized cost.

Item_____Cost $_____

Item_____Cost $_____

Item_____Cost $_____

Total amount for additional items $_____

The amount being used to reduce the capitalized cost $_____
added to the cost for the additional items should be
the same as your initial payment.

10.   Amount you're financing (total capitalized cost of $_____
lease MINUS your initial total payment amount)

11.   Cost of borrowing money (the interest rate)   _____%

To convert a money factor to an interest rate,
multiply the money factor by 2400. Leases don't
actually charge interest, but the cost of the money
needed to acquire the vehicle is reflected in the
payment you'll make.

12. Residual value of the vehicle at the end of the lease term (This will be specified in the lease contract. A higher residual value reduces your monthly payment.) $_____

13. Amount of your monthly payment $_____

    Total number of payments _____

    Total amount of payments (monthly payment x number of payments) $_____

14. Cost to break the lease early $_____

    If you decide to break the lease before the lease ends, you must return the vehicle to the leasing company and you'll be responsible for some or all of the remaining payments and the termination fee, if any. You would also have to pay for excess mileage charges, an amount for excess wear and tear, and a purchase option fee.

    Disposal fee, which is due at the end of the lease when you return the vehicle rather than purchase it $_____

Take This Second Look at Your Lease

15. Total capitalized cost (from line 8) $_____

16. Residual value (from line 12) $_____

17. The difference (line 15 MINUS line 16) $_____

18. Amount you'll pay each month under the contract's terms $_____

19. Divide line 17 (the difference) by the number of $_____
    monthly payments you'll make under the leasing
    contract

20. Subtract line 19 from line 18 $_____
    This is the amount you'll pay each month in rent
    (less taxes and other charges for any additional
    services). This amount includes the cost of money
    and profit for the leasing company. For leases calling
    for a single initial payment, compare that payment
    to the total amount in line 17.

CHAPTER

5

Buying a Used Car

In This Chapter

• • • • • • • • • • • •

- Why used cars and trucks can you save you money
- When used cars may not reduce your cost per mile
- How to avoid buying someone else's troubles
- Where to buy used cars
- How to test a used car or truck
- Why you should have a professional technician inspect the vehicle

Used-car salespeople have a saying: "Everybody drives a used car." True enough. Not everybody, however, buys a car that has been owned, registered and driven by a stranger. Still, if you look solely at total sales volume for a given year, at least four used cars are bought for each new vehicle purchased.

Buying a used vehicle has some obvious advantages and disadvantages. Perhaps the most compelling reason is to save money. Pocketbook considerations alone probably account for the popularity of used vehicles, even among people who easily could afford a new model.

The reason why a used car can be a good buy is simple. Depreciation – the loss of value that starts the minute a new car is driven off the seller's lot – takes its biggest toll during the first three years of a vehicle's life. It's not uncommon for a vehicle to lose half its value in that time; some lose 60 percent.

During this same period, most owners drive about 45,000 miles. That's only about one-third of a vehicle's potential mileage. So, buying a used car is a bit like purchasing three quarts of gasoline in a gallon container but only paying for two. You didn't get the whole gallon, but you got a great deal.

The savings don't stop with the purchase price, either. Used cars cost less to insure and can save you money on registration fees and annual taxes as well. The sales tax on a used vehicle is lower, too.

With the popularity of short-term leasing over the past decade, used-car customers have had ample supplies of low-mileage, late-model vehicles to choose from. These used cars often look new and perform nearly as well as their brand-new brethren, yet cost far less. And lots of older used cars are available – some that are very much used – starting at less than $3,000.

Finally, for people who find the overwhelming variety of new cars and trucks inadequate, the used vehicle market offers a broader selection of makes and models. It consists of just about every vehicle sold in recent years. And if you can't find exactly what you want today, just wait. Someone, somewhere will offer it for sale tomorrow.

The Disadvantages

If the advantages of buying a used vehicle are well known, so are the disadvantages. Surely you've heard many reasons for avoiding a used car or truck. *Used cars may not be the bargain you think they are. . . . You're buying someone else's troubles. . . . You don't know how long it'll last. . . . You're buying expensive maintenance and repairs. . . . The previous owner used the car to teach his son to drive, then loaned him the vehicle after he had his license. . . . You may buy an unsafe vehicle and then you're stuck with it.*

There may be elements of truth in these statements, both for and against used-car ownership. Let's look at them in greater detail.

'Used Cars Cost Less'

While it's true that almost all used cars cost less than a comparable new model, not all used vehicles cost enough less to justify buying one. If you plan to buy a car, either used or new, and keep it for as long as possible, and you want a make and model that holds its resale value, there's good reason to consider a new vehicle.

For example, if the 3-year-old car you want has depreciated only 40 percent while in the hands of its first owner, you could end up paying 70 percent of its original sticker price when you buy it used. The 10 percent difference between the 60 percent that the first owner received and the 70 percent that you will pay covers the dealer's costs and profit.

So why isn't this a good buy for you? A typical 3-year old used car has gone 45,000 miles and has a life expectancy of at least 150,000 miles. That means about 30 percent of its useful life, as measured in miles, has been taken by the first owner. If you're going to pay just 30 percent less for this vehicle than the first owner paid when it was new, you're not gaining much in this transaction. Clearly, on a cost-per-mile basis, you'd be better off buying another brand of car that depreciates faster. Fortunately, for used-car buyers, there are many models that do this while still delivering dependable service.

If, however, you're convinced that this model, which commands 70 percent of its value after three years of use, is for you, and prices for new ones have remained relatively stable for the past three years, then you can justify buying a new car — assuming, of course, that you can afford the higher price of the new vehicle.

Used cars that command 70 percent of their original price when resold, even when 3 years old, are called first-tier vehicles. They are excellent buys for their first owner and usually provide subsequent buyers with very good performance. They will not, however, deliver the same value for the dollar that many second-tier vehicles can provide.

Second-tier vehicles are those that are well designed and well made, yet, for some reason, don't generate enthusiasm among either new- or used-car buyers. As a result, they depreciate more than first-tier vehicles – often, much more. That makes them a much better value. You frequently can find vehicles that still have 70 percent of their useful mileage selling for only 50 percent of their original price.

Many second-tier vehicles are dependable, safe, comfortable and even fun to drive – and late-model examples sell for thousands of dollars less than first-tier vehicles of the same age and condition. This is where used-vehicle consumers get their money's worth.

'Used Cars Are Guaranteed Trouble'

Some used cars are nothing more than one continuous headache from the first mile to the last. They're undependable. They're money pits – you throw dollars in and, occasionally, get transportation in exchange. They don't run long between repairs – and cash infusions.

At least with a new car, you have a warranty and, depending on the state, the protection of a "lemon law." With a used vehicle, you're probably on your own.

Fortunately, this worst-case scenario is rare. The reality is that most used cars are very dependable. Not all are, of course, but there are steps you can take to weed out the duds before you buy. More on that later.

'Used Cars Don't Have the Latest Technology'

An older car certainly won't have the latest safety advances. Late-model used vehicles, however, may have all the features you want. Dual air bags are almost a given. Antilock brakes have been around a while too, so there's a good chance you can find a used vehicle that has them. Side air bags also are becoming common, as are electronic stability enhancement systems, traction control and advanced infant-seat mounting attachments. Generally, the more expensive the car was when new, the more likely it is to have these safety devices. Some moderately priced vehicles have them as well.

Selecting a Model

As with the purchase of a new car or truck, your search for a used vehicle should start with an accurate assessment of your needs and wants. See the new-car needs assessment in Chapter 1 for advice.

Next, set your budget. New-car buyers can spend this entire amount on a vehicle. The smart used-car buyer, however, uses 80 percent to 90 percent of the budget on the vehicle, taxes and registration and keeps the rest in reserve. Even for a late-model car, you should keep about $1,000 on hand for repairs and maintenance that you'll want to do shortly after buying the vehicle. For an older car, hold back $2,000.

Now you can start searching for a vehicle in your price range. As a used-vehicle buyer, you'll have many more options than someone who wants a new car. If your budget is $16,000, for instance, few brands or models will be beyond your reach. On the new-car lot, you could maybe afford a compact. On the used market, you have the luxury of choosing relatively new compacts, midsize sedans and even full-size vehicles. If you are willing to look at older vehicles, you can even find luxury models, including some pretty exotic foreign models that you'd never be able to afford new.

A new-to-you-but-still-used Mercedes-Benz, BMW or Jaguar gracing your driveway is a wonderful fantasy, but remember: the older the car, the more likely it is to need maintenance and repairs in the near future. And cars that were expensive new tend to be more expensive to repair as they age. Not only are the mechanical and electrical systems more complex, but you're less likely to find lower cost alternatives to factory replacements. And because those parts are produced in smaller numbers, they also tend to be more expensive. Finally, while there are any number of repair technicians who are good at fixing garden-variety Fords, Toyotas, Chevys and Hondas, there are far fewer wrench wielders who can tackle luxury and sporty brands. Expect to pay more for their services.

One way to help keep future repair and maintenance costs under control is to follow this rule: Buy no used car or truck that you could not afford new, if you doubled your budget. In other words, if you plan to spend $14,000, don't buy a car that sells for more than $28,000 new. This gives you a budget framework for future maintenance and repairs. If you're on a really small budget, you might want to stick to cars that cost no more than $20,000 when new, in today's dollars.

Research the Car

Local libraries can be a good place to start your research. They frequently stock buyers' guides, which contain full rundowns on all makes and models for previous years. If you want a 3-year old family sedan, SUV or minivan, for example, a guide from three years ago can give you an idea how the vehicle performed when it was new and how it stacked up against competitors.

Next, consult a used-car-pricing guide. Pick out models that performed well but have since depreciated the most. These are your best values, assuming they've stood up well to normal use.

Some buyers' guides outline repair costs. This is interesting information, but not always a predictor of what you'll pay to keep your car on the road. For example, replacement alternators can cost anywhere from $150 to $500. Don't automatically limit yourself to cars with the $150 alternator since the guide can't predict whether the alternator will fail. Just because you like the car with the $500 alternator doesn't mean you'll have to replace it, only that it'll cost $500 if you do. Besides, if the model with the $150 alternator experiences alternator failure four times as often − a point not mentioned in many guides − you're better off buying the car with more expensive parts. It helps to look at the frequency of repair record, which is available in some guides.

On www.aaa.com, you can research prices and vehicle history reports on the used cars you're interested in.

Where to Buy

Now it's time to see what's really out there at a price you can afford. Start by looking in the newspaper classified sections, used-car-shopping guides or on the Internet. You'll find four main sources of used cars. They are:

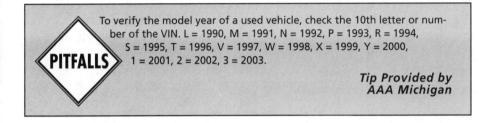

To verify the model year of a used vehicle, check the 10th letter or number of the VIN. L = 1990, M = 1991, N = 1992, P = 1993, R = 1994, S = 1995, T = 1996, V = 1997, W = 1998, X = 1999, Y = 2000, 1 = 2001, 2 = 2002, 3 = 2003.

Tip Provided by AAA Michigan

New-Car Dealers – Dealerships specialize in newer and, therefore, more expensive used cars. Many of the used vehicles they offer are late-model trade-ins or vehicles that have just come off lease. Since many leased vehicles are sold at auction, the dealer may not originally have sold or serviced the ones you see on the lot.

Just because you bought a used car that the dealer got from an auction doesn't mean you can't get its service history. If the previous owner or lessee used dealer service, the complete record of what was done to the car may be on the manufacturer's computer. Some manufacturers maintain a computerized service record system, which dealers can access through the vehicle identification number.

Nonetheless, since manufacturers usually offer their best, late-model off-lease vehicles only to franchised dealers, a new-car dealer's used-car lot is a good place to look if you want a late-model, low-mileage used car. Some vehicles you find here are still covered by part of the original new-car warranty. Many are even certified under a manufacturer's program that extends coverage to a second buyer.

Used-Car Dealers – Not affiliated with any new-vehicle franchise, used-car dealers usually specialize in older vehicles with higher mileage. What you find on these lots will almost always cost less than the used vehicles at the new-car place. But remember the risks of buying an older vehicle. In addition, some used-car lots are tenuous operations at best. They frequently fail, leaving buyers who have a claim based on a dealer-issued warranty with no place to turn.

Private Parties – Individual owners also sell their cars. These deals are often called "casual sales." In the case of late-model vehicles, these cars often are in exceptionally nice condition and the owners want top dollar for them. In other cases, the owners simply want – or need – to sell and would like to get a little more than a dealer offered as a trade.

> **<PITFALLS>** Usually you're better off avoiding vehicles that have been modified by a previous owner. Such modifications include the installation of aftermarket wheels and tires. These changes may have an adverse effect on vehicle ride, handling, safety and operation. They may also complicate future repairs.

When you look at a vehicle offered for sale by a private party, be sure to ask to see all the receipts covering maintenance and repairs. These will give you an idea of the problems that the seller may have encountered with the vehicle, as well as the maintenance schedule. Be suspicious if these records are unavailable or show gaps in either time or mileage.

Sometimes you can gauge the quality of a vehicle by the owner's demeanor and home, but don't count on it. More than one seller with an immaculate home has ignored vehicular maintenance for years. Likewise, many a slob proves to be a vehicle fanatic who has done everything by the book and has the records – albeit in jumbled order – to prove it. Remember, too, that private parties don't offer a warranty and some may not be what they seem. Abuses you should watch for are detailed in Chapter 14.

> **<PITFALLS>** Manufacturers attach a 17-character vehicle identification number, the VIN, to each new vehicle. If you come across a vehicle with a non-standard VIN – something with fewer than 17 numbers and letters, for instance – it may have been stolen, wrecked and rebuilt, plucked from floodwaters, or gone through some other process that prompted a state to issue a new VIN. Buyer beware.
>
> *Tip Provided by AAA Washington*

Auctions – From government agencies and businesses to dealer-only sales, most cars will be auctioned to a new buyer at some point in their lives. The place to go for the best price is a dealer-only auction. Unless you're a dealer, however, or know one who'll get you in and then bid for you, your chance of picking up a car here at the wholesale price is nonexistent. Not even dealers can get into all auctions. Some are held by automakers for their franchised dealers only. Lexus, for example, auctions its recently acquired lease returns to Lexus dealers only. If none of the Lexus dealers present want a particular car, it'll go to a multi-make auction where any dealer can buy it.

Before the auction, dealers can look at the cars and may be able to take them for a test drive. Generally, however, they rely on the seller to tell them about the car's condition. Once they buy the car, they look it over again before leaving the site. This is when they can note any problems and file a claim against a seller, if necessary.

At public auctions held by governmental agencies and businesses, the vehicles frequently are well used or even abused. Used police cruisers, cars from government agencies and confiscated vehicles are offered to the top bidder. Your chance to take one for a test drive is limited if not nonexistent. These sales are best for buyers who know exactly what they're doing.

Finding the Good, Rejecting the Bad

Realistically, you'll probably buy a used vehicle from a new-car dealer, a used-car dealer or a private party. No matter whom you buy it from, follow these rules:

- Before you buy a used vehicle without an extended warranty certified by the manufacturer, have an independent auto technician examine the vehicle thoroughly. You'll have to pay, but it's money well spent. No matter how much you like the car or how highly you regard the seller, have the car checked by a professional technician with no financial interest in the sale. Do this before you sign a contract or put down a deposit.

- Don't buy the vehicle first and then have it inspected by a technician, even though the dealer offers to take it back. Many such take-back deals only let you apply your payment to another car on the dealer's lot. Also, money-back guarantees often don't cover sales taxes, dealer fees or registration costs. Some dealers also deduct for the miles you drove while you had the car.

- If you're not comfortable telling the seller – perhaps a friend, family member or co-worker – that you want a technician to look at the vehicle, don't buy from this person. You might be better off buying from a stranger, so there's no danger of damaging a valued personal relationship if the deal goes wrong.

A professional auto technician's evaluation can cost about $100, so you should make every effort to eliminate cars that are likely to fail. You can do this yourself, even if you have no mechanical background or skills. Simply perform the following tests on every vehicle you consider buying. If you reject a vehicle that a professional would find acceptable, that's OK. There are lots of other good used cars out there. Some AAA clubs offer used-car inspection programs; check with your local AAA club for an Approved Auto Repair facility where they perform inspections. Only if you're looking at something rare should you consider having a professional evaluate a car or truck that fails one of the following tests.

Do-It-Yourself Evaluations

So you've never evaluated a used car. That's perfectly OK. You can still do a surprisingly good job. And since you'll have any vehicle that passes your examination checked out by a professional, your high-wire vehicle evaluation act has a good strong safety net beneath it. So, don't worry. Grab a flashlight, small mirror, measuring tape, tire-pressure gauge and weak magnet, then perform these steps one at a time.

Several of the following steps cover checks you can make to determine if the vehicle was in an accident and then repaired. Most body repairs, even those that are noticeable, will not detract from a vehicle's use, but some accidents cause significant damage. If repairs to parts and mechanical systems you can't see were not done properly, the vehicle could be unsafe. The professional technician you hire to check the vehicle should examine repaired areas of the body structure very carefully.

- Check for possible recalls of the vehicle you're considering by logging on to the National Highway Traffic Safety Administration website at www.nhtsa.gov. Click on Recalls, follow the prompts and enter the vehicle's year, make and model. Within seconds, you'll get a list of recalls. When you examine the car, record its 17-character VIN. Later, you can check with the vehicle's manufacturer to see if this particular vehicle was subject to any of the recalls on the government's list. If it was, you should then be able to determine if the vehicle was returned to a dealer for the necessary service.

- Pick the right day. You don't want to look at a car in rain or snow or in the dark. While you can shop for a used vehicle under these conditions, you don't want to start a thorough examination in bad weather or at night.

- Show up at least half an hour early if you have an appointment to see the car. Private owners may do all sorts of things to a car before a potential buyer shows up. They might warm up the engine to hide a cold start problem or empty the trunk of extra brake fluid and engine coolant used to replenish fluids because of leaks.

- Look at the car from a distance and from all angles in natural light. You may detect poor quality body work using this technique.

- From afar, you want to see that the proportions of the car are correct. While parked on a level surface, does the front or rear of the car tend to droop? From the front or rear, does one side seem to droop? Are all the body panels exactly the same color and do they reflect light the same way? If not, some body work probably was done. If the car is newer, you might want to reject the vehicle for this reason, even though most repairs won't affect your use of the vehicle. Body work on a relatively new car, however, reduces its value. The fact that the repairs are so visible suggests that the quality of the work was substandard.

- If the vehicle passes the visual test from a distance, it's time to take a look up close. Check again for any problems with the paint or body panels. Look down the sides of the car and examine the hood, roof and truck lid. Look at the car from a shallow angle. Often you can spot ripples in the surface or obvious fender or door alignment problems. Both are evidence of previous body damage and a poor repair.

- In addition to color mismatches, you want to look for uneven paint applications, differences in the paint surface texture, color shifts and overspray. Overspray is that little strip of paint on the edge of the door handle, molding, gasket or glass. It happens when the masking tape isn't aligned properly to keep paint off of the neighboring parts. Rubber blocks designed to hold the hood in proper alignment when closed also are subject to overspray, as are the rubber gaskets around the doors and trunk lid.

- Check all the gaps between body panels. They should be even and uniform. Run your finger along them to see how closely they're aligned. Check for differences in height as well as for varying distances between the panels. Make sure the gaps between the hood and the fenders are equal on both sides. Do the same exam on the trunk lid. Check the molding applications around the windshield or rear window as well. Uneven gaps often mean poor body repair. Repair after a front collision, for instance, might leave a gap that's thin between the hood and fender at the cowl but wider as you look toward the front bumper. If you suspect body damage, don't hesitate to open the hood or trunk and take some measurements. For example, the distance from the upper left corner of the trunk opening to the lower right should equal the measurement from the upper right corner to the lower left. You can take the same measurements at the hood opening. Variations should be minor, no more than one-eighth inch. Be sure that you measure precisely.

- If you're suspicious about a body panel, take out your weak magnet and see if it sticks to the surface. Many cars have some plastic or aluminum panels. However, if the panel is metal and a relatively weak magnet won't stick, you'll know that a repair shop used filler to straighten out dents or patch rusty areas.

- Open and close each door, the trunk and the hood. Make sure all the latches and hardware work smoothly and properly. While each door is open, use your mirror to look at its bottom for rust or mud. If there's not enough light, use the flashlight too. You shouldn't have to slam doors or lids for them to close properly. They also should move through their entire range of motion without binding or squeaking.

- Check all external lights and mirrors. Inspect wipers and washers.

- Look at the engine compartment. It should be free of oil and coolant leaks, which tend to trap sand and dust and keep it stuck to the motor. An older car with a pristine engine compartment, however, should generate a certain amount of suspicion. Some dealers simply clean the engine compartment of every car they offer for sale. Others reserve the cleaning for cars that need it. These cars had an oily mess under the hood, probably as a result of fluid leaks. If every used car has a completely clean engine bay, then the dealer probably gives them all a wash. If only a few show signs of a thorough scrubbing, think twice. Excessive leakage is not a good sign.

- While you're under the hood and the engine is cold, check all the fluid levels. Needless to say, nothing should be too low or too high.

- Engine oil should be reasonably clean, somewhere between the golden color of fresh, clean fluid and slightly darker — but not pitch black, except on diesels — shade of reasonably used oil. The dipstick should be free of varnish deposits and there should be no milky white foam visible anywhere on the dipstick or around the seal at the top. White foam means moisture in the crankcase. If you're lucky it's condensation. But it could also be engine coolant. If you find foam as well as water droplets on the dipstick, reject the car. If you find only foam on a car that otherwise seems to be a good buy, ask your technician to investigate the problem when he checks the vehicle.

- Engine coolant should be clear and colorful. Depending on the formula, it could be blue-green, yellow, orange or red. It should not be rusty or cloudy, dirty or muddy. If it is, reject the car.

- Power steering fluid should be properly filled. The pump, the hoses going to it and the point where these hoses meet the steering mechanism should be clean and dry with no oil or sand and dirt that leaking oil would attract. Some cars have a power steering reservoir that sits high in the engine compartment with only one hose leading from it. This is a remote fill point. Follow the hose down to the front of the engine to find the pump. The pump and the hoses going to and from it should be clean and dry. If you find power steering fluid leaks in a car that otherwise looks good, have a professional technician examine it.

- Automatic transmission fluid must be checked when the engine is hot and running to get an accurate reading. Even with the engine off, however, the fluid should be clear and, in most cases, light red. If it looks burned or black, is bubbly or seems to be leaking around the filler and check tube, be cautious. If the car looks OK otherwise, mention the transmission fluid to your technician when the car is checked. You can't always check the automatic transmission fluid. Some newer cars have sealed transmissions with no dipstick.

- Battery electrolyte should be clear and above the plates. The battery case should be clean and the terminal connections should be tight and free of frothy corrosion. The battery should be firmly mounted to the battery tray so it won't bounce around on a rough road. If the battery is one that cannot be opened, check its test-eye.

- Check the belts and hoses. Belts should be free of major cracks and reasonably tight. They should not look glazed or polished. When squeezed, hoses should be flexible but firm. If they feel spongy or are brittle, they need replacing. They shouldn't leak where they're attached to the engine or radiator.

- While you're under the hood, look for signs of damage or recent repairs. Wiring harnesses that have been broken apart and then sloppily re-bound, for instance, should make you somewhat suspicious.

- Examine the interior. Use a mirror and flashlight to look under the instrument panel and seats for mud or rust. Either could suggest that the car was in a flood, which can cause years of electrical problems. If you find mud or rust, reject the car.

- Examine the pedals, the driver's seat and the driver's armrest pad. They won't show signs of wear for 60,000 miles or more. If they're severely worn but the odometer shows low mileage, be suspicious. Check seat operation and seat belts.

- Check the operation of all windows, the tilt wheel, hood latch, trunk release, cigarette lighter and clock.

- Verify that all accessories work properly.

- The trunk should be clean and dry. Remove the spare tire to look for moisture and rust at the bottom. Check for jack and tools. Examine the spare.

- Check the tires next. The tread should be evenly worn and its depth should be ample. Use your pressure gauge to check the inflation of each tire, including the spare in the trunk. Grossly uneven tire pressures or a nearly flat spare suggest that the owner didn't follow the basic maintenance schedule very well.

- Now put the key in the ignition and turn the car on but don't engage the starter. All the warning lights should be on. If the "service engine soon," "ABS," "oil pressure" and "battery" warning lights don't come on (assuming the car has them), reject the car. Warning lights are designed to signal problems with the engine, electrical or braking systems. A light that doesn't come on is a red flag. The owner may have disconnected it because of a problem. Unscrupulous owners or dealers sometimes remove the warning light bulb on a car with a problem, then hope the potential buyer doesn't notice. Be aware, however, that some cars with a voltmeter and oil pressure gauge may not have warning lights for these functions.

- With the radio and the heater or air conditioning blower turned off, start the engine. The motor should be cold. Even so, the engine should start quickly with no more than two or three seconds of cranking. You shouldn't notice any unusual noises from the starting motor or the engine. Once started, the engine should settle down instantly to a smooth, steady idle.

- With the engine running and your foot on the brake, shift an automatic transmission through the gears. The transmission should engage quickly in either reverse or drive. A delay of more than two seconds suggests transmission trouble. It could be a simple problem such as a clogged filter screen or low fluid level.

- In a manual transmission vehicle, you should hear no unusual noises with the engine running and the clutch pressed to the floor. Shifting to neutral and releasing the clutch shouldn't cause any noise either.

- Now press hard on the brake pedal. You'll reach a point where the pedal stops moving toward the floor. Once you're there, press hard for a whole minute. Time the full 60 seconds on your watch. The pedal should not sink toward the floor or soften during the test. If it does, reject the car. In some cars with ABS, a pedal subjected to this kind of pressure will reach the floor. If the brakes seem to operate normally otherwise, have your service technician check the braking system.

> **SAFETY** If you want a truck with antilock brakes, determine what kind of ABS is on the vehicle. Some trucks offered only rear-wheel ABS when they were new. They'll have ABS symbols in all the right places, but rear-wheel ABS is not nearly as good as four-wheel ABS. The front wheels could lock in an emergency stop, causing you to lose steering control.

The Test Drive

Now take the car for a drive. Before you go, however, make sure the car is registered and insured or has an appropriate dealer's plate. This is especially important if you're buying from a private party.

In many states, private sellers will remove the license plate from the old car and put it on the new vehicle when they register it. When potential buyers want to test drive the old vehicle, they slap the plate that now belongs on the new car back onto the old car. If the police stop you, you'll be ticketed for driving an unregistered vehicle and possibly for driving without insurance. Take a couple of minutes to check the paperwork before you start out. It's worth it.

> **PITFALLS** If you are selling a vehicle, remember to keep insurance on the old vehicle after you get your new car or truck. That way, when a potential buyer takes it out for a test drive there will be coverage. Never let a potential buyer take the vehicle out alone.

The car should perform well with the engine cold and should continue to run well as it warms up. The test drive should be long enough to bring the car's engine up to full operating temperature. You'll want to drive the car much the same way as you plan to use it. But spend some time on the highway too, even if you don't do a lot of highway driving.

Highway driving often reveals problems that remain hidden at lower speeds. These problems could include vibrations from the drivetrain, wheels or tires or overheating that occurs only at higher speeds.

As you start, be aware of how the engine and transmission operate. Acceleration should be smooth. The transmission, whether manual or automatic, should shift properly. The engine and drivetrain should be free of vibration and roughness during both gentle and more rapid acceleration. If the vehicle has a manual transmission, the clutch should engage smoothly.

Head for a straight, smooth, flat, lightly traveled road and see if the car pulls to the left or right. Here's how: Bring your speed up to 45 mph and loosen your grip on the steering. Don't completely take your hands off the wheel, of course. Any tendency to pull should be investigated. Maybe it's nothing more than a minor alignment problem. Or maybe it's evidence of improperly repaired crash damage.

Now make sure there's no one behind you and — maintaining your light grip on the wheel — apply the brakes firmly enough to stop quickly. Don't, however, simulate an emergency stop. As with your first test, the car should not pull in either direction. You should notice no vibration in the brake pedal or steering wheel, nor should you hear any squealing.

As you drive, note any unusual vibrations or noises. Smooth roads are best for this test. Be sure to accelerate briskly onto a limited-access highway at least once. Again, the engine should be free of vibrations and the transmission should shift smoothly.

Once you're satisfied that the car performs properly, head back to the seller's base. When you arrive, let the engine idle as you check all the lights and accessories. Everything should work properly, from windows to directional signals. Do your checks in a logical order and keep an eye on the engine temperature gauge. It should remain rock steady, even with the air conditioning going on a hot day. If the engine temperature begins to climb, or if you run into several non-working accessories, reject the car.

A vehicle that passes all of these tests is probably a very good buy...but not always. That's why, once you find a car that you can afford and that passes these tests to your satisfaction, you should arrange for a professional technician to take a look, too.

Your technician should drive the vehicle to make sure that it operates normally. Then the technician should examine the car on a lift. This is the only way to get a good look at the fuel tank, fuel lines, exhaust system, suspension system, tires and brake lines. While the car is on the lift, each wheel should be pulled and the brakes examined. The technician should also search for evidence of improper body repair work and rust.

With the car on the ground, the technician should scan the computer for any trouble codes, then run the engine with an engine analyzer attached. Exhaust gasses should be checked and a proper compression test performed. This compression test means removing the spark plugs and using the starting motor to turn the engine over while a compression gauge records the pressures. Do not accept an engine balance test as a substitute for a proper compression test.

Finally, a complete under-the-hood inspection is a must. The technician should record all findings in writing. Any problems should include a repair estimate. Now it's time for the technician to render a judgment. One of three things will happen:

1. The car will be an absolute gem with few problems or no problems at all. Armed with this knowledge, you can buy with confidence.

2. The car will be a dud. It has lots of problems you missed, and it would cost a bundle to fix. Keep looking. Learning this now, before you sign a contract, could save you thousands of dollars, not to mention the inconvenience of having an unreliable car.

3. The car is basically good, but it has some problems. While nothing major stands out, there are some things you should address. Perhaps the shock absorbers are worn, the exhaust system is almost rusted through or a brake line is frayed. Armed with this knowledge, you can go back and negotiate a better price so that you can then do the repairs yourself, or you can insist that the repairs be made before you buy the car.

Occasionally, an owner or dealership will refuse to let you have your technician inspect the car. This is an absolute deal-breaker. The classified section is full of used cars. You don't need to buy this one. Shop elsewhere.

Certification Programs

Some cars and trucks, usually low-mileage vehicles that were leased by the automaker's captive leasing company, are certified under programs that extend the warranty coverage to the second buyer. In some cases, the drivetrain, the engine, transmission, differential and drive shafts, may be covered for up to seven years or 100,000 miles. Other late-model cars and trucks may come with significant portions of the original warranty available. Even these cars should be checked by a professional auto technician so that you can be sure there's no significant body damage or poor body repair work. A second opinion never hurts.

Certification programs are a good idea. Check on the premium you'll pay for coverage, however. Understand that these programs were created to help manufacturers sell large numbers of off-lease cars at a higher price. In many cases, automakers wanted to minimize losses caused by guessing too high on the vehicle's residual value.

Certifications often cover expensive items that don't usually break, such as engines, while leaving it up to the second buyer to fix air conditioning systems, electrical accessories or antilock brake system components – all of which are expensive and more likely to fail. If you buy a car under one of these programs, be sure that you read and understand what is and is not covered. If the program includes an extended warranty that offers true bumper-to-bumper coverage, you've found an excellent buy.

Certification programs usually start counting from the time the car was first placed in service. The promise of 70,000 miles of engine protection, for example, means a total of 70,000 miles – not another 70,000 for you after you buy the car. If the vehicle you like has traveled 30,000 miles, you're getting 40,000 more miles of coverage. There is nothing wrong with this, of course, but don't be misled.

For used-car buyers who want a safety net, an extended service contract – sometimes called an extended warranty – may be a useful purchase. This is especially true if a large repair bill would spell financial disaster for you. When you compare programs, read the terms carefully. Interestingly, simple terms that promise to cover all engine parts often are better than contracts that spell out in excruciating detail all of the covered items. These lists may leave out just enough to cost you a small fortune if you have a problem.

Be especially careful when reading the terms for consequential damages. If a major engine problem is caused by the failure of a non-covered part, some policies declare that none of the damage is covered.

Before buying any extended service contract, read the policy and compare it to others. In most areas, AAA offices offer these policies to members at member-advantage pricing, as well as to the general public. Some insurance companies also offer them.

Remember that the policy will be no better than the company that issues it. Many consumers have been left high and dry by companies that went out of business.

The Case of the Missing Title

Often when a private party wants to sell a car, he or she won't have the title. The title is documentation provided by the state government that declares that this person really owns the car and has a right to sell it.

When a bank or other lender finances the purchase, however, the lender holds the title. This lender is listed as a lien holder on the title.

The title serves as security for the lender. The only way the current owner can sell the car is to turn over the title to the new owner. And, the only way he or she can get the title is to pay off the loan.

This creates a problem for you, the next buyer. It would be nice if the current owner could simply go to the bank, withdraw the money from savings, pay off the loan and take the title. Many sellers, unfortunately, simply don't have the money.

You see the problem. You don't want to part with your money until you get the title. But the current owner can't obtain the title until you give him or her the money for the car.

How can you protect yourself in this situation? In most cases, the lien holder can confirm, in writing, how much is needed to pay off the loan. This sum is called the "buyout amount." You can then write your check for this amount, payable to the lien holder. If you're paying more for the car than the seller owes, you can make a payment for the difference – the asking price less the buyout amount – directly to the seller.

Once the lien holder receives your payment, he or she sends the title to the current owner, who must then sign it over to you. At this point, you can complete the transaction.

A more troublesome transaction involves a lien holder who is owed more than you are going to pay for the car. In this case you make your check out to the lien holder. Then you must insist that the owner provide a cashier's check to the lien holder for the difference. You then send both checks to the lien holder.

Under no circumstances should you accept a personal check from the current owner to pay off the amount of the loan. If the check fails to clear, you'll have to make up the difference to obtain the title.

Considering the added complexity, you might not want to buy a used vehicle if the current owner doesn't have physical possession of the title. Or you might reject the purchase if the buyout amount exceeds the purchase price of the vehicle.

Incidentally, even dealers sometimes have a problem obtaining a clear title. It is one of the nightmares of the used-car trade. Buyers have been kept waiting for months while lost titles are replaced or problems with final payments are cleared up. Be very careful when you deal with titles held by third parties.

When it comes to used cars and trucks, the good news is that you can afford to be selective. There are literally thousands of available models out there, each with an eager seller in search of a buyer. Never be afraid of letting one get away.

Used Vehicle Checklist

Current owner is_____

Current registration (if a private party)	Valid ❏	Invalid ❏
Car is insured	Yes ❏	No ❏

Title held by_____

Title is clean (i.e., not a lemon law buyback, salvage, etc.)	Yes ❏	No ❏
Reviewed Technical Service Bulletins for make and model	Yes ❏	No ❏
Reviewed Recalls for make and model	Yes ❏	No ❏
Reviewed owner's service record (check receipts for private party sale; dealership or manufacturer records when possible)	Yes ❏	No ❏

Visual Examination (Appearance problems include uneven gaps between panels, rippled sheet metal and other problems you observe.) Check if no problem is found.

	Appearance Problems	Color Mismatch	Over-spray	Rust	Operation Open/Close
Left front fender	❏	❏	❏	❏	Front Rear
Left door(s)	❏	❏	❏	❏	❏ ❏
Left rear fender	❏	❏	❏	❏	

	Appearance Problems	Color Mismatch	Over Spray	Rust	Operation Open/Close
Truck lid/ tailgate	❏	❏	❏	❏	❏
Rear bumper	❏	❏	❏	❏	
Right rear fender	❏	❏	❏	❏	Front Rear
Right door(s)	❏	❏	❏	❏	❏ ❏
Right front fender	❏	❏	❏	❏	
Hood	❏	❏	❏	❏	❏
Front bumper/ grill	❏	❏	❏	❏	Sunroof/ Convertible
Roof	❏	❏	❏	❏	❏

Tire Pressure/Condition/Inflation

	Tread depth	Pressure (cold)	Even Wear Yes No
Left front	_____/32nd inch	_____lbs/sq. in.	❏ ❏
Right front	_____/32nd inch	_____lbs/sq. in.	❏ ❏
Right rear	_____/32nd inch	_____lbs/sq. in.	❏ ❏
Left rear	_____/32nd inch	_____lbs/sq. in.	❏ ❏
Spare	_____/32nd inch	_____lbs/sq. in.	❏ ❏

Engine compartment check (only when engine is cold)

	OK	Low	High		OK	Low	High
Oil level	❑	❑	❑	Coolant level	❑	❑	❑
Power steering	❑	❑	❑	Brake fluid level	❑	❑	❑

Fluid Condition

	Acceptable	Not Acceptable
Oil (amber to dark brown, no froth)	❑	❑
Coolant (clear and clean, not foggy or dirty)	❑	❑
Brake (clear to light, not dark and opaque)	❑	❑

Battery

	Yes	No
Hold down tight	❑	❑
Cables tight	❑	❑
Connections clean	❑	❑
Electrolyte level good	❑	❑

(Note: Battery electrolyte is a strong acid. Use extreme caution when checking or have technician do it.)

Belts	Tension OK	Tension No	Cracked Yes	Cracked No	Worn/Glazed Yes	Worn/Glazed No
Serpentine	❑	❑	❑	❑	❑	❑
Alternator/water pump	❑	❑	❑	❑	❑	❑
Air conditioning	❑	❑	❑	❑	❑	❑
Power steering/air pump	❑	❑	❑	❑	❑	❑

Hoses	Firm	Spongy	Brittle	Bulging	Cracked
Upper radiator hose	❏	❏	❏	❏	❏
Lower radiator hose	❏	❏	❏	❏	❏
Heater hoses	❏	❏	❏	❏	❏
Reservoir hoses	❏	❏	❏	❏	❏

Instrument Panel Functions

Turn on key, but do not start engine. (Note: Not all warning lights will be present in all vehicles. "Check Engine" light may be labeled something else. Review the owner's manual.) Check for:

Engine Off	Yes	No	Not Applicable
Oil warning light on	❏	❏	❏
Or oil pressure gauge at zero psi	❏	❏	❏
Battery light on	❏	❏	❏
Or voltmeter at 12 to 13 volts	❏	❏	❏
Temperature gauge at "low"	❏	❏	❏
Temperature warning light on	❏	❏	❏
Brake warning light on	❏	❏	❏
ABS light on	❏	❏	❏
Traction control light on	❏	❏	❏
Check engine light on	❏	❏	❏

Engine Off	Yes	No	Not Applicable
Electronic odometer (no letters or symbols)	❏	❏	❏
Mechanical odometer (numbers spaced and aligned properly)	❏	❏	❏
Other warning lights	❏	❏	❏
_____	❏	❏	❏
_____	❏	❏	❏

Start Engine	Yes	No	Not Applicable
Oil warning light goes off promptly	❏	❏	❏
Or oil pressure gauge goes to normal range	❏	❏	❏
Battery light goes off	❏	❏	❏
Or voltmeter goes to 14 to 15 volts	❏	❏	❏
Temperature gauge at "low"	❏	❏	❏
Low temperature warning light stays on	❏	❏	❏
Brake warning light goes off	❏	❏	❏
ABS light goes off	❏	❏	❏
Traction control light goes off	❏	❏	❏
Check engine light goes off	❏	❏	❏

Start Engine	Yes	No	Not Applicable
Starter makes no unusual noice	❑	❑	❑
Engine is quiet within two seconds of start	❑	❑	❑
Other warning lights operate correctly	❑	❑	❑
_____	❑	❑	❑
_____	❑	❑	❑

Equipment	Works Correctly		
	Yes	No	Unsure
Driver's seat adjusts	❑	❑	❑
Passenger seat adjusts	❑	❑	❑
Interior lights	❑	❑	❑
Instrument lights	❑	❑	❑
Wipers (all speeds)	❑	❑	❑
Washer function	❑	❑	❑
Rear wiper	❑	❑	❑
Rear washer	❑	❑	❑
Heater	❑	❑	❑
Air conditioning	❑	❑	❑

Equipment	Works Correctly		
	Yes	No	Unsure
Defroster	❏	❏	❏
Vent system	❏	❏	❏
Blower (all speeds)	❏	❏	❏
Rear defrost function	❏	❏	❏
Radio	❏	❏	❏
Cassette/CD Player	❏	❏	❏
Driver's window	❏	❏	❏
Right front window	❏	❏	❏
Left rear window	❏	❏	❏
Right rear window	❏	❏	❏
Power/remote mirrors	❏	❏	❏
Door locks (all doors)			
Other accessories	❏	❏	❏
_____	❏	❏	❏
_____	❏	❏	❏
_____	❏	❏	❏

Lights (Check for brightness and proper operation. Light output from left and right bulbs should be adequate and matched. Check rear turn signals and brake lights with taillights on and off. Look for condensation — water droplets — under the lenses. Not all cars will have front/rear fog lights.)

	Works Correctly		Lens Unbroken/ Not cracked	Condensation	
	Yes	No		Yes	No
Headlights low beam	❏	❏	❏	❏	❏
Headlights high beam	❏	❏	❏	❏	❏
High beam indicator on instrument panel	❏	❏			
Front parking lights	❏	❏	❏	❏	❏
Front left side marker	❏	❏	❏	❏	❏
Front right side marker	❏	❏	❏	❏	❏
Fog lights	❏	❏	❏	❏	❏
Left front turn signal	❏	❏	❏	❏	❏
Right front turn signal	❏	❏	❏	❏	❏
Taillights	❏	❏	❏	❏	❏
Left rear side marker	❏	❏	❏	❏	❏
Right rear side marker	❏	❏	❏	❏	❏
Brake lights (include center unit)	❏	❏	❏	❏	❏

Lights	Works Correctly		Lens Unbroken/ Not cracked	Condensation	
	Yes	No		Yes	No
Left rear turn signal	❏	❏	❏	❏	❏
Right rear turn signal	❏	❏	❏	❏	❏
Backup lights	❏	❏	❏	❏	❏
Rear fog lights	❏	❏	❏	❏	❏
License plate lights	❏	❏	❏	❏	❏

Engine Running and On the Road	OK	Not OK
Engine idles smoothly	❏	❏
Engine idles at proper speed	❏	❏
Car accelerates smoothly	❏	❏
Car runs smoothly/quietly at speed	❏	❏
Transmission shifts smoothly, clutch engages smoothly (manual)	❏	❏
Car does not pull left or right on flat road	❏	❏
Car does not pull left or right while braking on flat road	❏	❏
Steering wheel does not vibrate at speed	❏	❏
Braking does not cause vibration	❏	❏
Engine temperature is normal after a few miles	❏	❏

Engine Running and On the Road	OK	Not OK
Oil light does not flicker while idling after engine is warm	❏	❏
With car stationary, turn steering wheel from lock to lock and check for smooth steering operation	❏	❏
Check engine light does not come on	❏	❏
Engine does not overheat on highway	❏	❏
Engine does not overheat while idling after warming up	❏	❏
No odors (coolant, burning, etc.) inside or outside after drive	❏	❏

USA Motors
100 Main Street
Anytown, VA 21234
(800) 555-1234

Sample Dealer Sticker

VIN : 1J4GZ58S7SC509327   Stock # : 33

1995 JEEP
GRAND CHEROKEE-6 CYL.
SW 4D LAREDO 4WD
46,750 Miles

---OPTIONAL EQUIPMENT---

Power Seat	$	75	Winch	$ 375
Alum/Alloy Wheels	$	50	Compact Disc Player	$ 50
AntiThft/Recover Sys	$	50		

N.A.D.A. RETAIL INCLUDING OPTIONS*   **$ 16,650**

---FEATURES AND ADJUSTMENTS---

Bucket Seats	Cargo Net
Custom Paint	Digital Clock
Disc Brakes	Floor Mats
Fog Lights	Fuel Injection
Intermittent Wipers	Keyless Entry
Locking Fuel Cap	Lumbar Support
Map Lights	Pinstriping
Power Mirrors	Rear Window Defroster
Rear Window Wiper	Rust Proofing
Tachometer	Trip Odometer
Vanity Mirrors	

RETAIL INCLUDING FEATURES & ADJUSTMENTS   **$ 16,650**

USA Motors price **$ 17,900**

CHAPTER

6

Selecting a Vehicle for a Beginning Driver

In This Chapter

• • • • • • • • • • • •

- When your teenager does not need a vehicle
- What to look for in a car for a teenager
- Vehicles and models to avoid for the beginning driver

For many teens, the prospect of acquiring their first car is exhilarating. But for parents, the prospect of their teen behind the wheel often causes the most worry. Their concern is not misplaced. No age group has a worse driving record than teenagers. Their lack of driving experience and willingness to accept high levels of risk are visible in the statistics that track motor vehicle deaths by age. Each year in this country, 30 out of 100,000 16- to 19-year-olds die in motor vehicle crashes. That compares to 13 motor vehicle deaths per 100,000 people in the 50- to 54 year-old age group.

It isn't an encouraging picture. No wonder parents worry about their teens and the cars they drive. But you can limit the risks your teens face.

Just as children get better at playing soccer or piano with practice, so, too, should their driving improve with practice and experience. A kid with a freshly issued license probably won't be able to tackle complex traffic situations with the steady hand of a more experienced motorist. One way parents can help is to limit a younger driver's time in traffic while they gain driving experience and maturity.

> **SAFETY** While teenage drivers often show poor judgment, teens who are in the passenger seat may have a better understanding of what constitutes safe driving. One driving instructor asks his students if they've ever been frightened while riding with another teenage driver. In most classes, 100 percent of the teens say yes, and many volunteer that some of their friends are so reckless that they refuse to ride with them.

One of the best ways to do this is to keep children from having their own car. Let them borrow a family vehicle – under appropriate guidelines, of course – on those occasions when they need to go somewhere. The teen will be safer and your family will save a considerable amount of money, since supporting and insuring a separate car for a teen is an expensive proposition.

Don't accept the circular argument that teens use to justify getting their own vehicle: the part-time job. Most of the paycheck will go toward the purchase and maintenance of the car. Without the car, your teen wouldn't need to work nearly as many hours at this job. And without having to work all those hours, your teen definitely won't need the car. As one employer whose business depends on part-time teenage labor put it, "I love it when a good worker tells me he just bought a car. I know he'll need to work a lot more hours." Yes, he will. Cars are expensive.

Still, there are circumstances under which teens need their own vehicles. You may live in an isolated area far from public transportation and opportunities to carpool. Or your teen may need transportation to classes, lessons or football games when no family member or friend can provide it. In such cases, putting a teenager on the road in his or her own car is appropriate. Nonetheless, it is always wise to couple this privilege to certain standards, such as maintaining a high grade point average, completing chores at home and avoiding accidents and tickets.

If you find yourself thinking that a car for your teen is a good idea, understand that selecting the right car is important. You want a safe vehicle, of course. But what constitutes safety in a vehicle for a teenager?

Five rules can guide you in choosing a safe vehicle for your beginning driver. These rules, incidentally, also apply when picking a family car that teens will borrow if they don't have their own vehicle.

1. The car should handle safely, especially in an emergency. This does not mean that you should buy your teen a sports car. Just the opposite. The lightning-fast reflexes and ample power that make a good sports car so enjoyable for an experienced driver are often just what a teen does not need.

What you are looking for is a car that is stable in a straight line, yet easy to turn when necessary. In addition, the vehicle should remain stable during an emergency lane change or when the driver has to stop quickly while turning.

A beginning driver at any age is poorly equipped to handle a car with a rear end that suddenly wants to slide out in the middle of a corner. This tendency, called oversteer, is best avoided. By the same token, excessive understeer – the tendency to continue to travel in a straight line even though the driver is turning the wheel to take a corner – also is not desirable. Mild understeer, however, is often considered a stabilizing factor in vehicle handling.

The vehicle also should have a relatively low center of gravity. Cars generally have a lower center of gravity than a sport-utility vehicle or pickup truck. A lower center of gravity helps your teen avoid rolling over in a skid or a crash. Unfortunately, rollovers are becoming increasingly common, in part due to the greater popularity of SUVs and compact pickup trucks.

Devices that help a driver maintain control are especially important in a teen's car. Antilock brakes and traction control, for example, are very desirable options in a car with a new driver in the household.

2. The car should offer good crash protection. Statistics clearly show that teens are much more likely to bend some sheet metal during their first two years of driving than are experienced drivers. Any vehicle you help your teen select should provide superior levels of crash protection. The vehicle's performance in NHTSA's full-frontal-barrier crash tests and IIHS' offset-barrier crash tests are particularly important, since teens often collide with immovable objects after leaving the road.

Many parents want to get their teen the biggest, heaviest car or truck available. In a barrier crash test, however, the added weight can work against the best interests of the occupants. In a collision with an immovable object, all that extra weight means that there are more forces for the structure to handle. In a crash with another vehicle, however, added weight and size are almost always on the side of the passengers in the heavier, larger vehicle.

The car also should have air bags. They're standard on new cars, and even older cars often have them. Other safety devices to look for include height-adjustable shoulder belts, shoulder belts (not just lap belts with no shoulder harnesses) for the rear seat, and head restraints that can be adjusted properly and locked in place. However, despite the suggestion that the rear seat have shoulder harnesses, parents should forbid teens from carrying more than one passenger in almost all cases.

3. The car should be large enough to afford a good level of protection in a crash with another vehicle, but small enough to be easy to maneuver. Few truck drivers learned to drive on a big rig. They almost always started on

SAFETY Despite state-imposed age restrictions on driving, you as the parent must determine whether your teen is ready to get a license or have a car. Many teens lack the maturity and experience to be good drivers, even though they've reached the age when the state will grant them a license. It's your call.

something smaller and worked their way up. Similarly, putting a beginning driver in a big, unwieldy, hard-to-control car or truck is often just asking for trouble. However, parents also should avoid subcompact and compact models.

4. The car should not be too powerful. Buying your teen a high-performance vehicle shows poor parental judgement. Typical teenage clumsiness – professional driving instructors says it's not unusual for teens to confuse the accelerator and brake pedal – suggest that a lot of power just isn't desirable in a car for beginners. Most cars and trucks in good condition have more than enough acceleration to keep a beginning driver safe.

5. The car should be reliable. Teenagers can easily become victims when a car breaks down. Reliability, however, requires good maintenance.

While these five rules strike most people as reasonable, there is often one overriding requirement for a teenager's car: it has to be cheap. Fortunately, there are some cars that meet these requirements and also are reasonably priced. Unfortunately, few of them would top a typical teen's list of desirable rides. For example, 1995 and newer Chevrolet Lumina sedans and 1994 and newer Ford Taurus sedans and wagons have done well in crash testing, are of reasonable size and offer good handling; the Taurus is a bit better in this department than the Lumina.

In the case of the Lumina, parents should avoid the optional 3.4-liter and 3.8-liter V-6 engines. The standard 3.1-liter V-6 has more than enough pep for a teenager. Similarly, Taurus buyers should bypass the 3.8-liter V-6 models in favor of cars with the 3.0-liter V-6. The Plymouth Acclaim with the non-turbocharged four-cylinder engine also is economically priced, though its three-star rating for the front-seat passenger's position in NHTSA's full-barrier crash test is not good enough for some parents. The driver's position earned four stars. Five stars is the best score.

The 1994 to '97 Honda Accord is another potentially attractive car, although it's likely to cost more than a comparable Ford, Chevrolet or Plymouth. It, too, earned four stars for protecting the dummy in the driver's seat and three stars for the protection of the dummy in the passenger's seat in NHTSA's crash test. The 1992 to '96 Toyota Camry is another good choice when equipped with the four-cylinder engine. It earned the same four-star-for-the-driver and three-star-for-the-passenger crash test score. In newer Camrys, the passenger-side crash test rating improved to five stars. Other cars that acquit themselves well in the federal crash test and offer good handling for a beginner include older 200- and 700-series non-turbocharged Volvos.

What Not to Buy

Domestic muscle cars from the late '60s and early '70s have started to become popular with some teens. They are relatively inexpensive and large enough to suggest a safety advantage in a collision with another vehicle. However, most of them also handle poorly, demonstrate poor braking characteristics, are completely devoid of current safety technology and have entirely too much power. Their big engines not only provide blistering acceleration, they also consume large quantities of gasoline. Add in aging components and, in some cases, older approaches to body design that may compromise safety in a crash, and you should reject these models for teenage drivers.

The grandparents' 20-year-old sedan is another example of a car that you probably should reject. Again, its age means that it will not have air bags or antilock brakes. Choose something newer.

Carefully consider any convertible. The canvas top offers no rollover protection and most convertible bodies are structurally weaker than comparable coupes or sedans from the same manufacturer.

Cars from the late '80s and early '90s with automatic seat belts should cause parents some concern as well. These automatic belts came in two forms. In one, the power-operated shoulder belts automatically go into action when the car is started and follow a track that outlines the upper opening for the door. Their major weakness: you have to remember on your own to fasten the lap belt.

The lap belt is critical because a shoulder harness alone can be exceptionally dangerous in some crashes. Yet many people forget to buckle the lap belt and are severely injured or even killed in a crash that they might otherwise have survived.

Another passive-restraint design from this period consists of mounting the combination seat belt and shoulder harness to the vehicle's front doors. While most people buckle and unbuckle these combination belts each time they get in or out of the car, they were designed to be buckled once and left alone. There is enough webbing on the spools to allow the door to be opened with the seat belts fastened. Unfortunately, that also means that if the force of a crash opens the door, the seat belt's effectiveness is lost. A variation on this design mounts the shoulder belt in a fixed position on the door. Carefully consider this design, too, since it usually requires that the separate lap belt be fastened manually.

Avoid compact sport utility vehicles with a high center of gravity, sluggish handling and poor brakes. These disadvantages easily outweigh the better view of the road that their higher seating position gives a driver.

Pickup trucks share some of the faults of compact SUVs. In addition, some teens may be tempted to carry friends in the open load box. This is extremely dangerous, and, in some states, illegal. Carefully consider these vehicles for your young driver.

High-powered vehicles, perhaps better thought of as toys for adults, are always inappropriate for teens.

More Safety Suggestions

Just as you should gradually expose teens to more complex traffic situations after they earn a license, you also should limit where they can go when they first get their own car. Inevitably, the handling characteristics and control placement in the new car will be different from the vehicle they're used to driving. It takes time to adjust.

In addition, parents must establish and actively enforce strict rules. They should understand that teens with their own car will drive more, which means that they will have more exposure to risky situations. One parent who bought a car for his twin daughters when they received their licenses was shocked to discover that they racked up 5,000 miles in their first three months. He immediately stepped up his level of supervision.

Parents also should limit the number of passengers teens can carry. The risk of crashing goes up significantly with each friend added to the passenger list. A summary of current research by the Insurance Institute for Highway Safety in June 2001 noted that crash rates for drivers 16 or 17 years of age go up more than 40 percent with just a single teen passenger in the vehicle. The risk more than doubles with two passengers and nearly quadruples when three or more teen passengers are in the car. Beginning drivers should drive alone. Those with more experience should be limited to one passenger. A crowd of teens can distract a beginning driver and might even goad him or her into attempting something unsafe.

Teens need to understand the importance of using seat belts and be required, as a condition of driving, to use them at all times. In a study conducted by the National Highway Traffic Safety Administration in 1995, researchers found that teens are less likely than adults to use seat belts, either as drivers or passengers. Of more concern for parents, the research shows that teens become less likely to buckle up as they get older. Seat belt use was greatest among 16-year-olds; it was lowest among the 19-year-olds in the study.

Draw Up a Contract

Many parents find it useful to write down the rules that a young driver must follow. These rules can be negotiated, and the responsibilities of both the teen and the parents should be spelled out. Here are some typical requirements for teenagers:

No drinking and driving is allowed.

There will be no unsafe vehicle operation.

Everyone in the car must wear seat belts at all times.

Curfew is 11 p.m. on weekends, 10 p.m. on weeknights.

There will be no long trips, for any reason.

No tickets or warnings are allowed.

SAFETY The ability to control one's emotions is key to being a safe driver. Parents who see emotional instability in their children should delay the licensing process. Teens who throw or break things when mad or frustrated, for example, should learn self-control before they learn to drive.

Breaking any of the rules must result in an appropriate punishment. For example, evidence of drinking or unsafe operation should mean suspension of all driving privileges for at least a year, even if no accident or police action resulted. A father who saw his 17-year-old son deliberately spin the tires on a family car when leaving a drive-in restaurant took drastic action. He physically took the boy's license and suspended his right to drive any family vehicle until he turned 21. He then stuck to this decision, even when the boy attended college. His siblings learned the lesson and established excellent driving records.

Parents should agree to either pick up teens or arrange for other transportation – no questions asked – if the kids believe they can't drive safely or are out with a driver who's not safe behind the wheel. Giving teens this safety net can save a life.

Parents also should agree to contribute toward insurance, maintenance and other expenses and should keep a close eye on the vehicle. Teens should agree to pay a share of the automotive costs, as well as to perform household chores associated with the privilege of getting behind the wheel.

To make the agreement official, parents and teens should sign it. Then, to keep it meaningful, they must live up to it.

Vehicle Use and Operation Agreement

We,_____

hereby enter into an agreement covering the use and operation of any vehicle

used by_____ .

You Will Be Required to Pay for the Following *(write in percent desired):*

_____ Cost of vehicle		_____ Vehicle registration
_____ Cost of fuel		_____ Maintenance costs
_____ Damage due to abuse		_____ Full insurance coverage
_____ Under-age-25 insurance costs		_____ Fines and penalties
_____ Collision damage		_____ Under-B-average insurance costs
_____ Costs due to driving record		_____ Other_____

You Will Be Responsible for the Following:

_____ Check fluids each fuel fill		_____ Inspect and check tire pressure
_____ Report unusual performance		_____ Clear or clean all windows
_____ Report when fuel is less than ¼ tank		_____ Do normal maintenance
		_____ Keep interior clean
_____ Wash and wax vehicle		_____ Other_____
_____ Have maintenance done		

Your User Privilege Will Be Linked to Your Grades In School and Performance at Home:

_____ Doing duties at home properly and on time

_____ Showing proper respect for parents and others

_____ Complying with family regulations

_____ Attendance, conduct and effort at school

The Maximum Number of Miles and the Maximum Number of Times You May Drive Per Week are *(related to grades):*

Grades:

A	_____ Miles per week	_____ Times per week
B	_____ Miles per week	_____ Times per week
C	_____ Miles per week	_____ Times per week
D	_____ Miles per week	_____ Times per week
F	_____ Miles per week	_____ Times per week

You Will Lose Your User Privileges These Numbers of Days or Months for Each Traffic Offense or At-Fault Crash:

First offense	_____ days/months	Preventable crash	_____ days/months
Second offense	_____ days/months	Serious violation	_____ days/months
Third offense	_____ days/months	Drugs or alcohol	_____ days/months

You Will Be Required to Comply With the Following Regulations:

_____ You will tell us destination and time of return.

_____ Safety belt will be fastened at all times.

_____ Every passenger must wear a safety belt.

_____ No drugs or alcohol in the car.

_____ You may not lend the car or allow others to drive it.

_____ You will call if more than 30 minutes late.

You Are Legally Responsible for Your Actions as a Driver.

We, As Vehicle Owners, Are Legally Liable for Damages Done By You As a Driver:

Signed on the _____ day of _____, 20_____

Parent_____

Parent_____

Son/Daughter_____

CHAPTER 7

Using the Internet

In This Chapter

• • • • • • • • • • • •

- What you can do
- Gathering information
- Why many dealers like it when you use the Internet
- Practical limits
- Sites to visit

For the auto industry, the Internet is like an elephant in the living room. While it's impossible to ignore and it prompts a lot of conversation, its ultimate potential is difficult to assess. Everyone agrees that the Internet is going to play an even bigger role in auto sales in the future. Just how big, or what that role will be, however, nobody knows.

In 2001, about half of all new-car buyers visited the Internet before purchasing a vehicle. In most cases, they logged on to garner information and make initial contacts with dealers. Since the Internet changes rapidly, updated information about car buying and researching can be found at www.aaa.com.

Surfing the Internet for auto information, however, is a challenge. Not that there isn't a great deal of data to be found, mind you. Quite the opposite. For most people, there's simply too much. Gathering Internet information has been compared to a thirsty man trying to get a sip of water by thrusting his cup into Niagara Falls.

There's so much automotive information that there are search engines devoted to the subject. You can find manufacturers' websites, dealers' sites and other automotive sites including AAA's. There are also clubs, auto magazines and chat rooms dealing with cars and trucks. Chances are, no matter what your questions, you'll find answers on the Internet. Just remember that not all the information you find there will be correct. It all depends on what you ask and where you look.

Visit a Manufacturer's Website

Manufacturers' websites let you gather all sorts of information on models you think you might like to own. Think of them as an online sales brochure. You can learn about body styles, trim lines, standard equipment and options. You also can research safety features offered as standard equipment or as options on the vehicles you like. Sometimes you can even look at paint colors and upholstery patterns.

Some automakers' sites allow virtual tours of interiors and engine compartments. Remember, however, that these tours often include optional accessories that you may not want. You'll also find a staggering number of specifications that spell out everything from engine size to the dimensions of the body.

Shopping on the manufacturer's website has significant limitations. You will not, for example, be able to learn whether you fit comfortably in a car or truck. You can't determine whether the driver's seat gives you a good view of the road in all directions. You won't be able to feel how the vehicle responds. And you won't be able to compare different manufacturer's vehicle models. In other words, the Internet will not take the place of visiting dealers and trying out cars in person.

Browsing the World Wide Web can, of course, make you far more knowledgeable about the vehicle you're interested in before you set foot in a showroom. Yet you may not have received accurate information, even at the manufacturer's website. For example, when you visit the dealer, you may learn that some options are mandatory, while others may not be available at all. A so-called mandatory option is a piece of equipment that shows up on the option sheet but ends up on every vehicle the manufacturer builds. You simply cannot buy a car or truck without this feature, even if you don't want it. This is often true of imports, although domestic manufacturers have also been known to dabble in this tactic, too.

The opposite of the mandatory option is the option that's simply unavailable, even though it is listed on the option sheet. In extreme cases, entire trim lines or drivetrain combinations that show up on the spec sheets aren't available for retail customers. Sometimes this happens because the manufacturer misjudges the demand for an item and orders too few from a supplier. The supplier may then be unable to build enough to meet the demand. Cadillac, when it first introduced its Night Vision option in 2000, faced this dilemma. So it rationed the number of cars with Night Vision that each dealer got during the year. Many people who saw the ads for Night Vision and wanted it were unable to get it.

Manufacturers also have simply stopped making some models with a specific engine or transmission. These components remain on the specification pages on the website, even though the product is unavailable. In other cases, specific combinations of options simply may not be available, despite their continued presence in the specs. The only way you'll know for sure is to contact a dealer.

Visit a Dealer's Website

Dealers, sometimes individually and sometimes as a group, are making increasing use of the Internet. Most provide a variety of information on the dealership, its history and its policies. Some even let you browse the inventory, both new and used. Want that pickup truck in plum? The dealer may list the color and equipment of every unit it has in stock, right on its website.

In addition, many dealers also invite you to make contact by e-mail. For customers who would just as soon not face a salesperson yet, or who don't have the time to shop the showroom, e-mail can be a convenient way to start the buying process.

Most dealers have learned to respond quickly by return e-mail rather than call until the customer expresses a willingness to talk in person. Many dealerships dedicate one or two salespeople to handling Internet customers.

For used car buyers in search of a rare model, the Internet is an exceptionally powerful tool. Its ability to search dealers' inventories throughout the country has changed the way many used cars are sold. It is not unusual to find dealers who ship rare, or difficult-to-find new or used cars across the country to satisfy eager buyers.

However, you should undertake a long-distance search for a specific vehicle only when all else fails. If you're interested in a relatively common vehicle, there's no need to look across the country when you probably can find what you need right around the corner.

Visit Third-Party Sites

If the information that the manufacturers and dealers provide is interesting, the facts, figures and opinions on third-party sites is often riveting. For example, some sites give both the manufacturer's suggested retail price and the dealer's invoice amount for the vehicle and each option. Others provide information on temporary factory-to-dealer incentives or holdback amounts that may not be widely publicized elsewhere. You won't find this information on the official websites of either the dealer or the manufacturer.

You also can find opinions on vehicle performance. As with other opinions, they may not be relevant to you or the way you intend to use the vehicle. In some cases, what you read may be completely invalid. On some sites, you never know the source of the comments, either positive or negative. Negative comments might come from a genuinely dissatisfied customer — all makers have them — or a competitor. A third-party site like www.aaa.com enables you to shop all makes and models and allows you to access information.

You Can Solicit Offers

One of the original promises of the Internet was that car buyers would be able to solicit offers from a variety of sellers eager for their business using a buying services website. The theory was simple. You want a new model and, through the Internet, you could invite bids from interested sellers. It certainly sounds nice . . . in theory.

Reality, however, turned out to be less compelling. First, the margins in the auto business are thinner today than they've ever been in the past. As a result, dealers simply don't have the leeway to make the price cuts many Internet customers expect.

Good dealers also know what price their competitors are offering. As a result, they know how far they have to go to stay in the game. Finding one dealer willing and able to sell you a new car or truck for thousands less than other dealers in your area is unlikely. If you have shopped three or four local dealers for a specific model and found prices pretty consistent, the chance that you could save a bundle by shopping on the Internet is small.

In fact, the Internet offer may be higher. Internet companies that recruit dealers into web-based marketing efforts charge the dealers for their services. As a result, dealers often charge their web-based customers more than they would someone who walks into the showroom. In this case, the Internet intermediary has simply added another layer of costs to the transaction. Increasingly, dealers see how inefficient the process is and they are refusing to participate.

When you request a quote for a specific vehicle, you may think that the car buying service is scouring the area and contacting many dealers to get you the lowest bid. Some companies do that. But others simply refer your request to a single local dealer. It's handed over to a salesperson, who either calls you or sends you an e-mail. The price may be startlingly good, merely competitive or even high. The only way to know for sure is do some additional shopping on your own.

Shoppers using bidding sites often demonstrate that they are market-savvy by offering quite reasonable sums for exceptionally popular and hard-to-find vehicles. In some cases they bid over the manufacturer's suggested retail price.

When you consider that, for some popular vehicles, dealers are willing to pay another dealer the retail sticker price, why should a dealer sell you the same car or truck for just $100 over invoice? It won't happen, regardless of the Internet's power.

What You Can't Do

Obviously, you can't drive a car over the Internet. For that, you still need to visit a dealer. You also can't buy a car directly from the manufacturer. In most states, dealership franchise laws prohibit a manufacturer from making a direct sale to a customer. This is true for new cars and trucks and also for used vehicles that the manufacturer owns – returned lease vehicles, for instance. While manufacturers may list their off-lease inventory on some websites, in some states they're not allowed to set a price for a retail customer. Since dealers and dealer organizations keep in close touch with their state legislators, don't expect this situation to change anytime soon.

In other states manufacturers are allowed to offer a car or truck to a retail customer at a specific price. They then arrange for delivery through a local dealer.

Ultimately, you'll end up dealing with a dealership even if you make all the arrangements over the Internet, so remember that you won't be able to get that all-important feel of the place by looking at a website and exchanging e-mails. You can't feel the pace of operations. You can't see the condition of the repair shop or overhear how service advisers and the service manager interact with customers and each other. You also won't be able to talk with service customers.

Is the atmosphere friendly? Do people, both customers and employees, seem happy to be there? The answers to such questions often can tell you whether you really want to do business at that dealership. You'll never learn the answers to these questions through an exchange of e-mails.

Nonetheless, if you've recently driven a car, perhaps as a rental, and are sure you know just what you want, you can go from initial contact to final contract using only the Internet. You should be able to do it all without visiting a dealership or having a face-to-face meeting with a salesperson. While such transactions are rare, they're not unheard of. Some dealers even deliver the car right to your front door, so you won't have to see the dealership until you need service. And if the dealership also picks up and delivers vehicles for service, you may never have to see the place at all.

What Dealers Think

It might surprise you to learn that many dealerships appreciate the contribution that the Internet makes to the way they do business. Many dealers have discovered that the widespread availability of pricing information makes it easier to sell a car, since customers no longer suspect the dealers of racking up profits of thousands and thousands of dollars on each new vehicle. On the majority of new cars and trucks, the difference between the dealer's invoice amount and list price ranges from just 8 percent to 15 percent. That means that most dealers don't have a tremendous amount of room to maneuver on what they have to charge you for the average $24,000 vehicle.

One reason that sticker prices have shown relatively small increases in recent years is that manufacturers have been raising the price that dealers pay for vehicles faster than they've been raising the price you see on the sticker. In other words, manufacturers have been cutting dealers' profit margins, in some cases by significant amounts.

That dealers have become a little cynical is understandable. What this means to consumers can be illustrated by what happened when a manufacturer introduced a new vehicle to replace a popular older model. With much fanfare, the manufacturer proclaimed that it was holding the line on pricing. The suggested retail price did not go up, despite the fact that the automaker made numerous improvements to the vehicle and offered more standard equipment on this new model.

Unfortunately, customers who shopped for the older model and decided to wait for the new, improved version discovered that the new model's selling price went up by about $3,000. How was this possible?

First, the manufacturer, in order to keep sales of the older model humming along when everyone knew a new version was just around the corner, offered some significant factory-to-dealer incentives. Averaging about $1,500 per car, they allowed dealers to lower the selling price of the existing model.

There were no such incentives on the new model, of course. So, immediately, dealers had to charge $1,500 more for it. In addition, the manufacturer also cut the dealer margin on the new model by 6 percent. That represented another $1,500 price increase on this $25,000 car. While the sticker price did not go up, the real selling price of the new model was markedly higher than that of the vehicle it replaced. Considering the improvements to the design and the added equipment, the manufacturer easily could have justified a list price increase. Instead, it chose to state that the pricing had remained stable, when in fact it had not.

Thanks to sites that spelled out the pricing strategy of this manufacturer, most customers knew exactly was what happening. In the absence of that kind of impartial information, people who went to a dealership expecting to buy the new model for the price of the old one might not have believed that the dealer's cost had increased so substantially. With independent corroboration delivered via the Internet, most dealers found customers were understanding – if not appreciative – of the price increase.

Sites You Should Know About

Here are some sites that can help you in your Internet browsing for a new vehicle. First, we list automakers' sites. AAA cannot guarantee the accuracy of everything you find on these sites, nor does AAA necessarily agree with their content.

Manufacturers' sites give facts and figures on all their models and the locations of their dealers. Think of these sites as electronic sales brochures.

Acura	**acura.com**
Audi	**audiusa.com**
BMW	**bmwusa.com**
Buick	**buick.com**
Cadillac	**cadillac.com**
Chevrolet	**chevrolet.com**
Chrysler	**chrysler.com**
Daewoo	**daewoous.com**
Dodge	**4adodge.com**
Ford	**ford.com**
GMC	**gmc.com**
Honda	**honda.com**
Hyundai	**hyundai.com**
Infiniti	**infiniti.com**
Isuzu	**isuzu.com**
Jaguar	**jaguarvehicles.com**
Jeep	**jeep.com**
Kia	**kia.com**
Land Rover	**landrover.com**
Lexus	**lexus.com**
Lincoln	**ford.com**
Lotus	**lotuscars.com**
Mazda	**mazdausa.com**
Mercedes-Benz	**mbusa.com**
Mercury	**ford.com**
Mitsubishi	**mitsubishicars.com**
Nissan	**nissan-usa.com**
Oldsmobile	**oldsmobile.com**

Pontiac	**pontiac.com**
Porsche	**porsche.com**
Saab	**saabusa.com**
Saturn	**saturnbp.com**
Subaru	**subaru.com**
Suzuki	**suzuki.com**
Toyota	**toyota.com**
Volkswagen	**vw.com**
Volvo	**volvocars.com**

Type in "cars" or "automobiles" using any Internet search engine and you'll be overwhelmed. We tried it and got more than 1.1 million hits. Checking them all out is out of the question. Some, of course, are more useful than others. Here are a few that we think are worth exploring.

aaa.com – Direct access to AAA and all of its services, including the club and offices near you. The car-buying section has a new-vehicle buying tool, use-car prices and access to VIN history reports. There's also information on vehicle insurance and financing.

aaafts.org – This site for AAA Foundation for Traffic Safety gives you up-to-date information on many safety issues.

alldata.com – Useful technical tips and a listing of recalls and technical service bulletins (TSBs) by title. For vehicle owners experiencing a hard-to-solve problem, the TSB list may offer some new possibilities. If you're buying a used car, it doesn't hurt to check the TSBs first.

auto.com – KnightRidder's site for auto news and reviews.

autoguide.net – Includes a bidding service for buyers of new vehicles, plus related information.

autonews.com – The site for *Automotive News*, a major industry publication. This is where you can read up on what's happening from the manufacturers' and dealers' perspectives.

autosite.com – Specifications, including some pricing information, for all makes and models. Has a useful listing of up-to-the minute rebates and incentives, plus opinions from the auto press on various makes and models.

carfax.com – Carfax checks vehicle titles for a fee. Submit the vehicle identification number for the car you want and the site will find a branded title or odometer inconsistencies, if they exist.

cars.com – A listing of available used cars, which can be sorted by brand, model and geography. Highlights include pricing information, a used-car value guide and access to content by the crew at NPR's popular Car Talk program.

digital-librarian.com/cars.html – A good listing of, and direct links to, many popular auto websites, including manufacturers' sites, auto publications and businesses that sell parts and accessories.

highwaysafety.org – Access the offset-barrier crash test results performed by the Insurance Institute for Highway Safety, as well as other information.

kbb.com – Kelley Blue Book information on new and used car pricing. New car pricing information includes the MSRP and dealer invoice amounts.

nhtsa.gov – Lists the latest results from frontal and side crash testing and rollover information from the National Highway Traffic Safety Administration. Also gives access to all safety-related recalls by year, make and model.

thecarconnection.com – Information of use to buyers, including pricing data, as well as news for the auto enthusiast. It's mostly industry information.

wardsauto.com – Auto industry news and statistics; probably of greater interest to the auto enthusiast.

CHAPTER

8

Financing the Purchase

In This Chapter
• • • • • • • • • • • •

- How to determine what to pay
- What lenders will look for in your application
- When you should not pay cash
- How lenders use your credit report
- How to determine which factory incentive is best for you
- How to finance a used vehicle

New cars are wonderful. Paying for them is not. That's how most people feel when they walk into the showroom and look at the stickers on the windows. If you haven't been car shopping in a while, the term "sticker shock" probably still applies, though recent price increases haven't been nearly as steep as they were in the late 1970s and early '80s when the term was coined.

Prices for some cars and trucks have actually come down lately as manufacturers struggle to stay competitive in a crowded market. Nonetheless, the average cost continues to climb, reaching more than $24,000 in 2000.

How Expensive a Car Should You Buy?

The maximum you can afford and what you should budget are two entirely different matters. Many consumers skip over the question of "How much should I budget?" and jump immediately to "How much can I borrow?" The answer is often, "More than you should spend."

Most financial advisers suggest spending no more than three or four months of gross income on a new car or truck. Gross income is your pay before anything is deducted, not the amount you take home. By that standard, a household with an income of $60,000 a year should spend no more than $15,000 to $20,000 for a vehicle.

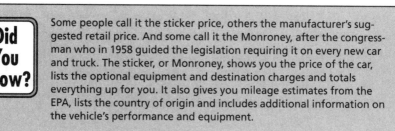

Did You Know? Some people call it the sticker price, others the manufacturer's suggested retail price. And some call it the Monroney, after the congressman who in 1958 guided the legislation requiring it on every new car and truck. The sticker, or Monroney, shows you the price of the car, lists the optional equipment and destination charges and totals everything up for you. It also gives you mileage estimates from the EPA, lists the country of origin and includes additional information on the vehicle's performance and equipment.

Auto industry calculations, however, indicate that the average family now devotes approximately 25 weeks – nearly six months – of pay to the purchase of a new car or truck.

Regardless of the formula you use to determine what you can afford, one fact is clear: The average American family – with a household income of approximately $41,000 a year – may not want to buy an average new car costing $24,000.

Most lending institutions have guidelines governing how much of your gross income you can devote to debt repayment. When the amount you owe approaches 28 percent to 33 percent of your gross pay, most banks won't approve an additional loan. Like the bartender who cuts off an overindulging patron, the bank figures that once your debt payments reach that level, you've had enough.

As income goes up, guidelines often become more lenient. A household that brings in $250,000 a year can afford to devote a higher percentage of gross income to debt repayment without encroaching on the grocery money.

So what's considered debt repayment? According to most lenders, housing costs – rent or mortgage payments that cover principal, interest, taxes and insurance – top the list. Also included are student loans, credit cards or other revolving debts, medical bills and payments for any other debt you may have accumulated. If you cosigned for a loan for someone, the financial institution may assume that the other person will default and that you'll have to pay that debt, too.

Using this formula, a family with an annual income of $50,000 could devote about $15,000 a year – or about one-third of the total – toward installment debt. If the family already has a mortgage payment of $800 per month, that claims $9,600 of the available $15,000.

Therefore, this family could borrow enough to generate about $5,400 more in debt repayments each year. That comes to $450 a month.

How much could the family borrow and still make a $450 a month payment? That depends on the interest rate for the loan and the amount of time they take to repay it.

For example, if they borrow $10,000 at 7 percent over two years they will pay $447.73 per month. That keeps them under the $450 ceiling that many lenders would impose.

Increase the debt to $20,000 at 7 percent and they will need four years and four months to repay the loan and stay under the $450 a month ceiling. Fifty-two months is a long time to make payments of $450, yet many people do it to buy a car or truck. Extend the loan to 60 months, and keep the payment at $450, and they could borrow $22,725 at 7 percent interest.

Obviously, the interest rate for the loan is a critical factor in these calculations. If, for some reason, the best rate you can get is not 7 percent but 9 percent, monthly payments on a four-year $20,000 loan would go from $479 to $498. Adding the car loan at 9 percent to the existing mortgage would bring the total debt repayment to 31 percent of the family's income. A bank that allowed up to 33 percent of gross income for debt repayment might grant the loan. If the bank has the stricter 28 percent guideline, however, the family should expect to be rejected. Incidentally, that increase in the interest rate from 7 percent to 9 percent would add $912 to the total cost of the loan.

Unless you are planning on financing 100 percent of the purchase price, what you borrow is not going to be the total that you pay for your new car or truck. Financial institutions like to see a down payment. They believe it commits you more firmly to the purchase, suggesting that you'll be more likely to make the payments on time and less likely to default. As a result, some attractive interest rates require a down payment.

Did You Know? Different banks define "100 percent financing" differently. In some cases, 100 percent financing means that you can borrow the entire cost of the car or truck – but you'll have to pay taxes, delivery charges and registration fees in cash. On a $20,000 vehicle, such costs can add $2,000 to the purchase price, depending on the sales tax rate in your jurisdiction. Other financial institutions, however, finance these additional charges as part of its 100 percent financing offer. Before applying for a 100 percent loan, expecting to take delivery of a new car or truck on your signature alone, ask what the loan really covers.

If, down the road, you default, your down payment gives the financial institution an added level of protection. For instance, if the car is repossessed, the bank may be able to sell it for enough to cover what you still owe. Without a down payment, it's unlikely that the lender could cover the amount due if the default occurs early in the life of the loan.

This problem for lenders occurs because new vehicles depreciate rapidly. It's not unusual for a $20,000 car or truck to be worth $2,000 to $3,000 less than its purchase price after just a few days of normal driving. If you financed 100 percent of the price, you almost immediately owe more than the vehicle is worth on the open market. In other words, you're "face down" or "upside down" on the transaction. Some in the business would say that you're "buried face down." If the buyer made little or no down payment and defaults early on, the lending institution is pretty much guaranteed to take a loss.

Finance 100 percent of your purchase and you will probably be "face down" for more than a few years. How long depends on how much the vehicle costs, the length of the loan and how quickly the vehicle depreciates.

> **◇ PITFALLS**
>
> When you buy or lease a car after making a small down payment, there will be a period of time when you will owe more than the car is worth. If, during that time, the car is completely destroyed in an accident, or it's stolen and not recovered, the insurance company will pay you only what the car is worth, not what you owe. You will have to make up the difference, which could be thousands of dollars. To protect yourself, you can buy gap insurance from the finance or leasing company. But this is usually quite expensive. For a lower-cost alternative, talk to your insurance agent.
>
> *Tip Provided by AAA Cincinnati*

To shorten the time that you're "face down" after borrowing the entire purchase price, be sure that you pick a vehicle that tends to hold its value better than competitive models. Then shorten the repayment period of the loan. Buyers who finance 100 percent over a five-year period can often be "face down" for three years or longer.

If you don't meet one lender's strict guidelines, shop around. There are any number of lending institutions that will bend the debt-to-income guidelines, or even break them entirely. At the same time, they'll increase the interest rate to cover the heightened risk of the loan going sour.

This leads us to another suggested guideline: just because you can borrow a large amount of money does not mean that you should. Somewhere, there is a lender who does not care about your welfare or solvency. It is up to you to determine what you can spend, develop a budget and stick to it.

People often don't even recognize the source of their money problems. One caller to a radio talk show on personal finance posed this question. "My husband and I have an income of $33,000 a year. Our only two debts are a mortgage of $600 a month and a car loan on which we owe $17,000. We're barely making it from month to month. Should we sell the house?"

"No," said the host. "You should sell the car." No matter how attractive the vehicle, buying a more expensive car than you can really afford is a sure way to create financial agony.

Paying Cash

Perhaps the most obvious way of putting that new car or truck in your driveway is to pay cash. Think of it: 100 percent down, easy monthly payments of zero. And it sounds even more appealing when you realize that you won't pay a penny in interest, as you would on a loan. However, economists say that a cash buyer should recognize the concept of opportunity costs.

Simply put, opportunity costs are another way of saying that you can't have your cake and eat it too. Take $20,000 out of the bank to buy a new car and you lose the interest income the money would have generated. In a certificate of deposit earning 6 percent, that comes to $1,200 each year, or $100 a month. If the interest is compounded daily, the total during the first year comes to $1,233 – all before taxes, of course.

Some buyers assiduously avoid debt and would never think about taking a car loan. Yet even these individuals should consider borrowing instead of paying cash, if the terms are right. For example, many automakers offer heavily subsidized finance rates to boost the sales of some models. Car makers often promote interest rates ranging from 0.9 percent to 3.9 percent.

If the model you like comes with a heavily subsidized interest rate, it may make sense to borrow the money even if you could pay cash. All you need to do to justify going into debt is confirm that the funds that you are keeping – in a bank account, for example – would earn more income after taxes than you'd pay in interest on the loan.

Here's how this works, before taxes are considered. Let's say that your $20,000 is in a CD earning 6 percent and that the vehicle you are considering has a subsidized 1.9 percent interest rate for 36 months.

If you pay cash, you will lose $3,944 in interest income – what your $20,000 would earn over 36 months if you left it in a 6 percent CD with daily compounding. Borrow the money instead at the subsidized 1.9 percent interest rate and you will make 36 monthly payments of $572. That means you will repay the $20,000 principal, plus $591 in interest charges. In this example, paying that $591 in interest will allow you to earn $3,944. You end up $3,353 ahead, before taxes, of course.

Year	Principal plus Interest Earned on 6 Percent for Money Left in Bank	Interest Earned on $20,000 in 6 Percent CD at Bank	Interest Paid on 1.9 Percent Simple Interest Car Loan	Advantage of Taking Subsidized 1.9 Percent Loan (pre-tax)
1	$21,236.63	$1,236.63	$323.24	$ 913.39
2	22,549.72	1,313.09	197.87	1,115.22
3	23,944.00	1,394.28	70.11	1,324.17
Totals	23,944.00	3,944.00	591.22	3,352.78
Loan Amount $20,000	Amount Left on Deposit $20,000			

Even people who dislike borrowing money should think about taking this loan. Of course, if a subsidized rate is not available, you'll need some very high rates of return on your cash to make borrowing attractive.

Before You Apply for a Loan

Your credit rating is very important when you apply for a loan. Many lenders use credit ratings to determine not just whether to grant the loan, but also what interest rate you'll pay. A less than stellar credit history may not scuttle your chances for obtaining financing, but it likely will force you to pay more for interest and increase your cost of ownership.

Perhaps most disturbing for loan applicants is the tendency of some financial institutions to entice borrowers with an attractive rate, then come back with a higher rate after the loan applications have been reviewed. Often, the credit reports are responsible.

Unless you have been lost and wandering in the desert for the past 10 years, your credit report contains a great deal of information about you. It will show your name, addresses for the last five years, employment history, Social Security number and date of birth. Credit reporting agencies do not verify the validity of any of this information. They rely, instead, on what you provided when you applied for credit in the past. If you filled out applications using different names – you might have used Elizabeth and Betty interchangeably, for example – confusion can result. Any errors you made in your Social Security number can complicate credit reporting as well.

In addition to personal information, you'll also find data about each obligation or debt in your name. Each account shows the date opened, the amount of the loan and your payment pattern. Credit card accounts also list the credit ceiling.

From public records, your credit report will contain information on bankruptcy, tax liens and any adverse judgments. Experian, one of the three major national credit reporting agencies, maintains information on tax liens for 15 years, bankruptcies for 10 years and other negative findings for seven years.

You'll also find the names of companies that have requested your credit report. A recent spike in activity often is a warning flag to potential lenders, who suspect that you're borrowing to the hilt for some reason. Unsolicited credit inquiries from companies that do mass-mailings for credit cards, however, should not count against you. If you had a credit problem in the past and disputed a report, your written statements and responses from the creditors are included.

Before applying for a loan, it's smart to verify that the information in your credit report is accurate. The three major independent credit reporting agencies are Experian, formerly known as TRW, Equifax and TransUnion. Unfortunately, finding out what one agency says doesn't mean you know what the other two have in their files. Each company maintains its own file on you, independent of its competitors. Credit reports are available to individuals for about $9 each.

If you've been subjected to a negative action based on your credit report, however, you have a right to see the report without paying any fee. Negative actions include rejection for a loan or credit card account or a change in interest or credit limit on a credit card account.

In their raw form, credit reports can be difficult for the uninitiated to decipher. That's why credit reporting companies include an explanation of what all those numbers and letters mean. It's not unusual for people who order a credit report to find errors. Incorrect entries often center on accounts that people have forgotten, but that remain open. Closing them can strengthen an applicant's standing in the eyes of a lending institution.

Other errors may be difficult or time-consuming to correct. Plan on at least 30 days – and be prepared to write several letters – to make changes.

More important to consumers is a credit scoring system developed by Fair, Isaac & Co. Using sophisticated mathematical models, these FICO scores, as they are called, are designed to predict whether an applicant will repay a loan in a timely matter. The system ignores marital status, age, salary and occupation and concentrates on payment history, amounts owed, length of credit history and types of credit in use.

> Different financial institutions price their loans according to many factors. All institutions, however, prefer to charge a higher interest rate than a lower rate on a loan. So banks and financing companies often make payments to third parties, such as dealers, who arrange loans based on the interest rate specified in the contract. The higher the interest rate, the more the lender will pay these third parties for serving as the loan originator. This gives originators an incentive to sell you on a higher rate of interest. Shop around to make sure you get the lowest rate possible.

Using these parameters, the company develops a three-digit score from 300 to 850 for each credit applicant. The higher the number, the more likely the applicant is to repay the loan. Until March 2001, however, individuals were unable to get their hands on their FICO score – despite the fact that many lenders relied solely on the FICO number when deciding whether to grant a loan. Fair, Isaac & Co. says that its scores are used in more than 75 percent of mortgage loan originations in this country, and that 70 of the 100 largest financial institutions use the numbers in their consumer credit decision-making processes.

The first – and as this is being written – only credit reporting agency to give consumers a chance to see their FICO score is Equifax. The company, which sells its reports for $8.50, is placing a 52 percent premium for including the FICO score. It also calls the resulting $12.95 price an introductory offer, suggesting that the cost may increase.

So far, the other major credit reporting companies don't offer the FICO numbers they develop based on the data in your file. As with credit information, which can vary from credit bureau to credit bureau, the FICO number developed by one agency isn't necessarily what the other two come up with.

While it will not provide you with a FICO number, Edmund's, which publishes both new- and used-car pricing information, has entered into an agreement with Fair, Isaac & Company to use some of the criteria that go into generating FICO numbers to grade potential applicants for a car loan. The interactive process is done over the Internet (www.edmunds.com). Participants will be placed in one of three tiers of credit worthiness and will then be given suggested interest rates that they should be asked to pay when applying for a loan, based on their score and home zip code.

In the past, automakers' captive financing divisions, as well as banks and loan companies, used FICO scores to determine which customers were the most creditworthy. These are the folks who always get the most favorable interest rates and terms. While the exact application of the FICO score is up to each lender, buyers with scores of 750 and higher are considered top-tier. Incidentally, a 720 happens to be the average score for all people with an Equifax credit bureau report.

Lower scores rank people in the second, third or fourth tier of borrowers. Those failing to make even this lowest grade are relegated to the subprime credit market. Tier one borrowers can expect to take advantage of the industry's most generous promotional interest rates. Those in lower tiers pay higher rates, sometimes in the low or mid teens. Sub-prime customers could expect to pay 18 percent or more in some areas, with the loan often contingent on the purchase of an extended repair contract.

In most cases, this extended service policy also is financed at the sub-prime rate. Lenders assume that any major mechanical breakdown not covered by an extended warranty would mean the borrower could lose the use of the car and then default on the loan.

You may request your personal credit report from these resources by writing to them, calling them or accessing their website:

Equifax Credit Information Services
P.O. Box 740241
Atlanta, GA 30374
1-800-685-1111
www.equifax.com

Experian
P.O. Box 2002
Allen, TX 75013
1-888-397-3742
www.experian.com

TransUnion LLC
Consumer Disclosure Center
P.O. Box 1000
Chester, PA 19022
1-800-888-4213
www.transunion.com

Taking a Loan

How much you pay to borrow money for your next vehicle is determined by the amount of the loan, the repayment period and the interest rate. Here are some examples of what a $10,000 loan can cost.

The first case shows what happens when a manufacturer provides a generous subsidy to lower the cost of the loan to 0.9 percent. While the chart projects the cost of this heavily subsidized loan over three-, four- and five-year periods, in most cases the low rates are limited to only two or three years.

In the second case, the 6 percent interest rate is exceptionally attractive and represents what might be available from an aggressive lender. A lender might offer such a loan to its best most creditworthy customers. It, too, might limit the term to two or three years.

The third example illustrates the costs associated with a higher interest rate loan.

Interest Rate (Percent)	Loan Duration (Months)	Monthly Payment ($10,000 Borrowed)	Total Interest Paid
0.9	36	$281.65	$ 139.40
0.9	48	212.18	184.64
0.9	60	170.51	230.60
6.0	36	304.22	951.92
6.0	48	234.85	1,127.28
6.0	60	193.33	1,599.80
10.9	36	326.91	1,768.76
10.9	48	257.97	2,382.56
10.9	60	216.93	3,015.80

It's easy to see that the higher the interest rate or the longer the loan, the more you pay in interest charges. Perhaps most interesting is the fact that as the loan repayment period lengthens, the monthly payment doesn't change much, even with large increases in interest.

Let's say that you apply for a manufacturer's subsidized 0.9 percent loan but don't qualify. The dealer then arranges a 10.9 percent loan for you. The resulting $46.42 per month jump in your payments – from $170.51 to $216.93 for a 60-month repayment period – may not seem important when all you can see is the glittering paint of that lovely new car on the showroom floor. However, over five years, that difference in the interest rate will add $2,785.20, or nearly 4 cents per mile, to your cost of ownership.

To reduce your interest expense when you borrow for a car, shop for the lowest interest rate you can find. Then put as much down as you can, either in cash, a trade-in vehicle or a combination of the two. Finally, do your best to keep the repayment period as short as possible, even though that means higher monthly payments.

Rebates

You've just seen a commercial for a new vehicle and you really, really want it. The ad says that you have a choice of 2.9 percent financing or a $2,500 rebate. Which is the better deal? The only way to answer that question is to crunch the numbers.

Determining your best option depends on how much you'll need to borrow, the interest rate of the non-subsidized loan you get and the length of the loan. Generally, smaller loans and shorter repayment periods make the cash rebate more attractive. Here are some examples for a $20,000 vehicle. Let's assume that if you take the rebate instead of the subsidized interest rate, you can get 7.9 percent financing from another source. We then assume that the $2,500 rebate is applied to the purchase of the vehicle. Also, the concepts of present and future value are not applied due to the short terms of the loans and the relative price stability that we've enjoyed in recent years.

	Loan Amount	Interest Rate (Percent)	Repayment Period (Years)	Monthly Payment	Total of Payments
Low Rate	$20,000	2.9	3	$580.74	$20,906.64
Cash Back	17,500	7.9	3	547.58	19,712.88
Low Rate	20,000	2.9	5	358.49	21,509.40
Cash Back	17,500	7.9	5	354.00	21,240.00
Low Rate	10,000	2.9	3	290.37	10,453.32
Cash Back	7,500	7.9	3	217.78	7,840.08
Low Rate	10,000	2.9	2	429.37	10,304.88
Cash Back	7,500	7.9	2	322.03	7,728.72

In each case, you are better served by taking the cash rebate, not the subsidized loan. However, if the best interest rate you can find independently is 12.9 percent, the picture changes.

	Loan Amount	Interest Rate (Percent)	Repayment Period (Years)	Monthly Payment	Total of Payments
Low Rate	$20,000	2.9	3	$580.74	$20,906.64
Cash Back	17,500	12.9	3	588.80	21,196.80
Low Rate	20,000	2.9	5	358.49	21,509.40
Cash Back	17,500	12.9	5	397.28	23,836.68
Low Rate	10,000	2.9	3	290.37	10,453.32
Cash Back	7,500	12.9	3	252.34	9,084.24
Low Rate	10,000	2.9	2	429.37	10,304.88
Cash Back	7,500	12.9	2	356.21	8,549.04

In this scenario, if you borrow the full amount, you're better off taking the subsidized interest rate. If you have $10,000 for a down payment, either cash or trade-in, however, the rebate is the better option – even with a 12.9 percent loan.

In many areas, AAA offices have auto loan specialists who can help you determine which option to take. Often you can get this information right over the phone.

Subsidized Loans

Subsidized loans are an effective selling tool. The lure of extremely low finance rates draws customers and improves sales. The manufacturers, who make these loans available through their captive financing companies, often place some significant limits on them, however.

For example, loan repayment periods may be exceptionally short, often no more than 24 months. Even with a low interest rate, a 24-month repayment schedule for the typical car loan would swamp most household budgets. In addition, manufacturers may not offer the interest rate on the model you want. Finally, the credit requirements for these low interest rate loans may be exceptionally stringent. Many consumers, even those who have never missed or been late with a payment, may not qualify.

Other Sources for Money

Most consumers are not limited to banks and loan companies when it comes to borrowing money. Here are some other options:

Home Equity Loan – Using the equity in your home to finance your new car or truck has two potential advantages. It might qualify you for a lower interest rate since your home secures the loan. You also might be able to deduct the interest on your income taxes. Buyers considering this option should consult a tax expert before signing on the dotted line.

The disadvantages include the imposition of service fees that some banks charge to originate these loans. In addition, the loan puts your home at risk if you can't make your car payments. Most people would rather lose a car than a home. With a home equity loan, it is possible to lose both.

Loan from 401k Plan – A 401k plan offered by many employers may let you borrow toward a purchase such as a new car. You then pay yourself back and – perhaps most appealing – these plans will also deposit the interest you pay on the loan into your account. In other words, you're paying yourself interest. Of course, if your 401k funds are particularly productive, you may lose money by not taking a standard auto loan from a bank. And if you leave your job, you'll probably have to repay the loan immediately or suffer some significant tax penalties.

Personal Unsecured Loans – For used cars that are older or have high mileage, a personal loan may be your only option. Many financial institutions refuse to loan money for cars that are more than 7 years old or have gone more than 100,000 miles. If the vehicle you want to buy falls into one or both of these categories, maybe you can find another bank with more generous standards. Or you may have to take a personal loan. Just remember that with no security other than your promise to repay, the interest rate will be higher than a regular auto loan that's secured by the vehicle.

Cash Advances from a Credit Card – Some people tap their credit cards for cash advances to pay for a new vehicle. Interest rates, however, are often very high. If you have too much available credit on your cards to qualify for a car loan, you can talk to a bank that rejected you for this reason. Ask if closing one or more of the revolving credit card accounts with a high line of credit would let you qualify for a secured auto loan. You could save a great deal in interest expense.

Other loan sources include borrowing against cash value that has built up in your life insurance policy, selling stocks or bonds and borrowing from friends or relatives. As with other forms of financing, all have advantages and disadvantages. For example, loans against life insurance could reduce the badly needed payment if the unthinkable should happen. Selling assets can trigger some significant capital gains taxes at the federal, state and local levels, while borrowing from family and friends can strain or even destroy relationships.

Financing a Used Car

The average new car costs $24,000, more than enough to prompt most buyers to consider their options for financing. The average used car is $14,000 – also high enough to make most buyers look for alternatives to paying cash.

Financing a used car is almost identical to financing a new one, with some significant exceptions. Primary among them is the fact that lenders consider used-car loans to be riskier, so they charge more to make them. Used-car interest rates often run 1 or 2 percentage points higher than a comparable new-car rate. Some banks charge even more, or couple the interest rate to the age of the car or the amount of the loan. The older the car, the higher the interest rate. Also, the lower the amount of the loan, the higher the interest rate may be. A higher rate helps defray a bank's fixed costs in reviewing and approving a loan that's so small it might not otherwise generate enough income to justify the effort.

Recognizing that cars have a finite life expectancy, many banks won't loan money on a vehicle more than 7 years old or with more than 100,000 miles on the odometer. In addition, many lenders shorten the maximum length of the loan period for older cars. For example, a bank may offer financing for up to 60 months on a 1- or 2-year-old model. Some banks even treat buyers of these cars to their new-car interest rate. Three- and 4-year-old cars

> More than one high-mileage driver has shown questionable judgment by taking an auto loan with a payback period that exceeds the useful life of the vehicle. An example: If a motorist drives 40,000 miles a year, a five-year loan makes little sense. Few new-car buyers keep their vehicles for 200,000 miles, which is when the loan would be paid. The chances are that this high-mileage driver will sell the vehicle before the third year is over, leaving two years to go on the loan and the possible need to finance both negative equity in the first car as well as the purchase of the next car. A loan term that exceeds the useful life of the vehicle can be a prescription for getting deeper and deeper in debt.

PITFALLS

may qualify only for 36- or 48-month loans; 5-year-old cars may require a 24-month repayment period.

As with interest rates, there are no hard and fast rules governing these policies. You may have to shop around to find a loan that meets your needs. Some banks, however, will waive their rules for a good customer or under special circumstances.

The amount that a financial institution will loan for a used car often is governed by "blue book" values. The *N.A.D.A. Official Used Car Guide*® or *Kelley Blue Book*™ loan amounts, which in theory are what banks will loan to borrowers, are 10 percent lower than the trade-in or wholesale value of most vehicles. This margin protects the lender if it has to repossess the vehicle. You can research loan amounts at aaa.com.

Many banks will loan more than suggested by the car guides – which is good for borrowers with little cash to put down, since the loan amount can be 20 percent below the suggested retail price. On a more expensive late-model luxury car, the gulf between a loan value and the suggested retail price can be $4,000 or $5,000.

Note that *N.A.D.A. Official Used Car Guide*® valuations are often high right across the board, with dealers offering current owners interested in trading cars in good condition less than the trade-in amount. They then sell these vehicles for less than the N.A.D.A. guide's suggested retail price. This lowers the 20 percent gap between the suggested loan amount and the retail price.

However, many banks will offer 100 percent financing on used cars, as well as on new vehicles. Check with the financial institution you plan to work with for the policies that will govern your loan. In some cases, 100 percent financing covers only the purchase price of the car. You're still responsible for taxes and registration fees. In other cases, banks will finance the entire transaction, taxes and registration included.

As with new car loans, a customer's total cost for interest expense on a used car loan is lower when the amount of the loan is kept as small as possible and the repayment period as short as possible. Shortening the repayment period may save a customer even more if the lender attaches a lower interest rate to the transaction because of the shorter term of the loan.

The lender will hold the vehicle title on a used car, just as it would on a new vehicle, until the loan is paid in full. Dealers are used to completing title applications that involve a lien and are generally trusted by banks and other lenders to handle the process properly. If they fail to do it right, the bank can always attempt to recover any losses from the dealership.

On the other hand, lenders regard casual sales with more suspicion. Casual sales take place between private parties – an owner who wants to sell a used car and the person who wants to buy it. Some banks won't finance these transactions, others will. If you think you'll buy from a private party, be sure to mention this to your lender when you call for interest rates.

If you find an exceptional used vehicle that would force a financial institution to break its lending rules, you should talk to the loan officer when you make your application. In most cases, loan approvals are still handled on an individual basis by people who genuinely want your business. Occasionally, a used car that is exceptional for one reason or another shows up on the market and commands a price much higher than the blue book value. Often these cars were bought by someone who kept them garaged and then, for whatever reason, rarely used them. One AAA club reports helping a member finance a 10-year-old luxury model with just 5,000 miles. In flawless condition, this car justified a higher-than-book-value price and, after hearing the details, the bank broke two of its rules to make the loan. The first was the seven-year age limit on used vehicles. Then it authorized a higher-than-book-value loan amount. These things do happen from time to time for customers who ask for special consideration.

Get a Loan Before You Find a Vehicle

Most people shop for a vehicle, then apply for a loan. There's nothing that says you can't reverse the process, however. Many banks and other lenders offer pre-approval, allowing you to go shopping knowing that you have the money. You'll know the amount of the loan, the time you have to repay it and the interest rate you'll pay. Most AAA clubs can do pre-approvals for you before you shop, so be sure to call your local AAA club first.

Pre-approval can give customers a sense of confidence when they venture onto the showroom floor. The fact that you've been pre-approved should give you more credibility with the dealership sales staff as well. They lose many sales when the customer, with whom they spent hours and who has signed their contract, fails to qualify for even a sub-prime loan.

Loan pre-approvals often serve to lock in an interest rate during a reasonable time period for shopping, usually 30 to 60 days. During that time, if loan rates go up, you enjoy the locked-in rate, as long as you find a vehicle and take delivery during the protected time period. Most lenders also will grant you a lower rate if interest rates drop while you shop. Check with your lender to determine what policies will govern your loan.

Refinancing

If you've already taken delivery of your new car or truck – complete with a very high interest rate loan – it's not too late You may be able to refinance. Call another lender.

Unfortunately, since your car is now used, many financial institutions won't give you a new car rate. Some lenders will, however, if the car is within the current model year or just 1 year old. Most banks insist that the current lender have the title, which can make it impossible to complete the transaction for several months. How long? It depends on how fast your state finishes its paperwork and generates a title.

Read Before You Sign

Be sure that you read and understand any loan agreement before you sign it. If you are unsure of any provision, or if you just want to review it at your leisure, the lender should allow you to take a copy of the contract with you. You can then have a friend, family member, lawyer or accountant explain terms and conditions you find confusing. Pay particular attention to any penalty or fee that will be charged if you pay off the loan early. You could end up paying the loan early if you decide to buy another vehicle, or if the car or truck is lost to an insurance settlement. Also examine how the bank computes its interest. Not all loans are the same.

Most consumers pay their auto loans early. Either they tire of the monthly payments, decide to trade or lose the vehicle through theft or a crash. If you're in this group of early payers, the way a lender computes your interest payments becomes an important consideration. Before you sign the loan agreement, see if it calls for interest payments to be computed as simple interest or the "Rule of 78s." Also known as the "Sum of the Digits" method of computing interest, it lets the lender front-load the interest payments. In other words, the lender can tack more of the total interest onto the early payments, unlike loans that use simple interest. To make up for the front-loading, the lender lowers the portion of each payment that goes to interest toward the end of the loan.

For borrowers who make each payment on time and don't pay early, whether a lender uses simple interest or the "Rule of 78s" makes no difference. Pay the loan off early, however, and you'll pay more interest under the "Rule of 78s," which effectively raises the rate of interest.

To determine which type of loan you're getting, read the fine print on finance charge rebates in the event the loan is paid early. If you don't understand the language, have a trusted and knowledgeable adviser review the contract with you.

AAA Financial Services

Because its members need access to loans that are fairly and uniformly priced, many AAA offices offer auto financing. In some cases, both AAA members and the general public are eligible for loans for both new and used vehicles. In addition, many AAA offices also can arrange home equity loans for consumers who prefer this financing option.

While a member of the AAA staff handles the application process, the borrower must meet the credit standards established by the financial institution that ultimately issues the loan. AAA does not decide an applicant's creditworthiness.

In most cases, borrowers can apply for their loans over the phone and the decision-making process takes only a few hours. Check aaa.com or your AAA club's publication for additional information.

Selecting a Dealer

In This Chapter

• • • • • • • • • • •

- What to look for when you shop for a dealership
- Why asking a friend about auto dealers probably won't work
- Outside sources that evaluate dealers
- Why you should have your car serviced where you bought it
- Checking the dealer's report card

Cars have improved a great deal in recent years. And so have dealers. Nonetheless, there are still enough differences, both among cars and dealers, to suggest that shopping for a good one is time well spent. And just as you want to find a car or truck that fits your lifestyle and budget, so, too, do you want a dealership that's responsive to your needs during the sales process and, more importantly, when it comes time for warranty repairs or service.

Finding a good dealer has become much easier. Competition, which makes dealers more responsive to their customers, is a wonderful thing. Manufacturers now monitor dealers closely, then reward the good ones and encourage the others to improve. While some dealers may not interpret the actions of the manufacturers in quite that light, the effect generally has been positive from the consumer's point of view. There's still room, however, for improvement.

How to Find a Good Dealer

When you search for a dealer, you should pay particular attention to the service department. While there's no need to take a new vehicle back to the dealer for the maintenance required to keep the warranty in effect – and many customers choose to go to independent garages for this work – you will return to the dealer for any warranty repairs. This is the only way the manufacturer will pick up the cost of the work.

To keep the warranty in effect if you use an independent garage for your vehicle's maintenance, be sure to follow the manufacturer's service schedules and keep all the receipts to prove that you had the work done correctly. Check the owner's manual to determine exactly what your vehicle's manufacturer requires.

With that in mind, finding a good dealer should not be difficult. Start by asking your friends and neighbors for dealers they think give satisfactory service. Be sure to ask them if they experienced any difficulties with their vehicles. Each manufacturer occasionally makes a car that turns in a less than stellar performance. If you can find a dealer who has been able to help a customer with a real problem, you're on the right track.

Many relatively ineffective dealers still enjoy the loyalty of customers who've never had a major problem with their car or truck. These customers should thank the manufacturer rather than the dealer for their satisfaction. It is difficult, but not impossible, to botch an oil change. Finding an elusive rattle or chasing down an intermittent electrical problem can be far more difficult for a service department. If you find customers who found a dealer who was able – or unable – to fix a hard-to-find problem, their experiences will be very valuable to you. A customer who can only report half a dozen satisfactory oil changes is far less informative.

Yet even these customers can give you useful information if you plan to use the dealer for all the servicing your vehicle requires. Ask them:

- Is the dealership's service department able to make appointments within a reasonable time period?
- Are the prices close to the estimates, or do they always call and ask permission to do additional work at an added cost?
- Is the work done right the first time, or are follow-up appointments often necessary?
- Does the dealer have to delay making repairs for lack of parts?
- Is the car ready when promised?
- Are the interior and exterior of the car kept clean while it is in for service, or are oily smudges proof that a technician has looked at the vehicle?
- Is it easy to drop the car off before the service department is open and pick it up after closing?
- If they have a free loaner program for service customers, can you *really* get the free loaner?

Once you have the answers to these questions from customers of various dealerships you're interested in, call the Better Business Bureau to check for complaints. You also may want to call the licensing board for dealers in your state to see if it keeps public files on complaints and other problems. Finally, if you don't know anyone who has used a dealership you are interested in, you can always ask complete strangers in parking lots who are driving a car with a sticker from that dealership.

Remember that it is a rare business that does not at some point have a dissatisfied customer. A few complaints do not suggest that the dealer gives its customers unsatisfactory service. Numerous complaints on file, however, suggest that there may be a problem.

The opinions of others, however, only go so far. Once you find dealers who seem to have satisfied your friends and neighbors, it's time to take a trip and see for yourself what these businesses are like.

Most customers enter a new car dealership through the front door and talk to a salesperson. There is certainly nothing wrong with that approach. But you can also enter through the back door — the one down in the service department — and start your visit there. You may get a reasonably good idea of how a service department is functioning just by looking around. Here are some points to consider.

- Is the shop area busy, yet also clean and uncluttered? A busy shop is usually a successful shop. The lack of dirt and clutter, which can accumulate quickly when servicing vehicles, suggests that management and employees take pride in their work and their workplace.

- What is the pace of the work? It should be steady and businesslike. Neither frenetic activity nor idle workers is desirable. Is the shop noticeably larger than seems to be justified by the volume of work and number of employees? A shop with only half of its bays in use suggests that service volume may have been higher at one time. If that's the case, why has it shrunk?

- Does the shop's test equipment look new and is it nicely maintained? Granted, you may have to look from a distance, since many shops have entirely rational rules that keep out non-service personnel. Nonetheless, having the latest diagnostic equipment is a must for solving many of the tough problems — rare though they may be — on today's vehicles.

- Are reference desktop computers available to the shop's personnel? Shop manuals and service bulletins these days are more likely to be on CD-ROM disks than in bound books. Easy access by the technicians suggests that workers have a better chance to do the job right the first time.

- Is the waiting room livable? Some dealers offer waiting customers comfortable surroundings. Others do not.

Before going to talk to a salesperson, ask one of the customer service reps or the service manager a few questions. Explain that you're considering buying a certain model and you need to know the following:

- What is the service schedule for this vehicle and how much will parts and labor cost?

- Does the service department recommend deviating from the manufacturer's suggested service requirements? If so, why and in what way?

- Does the manufacturer require any special lubricants or service procedures not generally available outside the franchised dealership network?

- Does the manufacturer make diagnostic information available to non-franchised shops? If the dealer says yes, verify that answer with your favorite independent automotive technician.

- What have customers who bought this model found to be problematic?

- Are there any service or repair procedures that this shop is unable to do? For instance, are wheel alignments farmed out to another service facility?

- What procedures does the shop follow for early drop-off or late retrieval of a vehicle? Is it possible to make a mid-day service appointment and wait for the work to be completed?

- How long does it take to get an appointment for standard service?

- Does the shop have evening and weekend hours?

- Does the dealership offer valet service, loaner cars or rentals? If there's valet service, does it go where you work or live? Will it take you to work and pick you up again later? If the shop offers rentals, what does it charge service customers?

- What is the training schedule for the shop's technicians and to what certification programs do they subscribe? Many service technicians are ASE certified. Review their credentials. Certificates are often posted for easy inspection. Does the staff collectively have a wide range of certifications and are they all current? If everyone is certified, but only in bodywork, who will do your fuel-injection adjustments and brake repairs?

- Is the dealer's repair shop an Approved Auto Repair facility? If it is, AAA has reviewed many of these matters and has delved into many more details of the shop's operation. You should also know that, as a AAA member, your local club will help resolve any dispute you have with the shop, as long as you identify yourself as a AAA member before repair or service work begins.

Service departments at dealerships are busiest first thing in the morning, when customers drop cars off, and late in the afternoon when everybody wants to get their cars back. Don't plan to have this conversation with the service writers during these hours. In the middle of the day, however, you should be able to get reasonable answers. If you can't find someone willing to talk to you before you buy, what chance do you think you'll have once the dealer sells you a car?

The Dealer's Report Card

Factories know exactly how their dealers are doing with customer service. How? They ask the customers. New car and truck buyers are one of the most thoroughly surveyed groups of people in the world. Manufacturers use this data to give their dealers a report card that shows how customers rated their service and how the dealer compares to other area dealers selling the same cars.

In some cases, this information, along with other aspects of the dealer's operation, is used to give dealers a superior rating that is publicly and proudly displayed. Ford's Blue Oval™ program and Chrysler's Five-Star™ dealers are examples. In other cases, the differences among dealers are kept confidential.

Even so, there is nothing to keep you from asking how the dealer rated in customer surveys. Ask to see the score. Manufacturers may rate dealers on a scale of 1 to 10 or 1 to 100. In addition, the report often tells how this dealership ranks compared to others in the area. There's no reason for you to deal with someone who falls well short of the competition.

There are, of course, reasons why a dealer might do poorly. One unreasonable customer can affect even a relatively large dealer's score for a time. In addition, customers sometimes fill out the surveys incorrectly. And some dealers manage to do better than they should have for other reasons. One, for example, offered customers who received the questionnaire a free oil service in exchange for completing the survey form.

It is important to select a dealer for both the quality of service you receive from the salesperson and for the level of service provided in the shop. While it is true that almost any dealer will service a brand it sells, no matter where it was purchased, they're understandably reluctant to handle adjustments and minor problems for customers who bought elsewhere. In many cases, such work isn't covered by the manufacturer's warranty. Instead, it's considered goodwill – which service-oriented dealers do at their own expense.

Even warranty service covered by the manufacturer is considered less desirable than off-warranty repair work. The reason: manufacturers often pay less for both labor and parts than would a regular customer. Manufacturers also are picky about the parts diagnosed to be bad. They want them back and often test them to see if the dealer's diagnosis was correct. If it wasn't, the automaker usually won't pay for the repair.

You can receive quality service and maintain your warranty if you have your car serviced elsewhere, as long as you keep the receipts proving that the proper work was done on time as recommended, but having the dealer do the service has advantages. Dealers often go to bat for their good customers when a problem arises that normally would not be covered by the warranty. A motivated service manager can act as your advocate and make a real difference in this case.

A good service department also is proactive – it looks for problems that your car or truck might develop down the road. Since the shop is compensated for repairs under warranty, technicians are often willing to look for problems before the warranty lapses. Don't assume they'll do this automatically, however. You may want to ask for an inspection just before your warranty is up, either because of time or mileage.

A good dealer can make all the difference in the level of enjoyment you have with your vehicle. Finding a good dealer is so important that if you end up looking at two different vehicles that perform similarly, you definitely should buy the one sold by the better dealer.

CHAPTER 10

Techniques of the Dealer

In This Chapter

• • • • • • • • • • • •

- How to select models for consideration
- Why salespeople do what they do
- How you can control the process
- What you can do to feel more comfortable
- How not to get rushed

This is it. The moment of truth. It's time to take a deep breath, gather your courage and cross the threshold into the dealer's showroom.

If you fear car shopping, we have good news for you: In all probability, you'll have a pleasant experience. Good dealers discovered long ago that it's more profitable to treat customers well. A professional manner and a gentle rather than high-pressure approach are more likely to lay the foundation for a long and profitable relationship. Today's salespeople work hard to be helpful and friendly.

Some things, however, don't change. Ultimately, a salesperson and the dealership have to make the sale or they don't make money. Treating you royally, being friendly and generally making you feel comfortable come to naught if you turn around and buy a car somewhere else.

Not only does the dealership make nothing if you walk away, the salesperson probably doesn't either. Many car salespeople work on commission, which means that their income is directly affected by your decision. If they're on straight commission, they earn nothing – not one cent – until you buy the vehicle.

In other words, you may feel some pressure, even in the friendliest showrooms. Once you announce you're in the market for a new vehicle, most dealers will want you to buy a car *now*. Not only that, they want to make a good profit.

You, on the other hand, want to pay as little as possible. Since you know that the bottom line is subject to negotiation, and that almost nobody pays the list price for a car or truck, you probably also feel a certain competitiveness with other customers. At the very least, you want to pay no more than other customers who are effective negotiators have paid.

Remember: You possess the ultimate weapon in this transaction. You can leave and buy a vehicle elsewhere. You can go to another dealership selling the same brand or buy a completely different car from another manufacturer. There are so many good models available in nearly every category that it makes little sense to fixate on a single make or model before signing the contract.

With that in mind, remember these rules:

- If you don't like the way you're treated, politely tell the salesperson that you are displeased, and why.
- If nothing changes, leave and don't return.

Just knowing that you can do this at any time should make car buying more comfortable.

What You and the Dealer Owe Each Other

At the dealership, you deserve accurate information delivered in a timely manner, as well as courtesy as the transaction progresses. In return, you owe the dealer the same honesty and courtesy. Unfortunately, many customers fail to live up to the standards that they demand from the seller. Auto salespeople have a saying: buyers are liars.

Good salespeople have developed ways to work around the fibs that customers mutter during the sales process. Your honesty, therefore, can be disarming. Besides, your failure to tell the truth – a technique recommended in some books on how to buy a car – just increases the stress of car shopping and can work against your best interests. Being truthful can make the process a great deal more enjoyable.

During the sales process, you will – by the very nature of the transaction and the number of dollars involved – have to disclose certain personal information to the dealership. However, the salesperson may ask you more than he or she needs to know.

In many cases, you can just say, "I'd prefer not to answer that. Why do you really need to know?"

In fact, very little personal information need be shared with the dealer, even after you decide to buy. If you're financing through the dealership, however, you will have to disclose your Social Security number, income sources, work history, number of dependents, and other debts and obligations to the person taking the credit application.

Even if you don't finance at the dealership, you'll often have to provide identification before taking a test drive. In some states, you also have to show a driver's license or some other form of ID before the dealership can complete the sales transaction.

The Sales Process

In many dealerships, you're assigned a salesperson as soon as you enter the showroom. You won't see the assignment take place, but it happens like clockwork. Usually it's done on a rotating basis. Say that eight salespeople are on duty when you drop in – then you realize that you entered the dealership by mistake. The salesperson assigned to you probably is out of luck. Eight more customers are going to have to come in before he or she has another chance to earn a commission.

This is why salespeople often approach customers too soon and too aggressively – at least from the customer's perspective. And it leads them to ask "The Seven Dreaded Questions". Don't worry. These queries aren't sinister and you can handle them easily if you know what to expect.

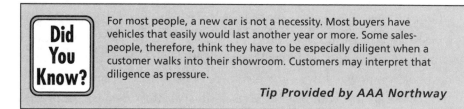

Did You Know? For most people, a new car is not a necessity. Most buyers have vehicles that easily would last another year or more. Some salespeople, therefore, think they have to be especially diligent when a customer walks into their showroom. Customers may interpret that diligence as pressure.

Tip Provided by AAA Northway

Question No. 1: 'Can I Help You?'

There you are in the showroom, looking for one specific model and probably not finding it. You were hoping to sit in the vehicle for a few minutes, just to size it up, then leave quietly. And here is a salesperson who manages to rip the cover off your stealth visit.

Accept it, the jig is up. You are going to have to speak to the seller. If you're like most customers, your response is going to be: "I'm just looking."

At this point, the salesperson can try to break the ice. Fortunately, the "Oh good, I'm just selling" response has fallen out of favor, as has the handshake technique in which the saleperson grabs your hand and won't let go until you say your name.

The salesperson can try some other technique to get you past "just looking" – or he/she can just back off. Backing off has become standard operating procedure in many showrooms. In some cases, salespeople wait until you give some sign that you want assistance. As a result, customers who used to complain of too much pressure are now likely to gripe about being ignored. They interpret this new posture as a sign that the dealership, for whatever reason, doesn't consider them a viable customer.

What's considered ideal treatment varies from customer to customer. You should be given a chance to look around without interruptions. Once you want help, though, the staff should be responsive.

In all likelihood, however, the salesperson will counter "just looking" by trying to draw you into a conversation about the kind of vehicle you want. At this point, you have a choice. You can stick to "just looking" and hope the salesperson disappears. Or you could say, "Right now, I'd just like to look, thank you." A clever seller will get the hint. Or you can go ahead and accept the offer of help.

Accepting assistance, in fact, is just what you need to do if you can't find what you want on your own. Tell the salesperson what you'd like to see. At a Ford dealership, for example, you could say, "I'm just beginning to shop for a compact sedan and, along with some other models, I want to consider the Focus. Today I'd just like to look at the vehicle and sit in it for a while to see if it's comfortable. If you could point me toward a Focus and give me your card, I'll call you when I need more help." You've been honest and polite and you should get what you want. If you don't, go elsewhere.

What to Expect on the Way to the Car

Good salespeople, however, will have additional questions. As they walk you toward the model you want to see, they'll work these inquiries into normal conversation – a technique intended to reduce the pressure you feel. Likely topics include:

- What other models are you considering?

- How long have you been shopping?

- When do you think you'll buy the car?

- Have you driven any of the models you are considering?

While you don't have to answer, there's probably no reason not to. Telling the truth often helps the salesperson give you valuable information. Say you plan to buy within 30 days. The salesperson then tells you that some manufacturer's incentives are scheduled to end in three weeks. Armed with this knowledge, you might want to adjust your time frame. Why wait for four weeks if you could save $1,000 by buying a week earlier?

Once you arrive at the car, your salesperson should show you around it briefly, demonstrate how to adjust the seat and steering wheel for maximum comfort and how to operate some of the controls. Then the salesperson should leave you alone to sit in the front and rear seats and get the feel of the interior. What happens next is up to you.

If you don't like the car – even for what seems like a silly reason – you can just leave. If you like the vehicle, however, you should plan to go back. You can go ahead and make an appointment to test-drive a demonstrator with equipment that closely matches the car you're interested in. Or you can call later, after you've looked at all the other cars on your list.

Question No. 2: 'Are You Planning on Buying a Car Today?'

While people often feel that this question is little more than a pressure tactic, it's really one of the easiest to answer. "No, today I am looking. I'd appreciate your answering some questions that will help me make an informed decision."

Most salespeople will help you. In some cases, however, you'll be turned over to another salesperson. You've apparently stumbled across someone willing to wait for a customer to come in and simply buy today. Perhaps the customer's car has been stolen or its engine has gasped its last. Whatever – these salespeople specialize in a certain kind of buyer: the one who needs to get transportation right now, rather than the best car or the best deal. For you, though, being turned over to another salesperson is the best thing that could happen.

Question No. 3: 'What Would I Have to Do to Get You to Buy Today?'

Understand that the salesperson's greatest fear is not that you won't buy a car, it's that you'll buy one somewhere else. Some other salesperson on another lot might ask you this question, or one like it, and succeed in making the sale.

Some customers – and maybe you're one of them – perceive this question simply as a pressure tactic. Whether you accept its legitimacy or not, your answer is simple: "There is nothing you can do, short of giving me the vehicle, that would make me stop looking today." Then you should continue asking the questions you need answered to make an informed decision.

Question No. 4: 'Will There Be a Trade-In?'

If you're just starting to shop, it's much too early to be concerned about the trade-in. Here's what you say: "Right now, I'm concentrating on choosing the right new car. Will you help me with that?"

When you get down to setting a price, however, the trade-in question has to be addressed. We'll show you how to deal with this issue – as well as explain why it's wrong to lie about your intentions, as some car-buying guides suggest – in the chapter on the pricing game.

Question No. 5: 'Will Someone Else be Involved in the Purchase Decision?'

On your preliminary outings, in which you simply look at the cars and see which models fit you and which don't, this information seems premature. Eventually, however, it could become a legitimate question for both male and female customers.

Women are often more than a little sensitive about this question. Improperly asked, it can imply "Listen sweetie, when it comes to buying a car, you're out of your league because you're a woman. Why don't you bring in your (pick one) father, husband, boyfriend, son, uncle, male friend and we'll get this deal done."

Women now buy about half of the new cars and trucks, so you'd think this attitude would have disappeared. In most dealerships, it has. But it's still fresh in the minds of many women who felt humiliated by it in the past. And they may find the anger returning, even when the sales representative poses a gender-neutral version of the question.

From the salesperson's perspective, however, this is important information. Good salespeople often can find this out without having to ask directly. For example, they may say, "Will there be any other people who'll drive this car regularly?" If you say yes, the salesperson can ask whether they'll also have a hand in the decision.

If others need to be involved, it's legitimate for the salesperson to want to address their concerns directly. Having all parties together also saves time.

Question No. 6: 'How Much Do You Want to Pay?'

In many respects, this is a terrible question for a salesperson to ask a customer. You, the buyer, probably think it's a trap. If you specify a price higher than the dealership would reasonably accept, you lose. If your figure is unrealistically low, you appear naïve, perhaps even foolish. You lose again.

No other business asks you to set the price you'd pay for its products and the dealership isn't really doing so, either. The salesperson knows what the price should be. From a tactical perspective, however, it makes no sense to reveal the amount just yet.

You, on the other hand, know very well that almost no car or truck is sold for the manufacturer's suggested retail price. And since you've done your research and obtained vehicle pricing information – from aaa.com, for instance – or the retail and the invoice prices for the car and each of its options, you know what the dealer paid for the vehicle in question. So what should you offer for it? Nothing. **It's not your job to set the price. It's your job to accept or reject the price offered by the dealer.**

Here's what you say: "I think you should tell me the lowest price you'll accept for this vehicle. I am not in your business. You tell me what you want and I'll decide whether I want to pay that price – after I check with a few more dealers. And just as I haven't told you what other dealers are asking for this car, I won't tell them what you want either."

Question No. 7: 'How Much a Month Do You Want to Spend?'

Monthly prices are always so much lower than total prices that you can't blame the salesperson for wanting you to think in those terms. Yet you must insist on thinking first of the total price and how that fits into the budget you've set for this major purchase. That means that before you enter a dealership, you have to do your homework and know how much you can afford. Stick firmly to your budget and insist on being told the true selling price of the vehicle, not the payments. Stay away from this tactic like the plague. Shop only on the basis of the total price, not monthly payments.

Controlling the Purchasing Process

Once you've done your research and found four or five cars that, on paper, meet your needs and fit your budget, try using this approach to complete your purchase.

Using conveniently located dealers, look at the vehicles on your list. Sit in the models, examine the control layouts and assess the blind spots. Check the seating position and the fit of the safety belts and head restraints. Make sure the seats are comfortable. Once you've done this for all the cars on your list, you'll find that you probably can eliminate at least one because it simply doesn't fit you.

This first visit is no time to take a test drive or talk fine points of options pricing and trade-in values with a salesperson. Confine your visit to examining the vehicle and making sure its overall design meets your needs.

Now consider the information you've gathered from your friends, acquaintances, your local AAA club, and regulatory or consumer reporting agencies on the dealers in your area that sell the vehicles you want to look at more closely. Pick dealerships that are conveniently located – very important, because you may want to go back when it's time for service. Since you probably already visited the dealership for your initial inspection, call the salesperson who helped you and make an appointment for a test drive. Arrive early so you can examine the service department first, if you have not done so already.

You may be surprised to discover that calling the salesperson who approached you on your initial visit gives you a good bit of credibility. Most people just toss the business card and start over with a new sales representative when they return for a test drive. Because you called your salesperson, he or she will take you more seriously as a customer. Your track record for being honest and doing what you said you'd do during the sales process may inspire the salesperson to be more helpful and forthcoming, too. A good relationship makes this purchase easier and lays the groundwork for smoother dealings in the future.

Be forewarned that if you want to play games, the dealership's personnel probably are far more skilled than you are. After all, they get more practice. Much more.

After test-driving the vehicle, you should thank the salesperson. Back in your car, you may want to make some notes on the strong points and weaknesses of the model you just drove. Remember that until you drive all of the cars on your list, it's too early to talk about pricing or trade-in.

After you drive them all, narrow your choices to the two models that seem most promising. Now it's time to obtain pricing reports that detail the invoice and list prices for the vehicles and each of their accessories.

Only now do you really know what you want. You also know – if you followed our suggestions in previous chapters – that these cars fit in your budget. You know you can afford the insurance and that their level of passive safety is adequate for you and your family. You have a good idea what you want to do with your current car and what it's worth. You know your credit standing and perhaps have been pre-approved for an auto loan. Only when all this is done is it time to start the pricing game.

CHAPTER 11

Options

In This Chapter

• • • • • • • • • • •

- Which options to consider
- Which options to reject
- Safety equipment that may be optional
- Options that may make you more comfortable
- Why some options can be hazardous under some circumstances

Not too many years ago, few cars came with the features that we consider necessities today. Forget power steering and power brakes, which were seen as frivolous gadgets two generations ago. Even such basic items as heaters, defrosters and directional signals were optional and often passed over by buyers who thought their money was better spent elsewhere.

Today's vehicles are far better equipped. Even many economy cars offer standard air conditioning, power windows and power locks. Power steering and power brakes are now installed on nearly every car and truck.

You'll still have options to consider when you go car shopping, though. Dealers install some of them, but most get put on the car as it goes down the factory assembly line. Options generally fall into five categories: safety, appearance, comfort and convenience, engine and transmission, and suspension, wheels and tires. We'll consider these by category, even though there's some overlap. For example, a wheel, tire and suspension package that offers sportier, more precise handling and better control could well be called a safety option.

Consider the optional equipment carefully when you order a vehicle. It's possible to add 50 percent to the price of some popular models simply by ordering an upgraded trim line and lots of accessories.

Tip Provided by
AAA South Jersey

Safety Options

That safety now helps sell new cars is of little doubt. But how much safety equipment is enough? The answer is up to you. Manufacturers offer a basic level of safety equipment, much of which is mandated by federal regulations. Additional equipment, especially in lower-priced vehicles, is optional. Here's a rundown of what you can expect:

ABS or Antilock Braking – ABS prevents the wheels from locking during a stop on slippery surfaces or in an emergency. This prevents skids and helps you stay in control of the vehicle. ABS may even shorten stopping distances, but that's not guaranteed. If better control and prevention of skids are advantages, the high initial cost, greater complexity and potential for expensive repairs as the car ages are disadvantages. In addition, ABS has a spotty track record when it comes to reducing crashes and insurance claims. Nonetheless, the added control that ABS affords a driver in a tight spot can be invaluable. If ABS is an option, give it careful consideration.

Did You Know?

Parents with children who are almost of driving age should keep this in mind when they go shopping for a new car or truck. One man, who had 13- and 14-year-old daughters, settled on a model with antilock brakes. It was a $600 option. Having competed in sanctioned auto racing for years and being skilled at threshold braking and avoiding skids during emergency stops, he originally felt that he didn't need the option. Then he was asked whether his daughters would drive the car after they got their licenses. They would – and ABS began to look like a pretty good idea after all.

Tip Provided by Automobile Club of Hartford

Brake Assist – Surprisingly, many drivers don't apply their brakes hard enough in an emergency or panic stop. Brake Assist was developed to take over for them. The system even discriminates between a brisk stop and an emergency stop. When it senses a real emergency, it applies full braking. It's standard on some luxury cars and a worthwhile option when available elsewhere.

Stability Control – When is a skid not a skid? When it's caught – often before the driver is even aware of a problem – and quickly corrected by an electronic stability enhancement system. The technology is complex but the results are worth it, especially for motorists who often have to drive on slippery surfaces. Standard on some luxury cars and trucks, this is another worthwhile option that's increasingly becoming available on lower-priced vehicles.

Traction Control – By regulating the engine's power output and selectively applying brakes to keep a wheel from spinning, these systems can help you keep going under less than ideal conditions. While no substitute for four-wheel or all-wheel drive, traction control can come close when the vehicle is equipped with the right tires for road conditions. Often a surprisingly economical addition to ABS brakes, traction control is usually worth the money.

Side-Impact Air Bags – While there's no federal standard either requiring side-impact air bags or governing their performance, initial side-impact testing suggests that they add a valuable margin of safety. Especially useful are air bags that protect the head and torso of the person sitting right next to the door. Some designs protect only the torso. But be careful: they can pose a hazard to children, who sometimes fall asleep in unusual positions while traveling. In some cars and trucks, rear air bags are available. As long as proper care is taken when seating children in the car, these are a valuable option.

Cargo Nets – The cargo compartment in a station wagon, SUV or mini-van is open to the passenger compartment. As a result, items stored in the cargo area can hit passengers in a crash even during a sudden, violent maneuver. A properly designed and installed cargo net helps prevent this from happening without blocking a driver's view to the rear. A net also can keep pets in the rear compartment. This is a valuable safety option.

Electric Rear-Window Defroster – If one is optional, buy it. Electric defrosters clear the rear window of dew and frost on the outside or fog on the inside. They are a must for good visibility under many difficult conditions. Some electric defroster systems also heat the outside rearview mirrors to clear them of frost or fog.

Limited Slip Differential – A common option on rear-wheel and four-wheel drive vehicles, limited slip differentials can keep you from getting stuck. In rear-wheel drive vehicles, however, they can complicate handling under some circumstances. They also require special fluids and may call for more frequent maintenance than the standard differential. Unless you often face slippery roads, you may not need this option.

Security System – Since a stolen car is more likely to be crashed, let's consider this a safety device. Factory-installed systems generally work well, although some failure modes will leave your car disabled and unwilling to start, even for you. Insurance companies sometimes give discounts for cars equipped with passive-security features. Some insurance companies only consider factory-installed systems worthy of discounts, although aftermarket or dealer-installed systems can work well. If you have one installed, try to determine the installer's track record. This can be more important than the system you choose. If possible, select a security system that can be installed by plugging into the existing wiring harness connections, rather than stripping insulation and physically cutting the wires.

Comfort and Convenience Items

In this category, the range of options is limited only by the manufacturer's ingenuity and marketing savvy. Carefully consider what you think you'll need and like before buying.

In-Car Navigation Systems – For drivers who frequently venture into unfamiliar territory, these factory-installed navigation systems can be quite valuable. Using global positioning satellite (GPS) technology and current maps stored on a computer disk, these systems show you where you are and how to reach your destination. In addition to an in-dash display of the mapping information, they also provide verbal commands – "Turn right in one-quarter mile," for example. The combination of the map and directions can be quite effective. The systems are expensive, however, frequently topping $2,000. And the routes they choose are not always the most efficient. Mapping information also needs to be updated regularly and maps for new areas are expensive. Still, knowing where you are and where you're going can be invaluable. It can reduce confusion at intersections and eliminate the need to stop, perhaps under risky circumstances, to ask for directions. Not all carmakers offer these systems, but there are after-market suppliers with models that fit any vehicle. Check out a system on a rental car – such as the "Never Lost" system in a Hertz rental – to help you decide if you really need it.

PITFALLS

Almost no option returns more at trade-in time than it costs when new. Don't buy unwanted items expecting to get your money back when you trade. It won't happen.

Tip Provided by
AAA Utica and Central New York

Telematics – These systems also use GPS technology to locate your car when you call a centralized service center. You pay a fee to subscribe to the service. When you call, the center can guide you to a destination, locate your vehicle and send emergency service or help you in some other way, such as making hotel reservations or pointing you toward the closest gas station.

The service center also can relay messages or give you information on local attractions. AAA's RESPONSE services center is one example; OnStar from General Motors is another. Using location technology allows a service provider to know exactly where you are even when you may not. Armed with this knowledge, telematics providers can proactively arrange for emergency service quickly or get directions any time of the day or night which enhances your safety.

Some manufacturers build these systems into their vehicles, but you can get the same services using a portable hand-held device. Portability allows you to access telematics services whenever and wherever you need them, whether you're in a car or not.

A system in the car can lock or unlock your car by remote control or trace your vehicle if it's stolen. Check the scope of the services and the subscription fees before making a decision.

Air Conditioning – Now almost universally installed at the factory, air conditioning offers several advantages besides the obvious comfort it affords on hot days. Air-conditioned cars often defog windows much more quickly than cars equipped only with a heater and defroster. Air conditioning also lets a driver keep all the windows closed, for safety and to reduce noise, which can cause fatigue. Interestingly, opening windows on the highway can reduce fuel efficiency as much as using the air conditioning, if not more so. Why? Because open windows increase aerodynamic drag. Expensive to add and sometimes expensive to repair, air conditioning is a matter of personal preference.

Upgraded Seating Packages – Try them for comfort and visibility before you buy. You may find the more expensive seating is less comfortable, affords less head restraint protection or interferes with your visibility. Then again, you may have problems with standard seating and find the optional interior setup preferable.

Leather Upholstery – A matter of taste. To many people, leather conveys a sense of luxury. Depending on the tanning process, the aroma also can be appealing. Leather does tend to be initially cold in the winter and hot in the summer. However, it allows some breathing for comfort, which vinyl does not, and generally wears well with minimal care. Is it worth $800 to $1,600? You decide.

Heated Seats – For relatively quick cold-weather comfort, electrically heated seats can be wonderful. Just push a button and in a few minutes the seat gets nice and warm. Unfortunately, some are slow to warm up, especially if you have heavy optional leather or cloth upholstery. Some cars also offer an electrically heated steering wheel. These generally warm faster than either heated seats or the heater itself and can make driving a cold car without gloves much more comfortable. Costs vary widely.

Power Accessories – Power windows, power mirrors, power locks and even power seats are increasingly popular. Power mirrors make proper adjustment of the outside mirrors quite easy, which is a safety factor. Power locks also can be considered a safety feature, since they let a lone driver lock all the doors with the simple push of a button. Power locks often are combined with keyless entry, another convenience. As for power windows, their convenience can't be discounted, but they're hardly essential. Some people need a power seat – which frequently allows a wider range of adjustment than a manual seat – to establish proper sight lines or adequate comfort. While these power accessories often are relatively inexpensive when the car is new, repairs can be costly.

Upgraded Sound and Video Entertainment Systems – Be guided by your needs and the cost. Just be sure to sample the product before you buy. More expensive systems are not always better.

Cruise Control – Reduces physical effort and prevents right-leg cramps on long trips. Cruise control also keeps your speed down – a safety factor – and can lead to more fuel-efficient operation. Improperly used – in heavy traffic, on curvy secondary roads or when there's limited traction – it can be a hazard. It's your choice. Use it wisely if you buy it.

Sunroof – The open-air sense of a convertible with the security and strength of a steel roof is the promise. What sunroofs actually deliver is pleasant enough, but hardly the equal of a true convertible. There are three types. One slides back inside the car, effectively reducing headroom. Others slide

PITFALLS

Try to avoid major non-factory installed options. Anyone, for example, can cut a hole and install a sunroof – but only a good technician can equal the job done at the factory. In addition, there's no factory warranty on aftermarket work.

Tip Provided by AAA Northwest Ohio

back outside the car, taking a far smaller toll on interior room and comfort. The least expensive type manually pops open or can be removed from the outside. The downside is, you can't close it quickly when the rain starts. Expensive to buy and repair, although fixes are seldom needed. Leakage is generally not a problem as long as drain tubes are kept clear.

Remote Controls on Steering Wheel – These let you change the radio station, advance the tape or CD, adjust the climate controls, or change the volume without taking your hands from the wheel or your eyes from the road. Probably a plus for safety and convenience, but not a major improvement.

Trip Computers – They often provide useful information, such as average or instantaneous fuel consumption, but operating them can be distracting.

Appearance Packages

Let your preferences be your guide, but bear these warnings in mind:

Rear Spoilers – These offer little or no value at current speed limits and can block visibility to the rear.

Aero-Packages – Usually consisting of under-bumper spoilers and lower side body cladding (also called a ground-effects package) aero-packages are easily damaged by curbs and road debris. Expensive to repair. They serve little or no practical function at highway speeds.

Alloy Wheels – Stylish, they are also fragile and easily damaged by pot-holes and curbs. Of course, steel wheels also are easily damaged by road hazards, but they typically cost less than $100 to replace. Alloy wheels usually start at $250 and some can cost much more. The lighter weight of alloy wheels has negligible effect on riding comfort and handling in most cars.

Non-Factory Roof and Grille Treatments – Fake convertible top applications and "classic" design grilles often require drilling holes in the body, which can lead to rust that the factory warranty definitely won't cover. Of no utility whatsoever.

Brush Guards – Ideal for trucks and SUVs that go off road, these are mere styling exercises for vehicles that stay on the pavement. Some of these guards can be knocked back into the sheet metal in minor bumps, increasing the cost of repairs.

Engines and Transmissions

Transmissions – Automatics are quickly taking over. Clutch-free driving has wide appeal and the engineers have significantly reduced – and in some vehicles even completely eliminated – the fuel economy penalty that automatics once extracted. A manual transmission can be a delight to use, or the clutch may be heavy and the shift linkage imprecise. Try the transmission you're going to buy with the engine you selected before you sign a contract. Automatic transmissions should offer at least four forward speeds, manuals five. In some cases you can find five-speed or six-speed automatics and manuals. Automatic transmissions generally are more expensive to repair and are more likely to need repair. An unskilled driver, however, can quickly reduce a manual transmission and its clutch to rubble. Repairs for manual transmissions also are expensive.

Engines – The standard engine is more than sufficient for most buyers. If you want more performance, however, bigger or more powerful motors are often available. In many cars, you may have to buy a glitzier model to get the friskier engine. In trucks, you often find a bewildering selection of power-trains to choose from. A skilled salesperson can be invaluable in helping you make the right choice. Manufacturers can increase engine performance by increasing engine size, adopting more expensive valvetrains, using some form of forced-air induction such as turbocharging or supercharging, or improving exhaust function. More powerful engines usually require more gasoline, day in and day out, so be sure you really want or need the extra performance. Recognize, too, that turbochargers can fail and are expensive to repair. If you want that added power so you can pull a trailer, make sure the drivetrain is up to the task. Turbocharged engines, despite producing more power, are often ill-suited for heavy loads.

Suspensions, Wheels and Tires

Suspensions – Some vehicles offer several suspension systems. Sport suspension upgrades generally make the vehicle ride more firmly and handle better. Simply put, a firmer ride results when the suspension components are stiffened. On rough surfaces, the ride in such a vehicle will be less supple and compliant over bumps. This can actually make a car or truck ride roughly. In other cases, it eliminates the bobbing up and down that sometimes occurs after the vehicle has struck a bump. This enhanced control can make some vehicles ride more comfortably. Is the better handling worth the firmer ride? You decide. Read the car-buying guides and try the vehicles before you buy. Generally, the firmer suspensions produce a safer, more stable, better-handling vehicle.

Wheels and Tires – Most cars come with all-season tires and serve the needs of their buyers well. Other cars offer performance tires as an option or as standard equipment. They provide better cornering grip and shorter stopping distances than all-season tires. Unfortunately, most perform very poorly in the snow. They also tend to be wider and to have a narrower sidewall and a lower aspect ratio, which makes the vehicle ride more firmly than it would with the standard tire. Vehicles with performance tires also tend to follow road imperfections – it's called nibbling – which can detract from directional stability. For most buyers, all-season tires are the best bet.

CHAPTER

12

The Pricing Game

In This Chapter
• • • • • • • • • • • •

- Why dealer profit margins are more important to the dealer than to you
- How to determine a fair price
- The role of rebates
- Determining dealer incentives
- What holdback is
- Why dealer invoice and dealer cost are not the same
- The best time to buy
- Why you must get it in writing

The pricing game is far more important to the dealer than it is to you. After all, a profit is all that the dealer has to show for the time and effort that went into selling you a vehicle. Granted, parts and service for your vehicle present additional opportunities for revenue, but there are no guarantees that you'll use the dealer's repair shop. This is why dealers work so hard to maximize profit on every sale.

Your contribution toward the dealer's profit is relatively small compared to the expenses you'll incur over several years of vehicle ownership. So when you think about it, this is a poor place to try to make or break your motoring budget. Not that you should pay more than you have to, of course, but a dealer's profit margin is often too small to make a significant difference in your overall cost.

As the AAA-Runzheimer International studies on driving expenses show, a new car is going to cost you 45 to 55 cents for every mile you drive during the first four years. Do the math: if you average 15,000 miles a year, you'll shell out at least $27,000 for transportation in those first 48 months. At 50 cents a mile, the cost is $30,000. And if your taste runs to luxury cars or larger SUVs or pickups, those costs can go even higher.

So what's the dealer's part in this equation? The spread from highest to lowest dealer price is about $700 in most areas for most typical family vehicles. Granted, $700 is a significant sum to most people – more than a week's pay for the average worker. In the big-car-owner picture, figuring costs at 45 cents per mile, it's a 2.6 percent difference in total expenses.

In many cases, you can easily save two to five times that amount simply by better managing your depreciation expenses. How? By selecting the right make and model and deciding how long you'll keep it. Check out Chapter 2 for more information on depreciation.

There are exceptions to this analysis, of course. Some dealers simply charge too much compared to other area dealers selling the same cars and trucks. Assuming the levels of service are similar and the location of a lower-priced dealer is convenient, the choice should be obvious. Even if the location is inconvenient, a sufficiently lower price can make choosing the inconveniently located dealer worthwhile.

Determining the Right Price

The concept of supply and demand is older than Adam Smith, who effectively explained its finer points back in the mid- to late 1700s. Simply stated – and applied to the act of car shopping – it goes like this: when the number of cars or trucks available exceeds the number of buyers who want them, the price goes down. When buyers demand more of a certain model than the manufacturer can produce, the price customers pay goes up.

As a car shopper, it's up to you to determine what constitutes a fair price in your area for the model you want. This book can't do it for you. Magazine articles can't do it for you. You have to go out and do the research – then decide if you want to pay that price or choose another model.

Once you determine which vehicle you want to buy, it's easy to discover whether a car is flying off the lot or stalled on the sidelines. Find recent copies of *Automotive News* or *The Wall Street Journal* – your library should have them – and look up the size of the unsold supply of a particular model, as measured in days.

Auto industry insiders think a 60-day supply for most models is ideal. This means there are enough unsold cars in dealers' inventories and in transit to meet customer demand over the next two months.

The makers of some unpopular, low-volume vehicles sometimes see the supply balloon to more than 100 days. In a few cases, manufacturers have reported nearly a year's worth of unsold inventory. Looking for a deep, deep discount? These are the vehicles you can expect to be marked down.

When you check the data, you'll undoubtedly find some vehicles in very short supply. Once supplies drop below the 30-day mark, you may have trouble even locating a dealer with a demo model for a test drive. Needless to say, there's little inventory on the dealer's lot. Often, even the models in transit are presold – in other words, dealers have deposits and signed contracts on every one of them.

If this happens when you're car shopping, you'll have to decide whether the vehicle is worth the higher price. Remember, you still have options. You can order a vehicle from another dealer and wait for delivery or simply choose another make and model.

Obviously, in a competitive market, a dealer who's drowning in inventory is more likely to be flexible on pricing than the one who has more customers than cars. And that's not all: the factory producing those less popular cars and trucks destined to sit in a lot awaiting buyers has an incentive to help the retail side.

The Pricing Waltz

Fortunately, there is a simple way to determine what the new car you want is worth on the open market: Ask the dealers in your area and perhaps beyond what they want for it. Remember, too, that there are significant regional differences in the popularity of many models. If business or pleasure travel takes you to a part of the country where supplies of a model you like are ample and demand is weak, you might be able to make a better deal there than at home. The seller should be able to arrange shipping – usually at your expense. Just make sure that the vehicle is insured while it's in transit and that you get the appropriate certificate of origin and the right paperwork so you can register the vehicle back home. If you drove to the area, however, you can always just drive your new car home.

Unfortunately, simply asking for a price is not as easy as it should be. Unless they know that every competitor is sticking to list price, dealers hate to give you their best numbers without a long, drawn-out effort on your part. This is the part of new car shopping that most people dread and dislike the most.

Dealers have a good reason for doing this, however. They'd much rather quote you a price and promise additional discounts when you're ready to buy than show their hand too soon. Why? Because they know you'll just go to a competitor and try to get something better. A dealer who offers you a fair price but maybe not the absolute lowest price could lose the sale to someone who undercuts by an insignificant sum. Dealers have seen buyers swayed by as little as $25 on a $30,000 vehicle.

Dealers also know that it's possible to lose a deal after the contract is signed. Some customers take the paperwork to other dealers and try to use it to negotiate an even lower price.

That's why dealers selling a model that's in ample supply hate to give you their best price until they're confident you're ready, willing and able to sign a contract right then and there. From your standpoint, however, such maneuvers make it difficult if not impossible to know whether you got the best price.

Try This Approach

Here's an approach that often works in a buyer's market, one in which supply is greater than demand: Approach several dealers, starting with the one where you did your initial shopping, and ask for a price. Since you were honest with this dealer and did what you said you'd do, you should have some credibility at this point. Ask for a price that's valid for seven days and let your salesperson know that you won't disclose it while you shop. Then contact additional dealers, either in person, by fax or over the Internet, and request a price for the identical model with the same options. Tell each dealer that price is important and that you plan to make your decision within the week. After a few contacts, you should have a good idea what your chosen vehicle fetches from paying customers.

Some dealers will ask what your lowest price is. Don't tell. Just say that you're not disclosing prices you've obtained so far – and won't reveal this dealer's price to others, either.

If you provide a dealer with your current low price, you just give the dealer a firm target. Let's say you're considering a car that stickers for $20,000 and that your lowest price so far is $18,400. This dealer might have been willing to go to $17,900, but now they offer to sell it for $18,200. You just shot down your chances of getting the better deal.

If you follow only one piece of advice when seeking prices from dealers, it should be this: Do not lie about prices you obtained elsewhere. Doing so will not only cost you credibility, it will suggest to the dealer, "Ah-ah. This customer wants to play games. Let the games begin." Who do you think is better at this particular competition? It's not you.

In some cases, dealers are perfectly willing to embarrass customers who fib. More than a few salespeople will call the competing dealership – the one that supposedly offered the wonderful price – while the customer sits right there listening.

In many dealerships you can expect to be "turned over" during your shopping foray. This means you'll be introduced to another salesperson or to a manager if things aren't going well from the dealer's perspective. Why? Because, the dealership reasons, another salesperson might prove more compatible with your personality and be more likely to make the sale.

Tip Provided by AAA Berkshire County

Some customers are so embarrassed that they stick around and buy a car from this salesperson.

Sometimes the low price isn't the result of a lie by the customer, it's a low-ball offer. A low-ball price is one that's simply too low. The dealership would never sell you the car for that amount. Its only purpose is to get you to come back after you do all your price comparisons. It's usually offered just as you leave. Say you get what you believe is the best price this dealer will offer, $17,300. Then as you leave, the salesperson says, "You go do your shopping. Just remember that when you're ready to buy, we can really offer you our best price. Keep the figure $15,800, in mind, give or take a little." So now you're thinking you can get your dream car for $15,800. You can't, of course, but this price becomes that benchmark — one that no other dealer can match because it's less than what the dealer pays the factory. After you shop — unable to equal the price, of course — you return to this dealership. Then the salesperson tells you that you can't buy the car for that price here either. The $15,800, give or take, turns out to be for a low-mileage used model or a stripped-down version of what you want. You were tricked — but the trick has gotten you back in the showroom where the salesperson can now try to sell you another vehicle. And it gives the dealership another chance to trim its $17,300 price. It's up to you to decide whether you want to deal with such an establishment. If you think you're getting a low-ball offer, the best response is to leave and not return.

Remember this, too: Dealerships compete with each other, sometimes vigorously, but the world of car selling and servicing is really quite small. Dealers are often friends. They play golf together. They go on factory junkets and socialize with each other. In most cases, salespeople at one dealership know the salespeople at other dealerships. Turnover is so high that salespeople with any experience in the field probably worked with the folks at the other dealerships. Dealers often buy or sell used cars or swap new cars with their competitors. They know what's happening in their market. You probably won't rattle them with stories of prices you got elsewhere – and they'll recognize a fake price instantly.

A popular vehicle in ample supply generally sells for $300 to $500 over invoice after negotiation. You should have determined the invoice price either by buying a pricing service report, which reveals the vehicle's invoice price and all its options, or searching on the Internet. If you asked several dealers for their best price – without tattling, of course – and you still can't get an offer in this optimum range, you have some decisions to make. If your heart is set on this car or truck, you can return to the most convenient dealer, or the one with the best service department, and make an offer that you think is fair. The dealer can then accept your bid, reject it or make a counter offer.

In a perfect world, you could just decide on the make, model and equipment you wanted and find many dealers in your area with numerous examples in stock. This is not a perfect world. Consequently, when you call around asking for quotes, you'll get prices on vehicles that are close to what you want but that differ in some details. This usually happens because the dealer doesn't have the exact vehicle that you want in stock. The price still can be useful, depending on whether the differences in equipment are important to you. For instance, one car has floor mats, the other doesn't. Just remember to take the equipment differences into account when comparing prices.

In some cars and trucks, however, equipment can make a big difference in the size of the discount dealers are willing to offer. A model with one set of options may be significantly harder to obtain than a version with almost identical equipment. The harder-to-find model won't be discounted nearly as much as its less popular sibling.

Significant differences in equipment and price may come up as well. Say you didn't want a sunroof, but the dealer gives you a quote on a vehicle with this $1,000 option. You might want to see if there's anything in the inventory that's closer to what you want. Or you could ask for a bid on a vehicle ordered to your specs. Or you could just ignore this dealer and consider the others.

In some cases, dealers are willing to swap accessories – wheels, for instance – from one car to another. You may find a car with alloy wheels on the price sticker but steel wheels on the vehicle. If so, you also should find an auxiliary sticker showing that the alloy wheels were deleted and their price subtracted from the total. The dealer may have swapped the alloy wheels for another customer. Just make sure that the right wheel and tire size is installed on the vehicle you're buying.

It's also possible that the factory made a mistake. For example, when leather upholstery became available on one popular family car halfway through the model year, the factory started producing cars with this option without adding it to the price sticker. The factory also forgot to charge dealers for it. That meant free leather – in theory a $1,200 option – for people who wanted it. But it also complicated life for dealers and customers who bought cars in transit. In many cases, the buyers wanted cloth upholstery – and according to the sticker, that's how the cars were equipped. To them, the prospect of free leather wasn't the least bit appealing. Many people blamed their dealers, but really it was the factory's fault.

Almost all dealers with a significant inventory want to sell you a car from stock, not order one. The reason is simple. Dealers borrow money to purchase inventory. Every month they owe the finance company interest on the loans for the vehicles that remain unsold. Therefore, if you want a truck in bright red and the dealer has one in dark red, you can expect the salesperson to make a real effort to sell you the dark red model. If the salesperson succeeds, the dealer gets out from under the loan.

Dealers also trade vehicles with other area dealers of the same brand to obtain just the color or equipment you want. That's why you sometimes see a vehicle at one dealership with a price sticker showing it was sold to another dealer in the next town or even another state. If the dealer with the dark red truck can trade with another dealer for your bright red model, then the dealer has effectively gotten the dark red model out of inventory and can stop paying interest on it.

If, however, you want a slow-selling model, the other dealer may not be willing to trade. Instead, the dealer may want to sell your dealer the vehicle that meets your requirements. That means your dealer can't reduce his inventory even though you're making a purchase. The other dealer may sell the car at invoice or even below, but this is still a far less attractive option for your dealer – and this will be reflected in the price you pay.

A Different Experience

When demand exceeds supply, you're in for an entirely different experience. If demand is strong enough, you may find that instead of looking for a discount from the MSRP, you'll be negotiating the size of additional dealer markup over MSRP. Dealers have many ways of boosting prices on a popular model, even in the face of objections from the manufacturer. Some dealers add expensive packages of equipment or services to every car in their stock. Fabric protection, pin striping and paint treatments can do wonders for the dealer's profit margin. If you don't want to pay for these questionable additions, the dealer knows that someone else will be more willing to fork over the extra money. Such is the joy of selling a model in peak demand.

You often see these extras on a dealer-installed price label that the dealership pastes to the window right next to the factory sticker. It lists all the little extras and shows how much they cost. It's perfectly legal.

Some dealers don't even try to camouflage their lust for additional profit. Their price stickers list only "ADM," or similar initials. In this case, ADM stands for "additional dealer markup" – in other words, extra profit the dealer can charge simply because demand for this vehicle is strong.

Additional dealer markup stickers are to be expected on extremely rare or popular cars. But you might find these stickers on cars that aren't in high demand. Here they serve a valuable purpose – at least from the dealer's perspective. Even if no competitor is charging comparable surcharges, the presence of such a sticker often prompts a buyer to start negotiating from this inflated sticker price. These buyers may end up paying MSRP or slightly below and think they've scored a major victory. They haven't.

With more and more customers starting their negotiations from the dealer's invoice price and working their way up, getting the customer to start negotiating at a higher-than-MSRP level often ensures higher margins for the dealer.

In other cases, the stickers are simply silly additions that allow a dealer to advertise "$6,000 discounts" in bold type on a model with barely a $2,000 profit margin. Such advertising is guaranteed to catch the attention of shoppers. Unfortunately, the promised savings are an illusion. Notice that in most of these ads, the price of the vehicle after the discount is never mentioned. You discover how unimpressive the "sale" price is only after you enter the showroom. Still, dealers who do this think they can sell a car to somebody hoping to go home with the bargain of the century. Don't be one of them, even if your old car won't start when you're ready to leave! Remember, it's not what you save, it's what you pay!

One Price Dealers — Version One

Recognizing that many new-car buyers simply hate the negotiation process, some dealers try to gain an advantage by offering a good price right up front. Sometimes called "no-dicker sticker" dealers, they often mark the discounted price on the vehicle.

This seems an honorable way to satisfy customers who don't want to haggle but don't want to pay list price either. Unfortunately, no-dicker sticker dealers have a tough time in the market. Competitors often underprice them just enough to make a sale. In addition, some no-dicker sticker dealers *will* dicker, if you push the issue.

One Price Dealers — Version Two

Then there are dealers who simply charge sticker price, no questions asked. What the MSRP says is what you pay. Saturn dealers are noted for doing this, although as sales softened there were rumors of some dealers cutting prices. In addition, faced with too many unsold Saturns, the factory has been known to offer what are, in effect, sale prices in the form of substantial lease subventions.

Seeing the success of Saturn dealers in customer satisfaction surveys, other manufacturers tried to force their dealers to adhere to the MSRP and dispense with negotiating. Often they do this by cutting the margin, or the amount of markup between the invoice price and the sticker price. Cut it thin enough and the dealers have to charge sticker price or go out of business.

Some customers genuinely appreciate not having to negotiate prices – even if it means that the dealer makes a far more impressive profit on each car. These customers take comfort in the knowledge that nobody else got a better deal.

However, even one-price dealers have to negotiate when you have a trade-in. Here, too, you have to do your homework to determine what your used car is worth. It's often valuable to compare prices at competing one-price dealers to see what they'll offer for your trade.

How to Handle the Trade-In

For many buyers, the trade-in is probably the most difficult part of the deal. It's also hard for dealers, who have to handle customers with unrealistic expectations of their trade-in's value.

Some consumer advocates suggest that you lie about your trade-in intentions. When the salesperson asks, "Will there be a trade-in?" these people say you should say no. This is one way to find out the real price of the car or truck you want to buy. It also helps you keep the three transactions – buying the new car, disposing of your old car and financing the deal – separate, as we suggested in Chapter 2.

But it complicates the purchase process. Just when do you plan to introduce the trade-in? Some customers wait until they go to pick up their new car to spring it on the dealer. Never, ever do this.

There are several reasons why you want to tell the dealer, truthfully, that you probably will trade your car. First, it's the honest answer to a question that, at some point, the dealer needs to know. In addition, if your car has some value and is a brand your dealer doesn't handle, the used-car manager may have to "shop the car." In other words, he or she will get on the phone and describe your car to dealers who sell that make and who should have a better idea of its value. Sometimes they discover that your car is more valuable than the used-car price guides say it is. In that case, the dealer can make a larger offer for your trade-in – which means a lower price on the total deal.

If you mislead the dealer by saying that your brother-in-law is going to buy your car, the salesperson won't do any of this background work. Then when you spring your trade at the last minute, you'll be at a real disadvantage. Adding the used car to the deal after you've reached a good and fair price for the new vehicle simply reopens the pricing negotiations. Many dealers do better in round two than they do in round one.

To keep the new-car and old-car deals separate and still stay honest, you should tell the dealer something like this: "In all probability I'll trade in my old car. However, I'd like you to keep the prices of the new and used vehicles separate. Let me know what I'd have to pay for the new model if I don't trade in my old car, and tell me what you'd pay me for my old car if I do trade it in."

Rebates and Incentives

A rebate is a factory payment made directly to the customer who buys a given vehicle. Usually offered during a limited time period, rebates are designed to spur sales of certain models and keep the factory assembly lines humming. Or they can help dealers clear the lots of a model that turned out to be a real dog.

An incentive is factory money designed to accomplish the same task, but rather than going directly to the customer, it goes to the dealer. With this extra money, the dealer can lower the price you'll pay, offer added incentives to salespeople to sell this model or just pocket the money.

In some cases, rebates and incentives can be substantial. On some slow-moving luxury models, manufacturers have offered up to $6,000 in cash – rebates, incentives or a combination of the two – to move the metal. It works.

When one manufacturer closed out one of its models, it offered a combination of rebates and incentives that let dealers advertise genuine $6,000 reductions on a car with a $22,000 sticker price. In these cases, dealers advertised both the discount and the final selling price.

Holdbacks

Many manufacturers offer their dealers holdbacks. This is money that will be remitted to the dealer once a vehicle is sold. Holdback payments effectively discount the invoice price that the dealer pays for the vehicle. The money represents additional margin for the dealer.

A few manufacturers – Volkswagen, Porsche and Audi – don't offer hold-backs. The other manufacturers do, and their payments range from 1 percent to 3 percent of the MSRP. In some cases, factories compute holdback using the base MSRP – in other words, options are excluded. In other cases, the total MSRP is used. Some manufacturers offer a smaller holdback and a 1 percent or 2 percent floor-planning allowance which is the interest that dealers pay on the loans used to buy vehicles on their lot.

Whatever its purpose, holdback effectively lowers the invoice price for the dealer, yet is not reflected in what you see on the MSRP.

Invoice vs. Dealer Cost

Holdbacks and occasional factory-to-dealer incentives are what's usually behind those ads that scream "lower than invoice" or "$1 over invoice." No dealer could stay in business by selling a car or truck for less than it costs wholesale or for only $1 more.

What this really means is that the invoice price is not what the dealer pays. The real cost is almost always less than invoice.

But the price of the vehicle is not the only cost associated with the sale. A dealer has to staff the showroom, handle the paperwork, pay the electric bill and keep insurance premiums current – yes customers do occasionally crash on test drives. You're expected to help pay for these expenses at a dealership, just as you help pay for overhead at every other company you do business with. The dealer has to make a profit, too.

A dealer's total cost for a car is something that accountants could argue about for some time. Just remember that what you end up paying has to cover costs and provide a margin of profit. This is only fair. Selling cars is not a non-profit game, nor should it be. When people tell you that you should be able to buy any car at or below invoice, they're not giving you solid advice.

The method of paying salespeople varies from dealer to dealer, but in some showrooms the salesperson doesn't get paid simply for getting you to sign on the dotted line. The sales representative's pay is based on the profit margin. In other words, the histrionics you sometimes see between the sales-person and the manager over the price of your deal may be just good – or not so good – theater.

Sometimes the selling and buying games have an element of bluff on both sides. Often, if you decide to leave, you'll be tackled – figuratively, not literally – before you get to your car. In other cases, you may get a call later from the dealership suggesting it can do better. Remember that once you leave or start to leave, the first party to blink is at a disadvantage.

In addition, a salesperson's frequent departures to "try to get you a better deal" may be carefully calculated to make you stew over the purchase. Just as in cooking, letting you stew is designed to soften you up. You can put an end to it by saying, "Rather than try to rush and end up with only a slightly better deal, take your time. Get me your best deal. Then call me with the final price. You have my number." Then leave.

Association Surcharges

Among the costs not reflected on the pricing report you obtained are association advertising surcharges. These are costs that a dealer in a given area must contribute to coordinated regional advertising campaigns. Costs are levied on each car sold in the zone. Dealers often add them to a dealer-installed price sticker. If they're legitimate, you should find the same price added to every comparable model sold by other dealers in the zone. If you don't find this price when you contact other dealers in the same area, you may have found a dishonest dealer. Or you may live on the border of two zones with two separate policies.

When to Buy

The traditional advice to shop late – late in the day, late in the week, late in the month and late in the year – isn't always valid. The theory is this: a dealer is most flexible when a deadline looms. Late in the day, the salesperson and manager want to go home, so they'll be more flexible. Choosing a career in car sales means long hours and many late nights.

Late in the week, sales managers may be facing sales goals they haven't met yet. The "we're falling short or our sales goals" mentality is more likely to kick in later in the month, however. And don't wait until the last day of the month. The sale won't be completed until the following month, so it can't count on this month's tally. All the pricing flexibility you were hoping to find — and that might have been available for four or five days before the end of the month — is now gone. Sorry, you waited too long.

Late in the year also presents problems for the customers. Surprisingly, some dealerships do a roaring business during December. The old saw, "you can't compete with Santa Claus," used to explain why the entire sales department went into hibernation for the month. Now there's a last-minute rush to buy business vehicles before the end of the tax year. In some show-rooms, the week between Christmas and New Years is an absolute mob scene. This is not the time to buy.

Did You Know?

Traditional sale periods such as President's Day, Memorial Day and Labor Day are still heavily promoted. Although you can still typically find good deals through these sales, they are not the only times that good buys can be found.

Monthly quotas for dealers mean that if a dealership finds that, as the end of the month approaches, it has not met its goals, it may offer buyers better incentives just to move vehicles off the lot.

Tip Provided by
AAA Southern New England

Late in the model year, which usually ends in September or October, can be a better time to shop. Soon-to-be-discontinued vehicles from last year are offered at attractive prices. The slightly lower price may be a trap, however, if you end up having to sell within a couple of years. Why? Because the price reduction that you enjoy by buying what will, in a matter of days, become last year's model may not cover the added depreciation you suffer if you have to sell in two or three years. Even though you bought late in the year, in two years the next buyer will consider your car three years old. You may end up short unless the discount is hefty when you buy the vehicle. Once a car or truck has passed the five- or six-year mark, its condition and mileage mean at least as much as its age and losing a year isn't as important.

This is why it's often more expensive to lease a car late in the model year. The leasing company knows that your three-year lease will leave it with a 4-year-old car or truck.

Buying late in the year also may mean you won't get a good deal on a popular import. As the year comes to an end and demand outstrips supply, just finding an acceptable model in a color you can live with may be the best you can do. In fact, this may be when you pay the highest price of all, simply because supplies are short.

Assuming ample supplies, you should be able to get a highly competitive deal any time you choose to shop. Certain circumstances – including zone sales efforts and a dealer's need to sell more vehicles now to protect future factory allocations – can affect prices on some models at a specific time. If you can take advantage of one of these opportunities, go for it.

Get It in Writing

Whatever the offer happens to be, if it's important to you, get it in writing. If the salesperson offers you a free loaner when you bring your car in for service for as long as you own the vehicle, get it written into the contract. If the offer is for delivery within a stated time period, get it in writing. If the offer is for free service after the sale, get it in writing.

Anything the dealership refuses to put in writing probably isn't a valid offer. Read the contract. It probably says that offers not written on the contract are unenforceable. This is fair, really, since it effectively short-circuits verbal misunderstandings – even out-and-out fibs by some customers – that can end in small claims court where it's your word against the dealer's.

> **PITFALLS**
>
> Ordering a specific car that has yet to be built? Be sure to set a time limit on delivery. While many custom orders are made by the manufacturer and delivered to the dealer and the customer in a timely manner, others are not. Set a time limit in the contract that, if not met, lets you cancel the order and get your deposit back.
>
> *Tip Provided by AAA Kansas*

Even if the verbal offer is sincere, if it's not written down and the people involved move on – as often happens in automotive retailing – their successors won't know anything about it. Get it in writing.

You'll want to have a copy of the contract you signed when you leave the dealership. Make sure that someone authorized to commit the dealership to the deal signed it. Salespeople often can't do this. It requires the signature of a manager or principal in the dealership. If you don't have this signature, you don't have a contract. All you have is an offer that the dealership is free to accept or reject. By the same token, you're probably free to withdraw, too, before the dealership accepts by signing the contract.

In many dealerships, the handwritten contract will be replaced by a neatly typed one that you sign when you close the deal. Make sure that the content of the typed contract agrees with the handwritten original, since the typed contract will supersede the first one. If the free loaner during service was written into the first contract but not typed in the second, you no longer have the offer in writing.

Buying Services and Other Options

In This Chapter
• • • • • • • • • • •

- What buying services generally do
- What to look for in a broker
- Why an auto broker who doesn't charge might not be a bargain
- How to spot a "bird dog"
- How some group referral programs work

Some people just hate negotiating the purchase of a vehicle. Is it any wonder then that some clever entrepreneurs have found a way for these folks to buy new wheels at a good price without the hassle of haggling with a dealer – and, in some cases, without even setting foot in a showroom?

This alternative to do-it-yourself shopping is called a buying service and it can take many forms. You can pay a company to find you the perfect new car and negotiate the price. Other companies charge the dealer for finding a buyer – that would be you, of course.

You also might find credit unions and some AAA offices that have negotiated prices at specific local dealerships for their members. In some cases, the prices are valid only for special sales; in other cases, the prices are effective all year.

If you lack the time or the will to go new-car shopping and are considering a broker, adviser or buying service, here's what you need to know.

Auto Brokers

Many companies call themselves auto brokers, but there's no nationally accepted definition of what an auto broker is or how one should do business. In many cases, state law governs their activities. In addition, automakers often discourage their dealers from working with certain types of auto brokers. And while many customers simply couldn't be happier with their broker, others have been burned – in some cases quite badly and in ways that they didn't even realize until several years later.

Generally, an auto broker is someone who knows the local market and who uses that knowledge to get clients a good deal on a vehicle. Brokers are paid for their services – which leads us to the first question you should ask of any brokerage company: who pays you and how much do you charge?

Don't engage any broker until you obtain at least two prices on your own. You're going to have to go to a dealer or two anyway to see which model fits you properly, so you might as well also get a price while you're there. Then you can determine how effective the broker is for you.

Tip Provided by AAA Nebraska

This a critical question, for it tells you how this person or company operates. Some charge a buyer a flat fee – which can be several hundred dollars – to find a car, set up the deal and negotiate a fair price. In other cases they may charge a percentage of the purchase price. Some combine the two, charging a flat fee plus a percentage of any price over a certain amount. Find out before you enter into any agreement with a broker.

Other companies work with a buyer – that's you – at no charge. Rest assured, however, they're not pounding the pavement out of the goodness of their hearts. These brokers expect to be paid by the dealers they work with. And many dealers are willing to pay their fee for finding them a customer. If a dealer doesn't want to pay a broker, the broker just moves on to one who will.

Of course, you still end up paying, you just won't know how much. Why? Because the dealer adds the broker's fee onto the price of the vehicle and cuts a check to the broker afterward.

Brokers can make their money a third way: charging both the buyer and the dealer. You, the buyer, pay up front. The dealer also remits a payment after you take delivery of your new car. Again, you obviously pay both parts of the broker's fee. And as with the broker who charges you nothing, you won't know what the total fee is.

This is not to suggest that a broker's services might not useful to you. Just recognize that, as is the case of Internet-based intermediaries, your decision to use a broker adds another layer – and another expense – to the deal. Of course, if the broker has the experience and knowledge to save you more than the broker charges, the service will save you money.

There's one additional wrinkle in the brokerage business. Some brokers take possession of the cars and trucks before their clients get them. Others simply hook the buyer up to a dealer who makes the sale directly. This difference can be significant.

If the broker takes possession of the vehicle – in other words, buys the vehicle and takes title to it before selling it to you – you're buying a used vehicle. In the eyes of the manufacturer, you're the second owner. In some cases, those exceptionally long warranties are offered only to the first owner or to a member of the first owner's family who buys the vehicle second hand.

Unless the broker is related to you directly, chances are you'll lose out on some of the time and mileage protection. Remember that the ads tout 10-year, 100,000-mile protection in large print – then in small print take it away from subsequent owners. These buyers may receive coverage only for a much shorter period. If the broker is the first owner, you may get stuck without the extended warranty. Do your homework to determine how your sale will be handled and whether it has any effect on the warranty coverage. These brokers are the ones the manufacturers discourage their dealers from using. They complicate everything from customer satisfaction warranty claims.

If you decide to use a broker who charges the buyer, expect to pay some money up front. In some cases, the money is refundable if you decide not to go through with the deal. In other cases, this is earnest money – cash that shows you're serious about the deal – and it's not refundable. This reassures the broker that you haven't sent him/her out to chase prices that you'll then use in your own shopping expedition or to confirm that a price you were quoted is good, perhaps even great.

Guarantees from brokers generally aren't very useful. Often they let you get your money back, minus the broker's fee of course, if you find a better deal. Finding a better deal, however, entails shopping for the vehicle yourself – which you hired the broker to do because you dislike it so much. It's highly unlikely that you'll ever uncover a better deal and get your money back, even if a better deal was easy to find.

Finally, unless you know just the car you want – perhaps you rented a half-dozen competing models while on business trips – you'll still end up visiting dealers for test drives. Brokers, for the most part, do not stock cars for you to see, sit in and drive. If the broker did all this, the broker would really be a used-car dealer, right?

Some brokers require you to give the exact specifications you want by option code. In other words, you can't just say you want the AM/FM/CD stereo. There might be two or three such radios. You have to know the ordering code, which usually is on the factory price sticker and also can be found on a car-buying tool such as the one at aaa.com. So in addition to visiting the car lot for test drives, you may go there to copy down order codes from the price sticker. You'll also need order codes for interior and exterior colors.

As long as you're at the dealership you might as well get a price, too. Who knows – it might be lower than the price of the car and the broker's fee combined.

The Bird Dog

Bird dogs aren't brokers, but they can play a big part in the success of some salespeople. A bird dog is someone who meets lots of drivers and could easily recommend a vehicle or a dealership. Automotive technicians, for instance, or gas station attendants who build up a rapport with their customers make good bird dogs. Many car shoppers ask such people for recommendations. Bird dogs often have an arrangement with a salesperson who slips them a payment if the customer ends up buying. So if a mechanic tells you to "Go see Al or Mary at XYZ Motors. They sell really good cars and have taken good care of some of my other customers," he may be telling you the truth. Or he may be engaging in a little paid advertising. Some really successful salespeople have a small army of bird dogs in the community.

Group Referral Programs

You already may be a member of an organization that has negotiated a reasonably good price on a new car or truck for you. How could this be? Some credit unions, unions, companies, social organizations and, in many parts of the country, AAA clubs negotiate prices with area dealers. If you aren't sure whether a group you belong to does this, ask.

Sometimes the deals are valid only for specific sales events. Credit unions, for example, often work with a handful of dealers who sell brands their members like and arrange good prices for specific dates, usually around holidays. The credit union hopes the members appreciate the service and, most importantly, apply for a car loan. Dealers hope to get new customers without having to advertise for them, which is expensive. In exchange for generating heavier traffic in the showroom, dealers are willing to cut their prices. And the members enjoy good deals without having to haggle.

Other organizations, including some credit unions and some AAA offices, negotiate with selected dealers for prices that are good year round.

Such arrangements work in a variety of ways. In some cases, the price – a certain percentage or dollar amount over invoice – is set on a model-by-model basis. Contracts often call for incentives to be subtracted from the invoice amount, but not the holdback. Under this type of arrangement, a Chevrolet dealer might agree to sell every Impala for 3 percent over invoice while a neighboring Ford dealer commits to sell every Taurus for $500 over invoice. Under some programs, the dealer will show the customer the invoice.

Not all cars and trucks in a dealer's lineup, however, are necessarily included. The Chevrolet dealer might exclude Corvettes or Suburbans, which are very popular and sell out easily.

Also bear in mind that different dealers handling the same brand may cut different deals with the organization. Two Toyota dealers, for instance, might agree to different markups for the group's members. If you're motivated only by the lowest price, you still have to do some shopping. And you'll probably have to visit each dealership. Most such agreements require the member to visit the dealership and speak with a specific contact person – often a manager who doesn't work on direct commission – to take advantage of the price. You also may have to call for an appointment.

Unless the dealer contact turns you over to another salesperson, don't assume that the first person who approaches you will be able to work the same deal. Salespeople, always eager to make a sale, might offer to help you even after you identify yourself as, let's say, a AAA member. "I can get you that deal," salespeople might say, even if that's not possible. Be sure to speak only with the designated contact for your group.

You also should recognize that these negotiated deals are not necessarily the best you can do. A good bargainer may be able to do better. It might require a lot of work to come up with a better deal, but you'll never know until you try.

You probably won't be able to try at the participating dealer, however. Often the contract with the group stipulates that there be no negotiation on the arranged price. Once you identify yourself as a member of the group eligible for the special deal, that's it. The price negotiated by your organization may be the only price you can get here. Remember that the reason for these deals and their main appeal is that they offer group members a good and fair price without having to negotiate.

Other Options

You also may be able to buy cars and trucks through discount or whole-sale clubs. Again, the price is set and the selection may be meager, but if they offer the vehicle you want at a price you like, it could be a good deal. Just remember the warranty restrictions and make sure that you're the first buyer.

As with brokers, discount and wholesale clubs probably have no demonstrators for a test drive, so you'll undoubtedly end up at a dealership. And as with Internet services, the retail outlet might end up adding another layer of costs to the transaction. So don't automatically assume that the folks who bring you great prices on paper towels bought by the case can work that same magic on a new car or truck. They might. Then again, they might not. The only way to find out is to go shopping and get some prices for comparison.

Staying on the Right Track

In This Chapter

• • • • • • • • • • •

- Avoiding problems before you buy
- Avoiding problems with contracts
- Protecting yourself when you order a vehicle rather than buy one from a dealer's stock
- How to tell when a private seller is really a dealer
- What to do about service problems after you buy

The vast majority of new and used vehicle sales proceed without a hitch. From the beginning of the transaction to the follow-up services afterward, not a single problem pops up that can't be easily fixed. Unfortunately, this isn't the case for every buyer. Just about anything can go wrong when you buy a vehicle.

Fortunately, most problems that buyers – or sellers, for that matter – encounter aren't the result of intentional deception, even though a very few people involved in troubled transactions do not act honorably and probably never had any intention of doing so.

In this chapter, we'll look at some of the problems buyers may encounter and explain what you can do to ensure that you don't fall victim to an unscrupulous seller, whether a private party or a dealer.

Are You Vulnerable?

Unfortunately, many problems seem to happen to the most vulnerable consumers. People with a poor credit history, for instance, may not be able to get a loan from any lender except one that specializes in the sub-prime market. If your credit is blemished and you can't find a loan through standard channels – banks and credit unions where most people borrow money – be careful when you arrange financing elsewhere. Check the terms and conditions and pay particular attention to the interest rate.

There's an old trick that, thankfully, has gone out of style. Almost. It's when a dealer tries to keep you in the showroom no matter what. Salespeople can't get you an answer quickly. The used-car appraisal takes an hour. And you're certainly not going to go anywhere until your car comes back. Each offer takes 15 to 30 minutes to review. The goal is to wear you down.

If you know your credit report is poor, consider avoiding loans entirely until it improves. Borrowing when you have a poor credit rating – assuming you can even get a loan – means you'll have to pay a higher interest rate. Instead, consider paying cash for a lesser, older or higher-mileage vehicle. Choose the right car or truck and you can not only save a great deal of money, but maybe mend your credit rating as well.

Another potential victim is the person whose needs outstrip his or her financial resources. Yes, it would be nice for a couple with a fourth child on the way to be able to buy a late-model, low-mileage minivan that is both comfortable and dependable. Their $5,000 budget, however, won't do the trick unless they get very lucky. Few do. Before you begin shopping for a vehicle, get your expectations in line with your financial capabilities.

Start by doing an accurate self-appraisal. Thirty days before you start shopping, check your credit report if you plan to finance. Make sure it's accurate. If it isn't, eliminating the errors could take a month or more.

Before You Sign on the Dotted Line

Problems you might encounter while vehicle shopping are almost too many to count and can occur at any point in the process. Most fall into three broad categories: misleading advertising, confusion over contracts and warranty problems. Other aspects of the transaction also merit careful attention.

Let's first look at some difficulties that can develop before and after you sign a contract.

Misleading Advertising

In some cases, sellers promote a vehicle in a confusing manner. Is the price advertised a purchase price or the total of all the payments generated by a lease? It should say in the ad. The advertisement also should specify whether the vehicle is new or used. Some places sell current model-year cars from fleets. That gem that you thought you were getting for a sweet price may turn out to be an ex-rental with 20,000 miles on it. While there's nothing wrong with buying a retired rental car, you shouldn't be enticed into the showroom believing it's a new vehicle.

If you find that you've been pulled into a dealership by misleading advertising, leave at once. If the ad was misleading, what else do you think might happen to you there?

Advertising is subject to state regulation, so it's difficult to make blanket statements of what's required. What we can say is that you should not be exposed to advertising that deceives you.

In fairness to dealers, advertising media – newspapers and broadcasters, primarily – can make mistakes. They might run the wrong ad or make a typographical error. When that happens and the mistake is significant, the paper or station usually acknowledges its error by issuing a letter that the dealer can post for people to see. You should not, however, come across the same error for several days or a week later in a new series of ads.

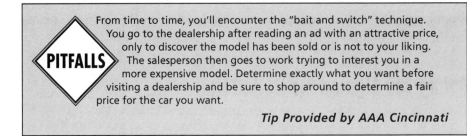

> From time to time, you'll encounter the "bait and switch" technique. You go to the dealership after reading an ad with an attractive price, only to discover the model has been sold or is not to your liking. The salesperson then goes to work trying to interest you in a more expensive model. Determine exactly what you want before visiting a dealership and be sure to shop around to determine a fair price for the car you want.
>
> *Tip Provided by AAA Cincinnati*

You should be able to buy a specific model that you see advertised at a specific price. In some cases, such as an inventory clearance or an end-of-the-model-year sale, be aware that the vehicle you want may be sold by the time you get there.

A sales reprepresentative who tries to dissuade you from buying or ordering a highlighted car or truck, however, might be pulling the old bait-and-switch routine. The ad lured you to the showroom. Now the salesperson wants to sell you a more costly – and, for the dealership, more profitable – model. If you run into a salesperson who makes it difficult for you to buy an advertised model, leave at once and do not return.

In some cases, you'll find a low price followed by the phrase, "Order yours for just…" and then the price. This means that the particular model is not in stock and is available only by special order. Waiting periods can be lengthy if the vehicle is in demand.

Perhaps one of the more misleading forms of advertising comes from "curbsiders." Buying a used car always entails an element of risk not present with a new car. Perhaps that's why many consumers feel more comfortable buying from a private party. They believe that another individual isn't nearly as likely to deceive them and that they can use basic people skills to assess the character of the previous owner.

They're also looking for a good deal. By buying from an individual, they expect to pay well below retail.

To exploit the appeal of private-party sales, some used-car dealers have begun a practice called curbsiding. They place short classified ads containing a brief description of the vehicle and a phone number in the used-car sections of newspapers. It looks just like an ad that might be placed by someone concerned about keeping down the cost of the ad.

How can you know if you are dealing with a dealer instead of a private owner? Here are some clues: First, if you see several used-car ads with the same phone number, you've almost certainly stumbled across a dealer.

Another sign is that you can't get through when you call. When you leave a message on the machine, you get a call back almost instantly. Be aware, however, that a private seller might use an answering machine to screen calls.

Another tip-off is that the seller asks you to go to a public place rather than a home to see the vehicle. In many cases, the seller will graciously offer to bring the car to you.

One way to be sure is simply to ask the seller directly if he or she is a dealer or working for one. Always ask who owns the car and who holds the title. Another tactic takes advantage of the fact that few curbsiders front just one car or truck. Whether you get an answering machine or a person when you call, simply say that you're calling about the vehicle for sale. Don't identify the make or model. A private seller knows what's in the driveway awaiting a buyer. A curbsider has to ask which model you want to discuss.

If you find yourself dealing with a curbsider, you have to decide whether you want to proceed. If you go forward, understand that you'll probably end up paying a bit more for this vehicle than you would if you were dealing with a private party. Dealers do have to make a profit. You might, however, get the added bonus of some warranty protection. In some states, dealers may have to provide a warranty. Private-party sellers almost never do. However, if you find curbsiding unacceptable, break off the contact and search elsewhere.

Before buying any used car, be sure to review the title history and safety recalls for that make and model. Also, have it checked by a technician whose opinion you trust. See Chapter 5 on purchasing a used car. And remember that some genuine private sellers can be dishonest. Some, in fact, are down-right criminal.

Contract Confusion

Just about any aspect of a vehicle sale can be subject to misrepresentation. It's your responsibility as the customer to make sure you don't become a victim. This means you have to read and understand everything on a contract or agreement form before you sign it.

Yes, you must read and understand the contract. It takes time, but do it anyway. If a sentence or paragraph doesn't make sense, stop and read it again. You could save thousands of dollars.

If you read the contract and find terms or phrases you don't understand, don't sign it. Have someone you trust – a banker, accountant or attorney, for example – review it and explain the parts that are unclear to you. Be sure to read every part of the contract. The backs of the pages often contain important information. If the salesperson won't let you take a copy of the contract to have it reviewed, don't buy a car there.

When it comes time to sign a contract, never sign anything with blank spaces where words or numbers could go. Make sure that every number is filled in, including the purchase price of the car, the trade-in allowance and – if the dealer is handling the financing – all of the terms and conditions of the loan. This includes the amount borrowed, the date of the loan, the interest rate and where and when you have to make payments. Take a calculator and make sure the numbers add up. It's surprising how many math errors you can find on sales documents. Again, remember that your money is at stake.

If you don't understand the numbers or you can't make them add up, ask for an explanation. If you don't understand the explanation, take the

PITFALLS Think that the manufacturer will bail you out if you get into trouble with a dealer? Don't count on it. Dealers are independent business people and often are protected by near-ironclad franchise laws. Manufacturers may have little influence over a dealer's actions in a single case.

contract to someone unconnected with the seller who can help you. If a sales-person is rude, condescending or abrupt when reviewing the numbers with you, remember that you can always go elsewhere.

You might be surprised to learn that auto salespeople don't always understand the numbers either. In some showrooms, a computer generates the figures and fills in the spaces based on the data entered by the salesperson. Fortunately, from the salesperson's perspective, few customers ask for a thorough explanation.

It's harder to slip something past a customer who says, "Wait a minute. I don't understand that," than one who pretends to understand for fear of appearing ignorant or foolish. Some contracts are difficult even for professionals to follow, so never hesitate to admit that you're in the dark. Make the seller give you enough light or enough time to figure it all out before you sign anything.

Always get a copy of what you sign. Find out beforehand if you'll be getting a carbon copy of the contract. Make sure that all the numbers and terms unique to your contract go through to all the copies. If you're getting a photocopy, make sure that the original contract copies well and that the copies you get contain all the terms on the front and the back of all pages. You should be able to get a photocopy of the contract with all the terms filled in before you sign the original. If the photocopier is out of service or the contract does not copy legibly, don't sign it.

Contracts often need to be revised during the sales process. You might change your mind and decide you want another color, for example. The car you want may be unavailable or arrive at the dealership damaged. Or it could be stolen before you pick it up.

Even without any of these problems, however, you still might be confronted with a replacement contract. Perhaps the first contract was handwritten. It may be superceded by a computer-generated, more legible replacement. Before signing the second contract, make sure that everything you wanted from the handwritten contract is included.

All those promises you've gotten in writing should be carried over. If they aren't, don't sign the replacement document. In addition, all options should be spelled out in descriptive terms as well as in the manufacturer's order codes. Are you really sure that accessory package "X4P" includes the sunroof you wanted and the optional interior lighting to make up for the dome light the sunroof eliminates? If not, then have the description of the option and all that it includes spelled out in plain language on the contract. Don't sign the new contract until this is done.

When contracts are revised, the newest contract by date and time is usually the one that governs the entire transaction. This means that all the extras you obtained and spelled out in the previous contract are gone if you sign a new contract without them. That would include, for example, that free loaner you negotiated when you return this new vehicle for service.

Conditional Contracts

In some cases, the wording of the contract makes the sale contingent on something else happening. For example, you say you'll buy the vehicle if you can arrange financing. If you fail, however, the contract may not be null and void. It simply might give the dealer the right to try to obtain a car loan on your behalf. If the dealer's successful, the sale goes through.

Make sure any conditional terms spell out all parameters of what can and can't be done. If your deal depends on financing, for instance, you should include an interest rate ceiling and the terms for the loan the dealer might be able to arrange. If you're unable to arrange financing at 7 percent, you certainly don't want to be saddled with an 18 percent loan.

Other contracts are conditional on the dealer being able to locate a vehicle and arrange delivery. Again, you don't want this to be an open-ended arrangement. You should specify a cutoff time so you're not in vehicular limbo for months. Custom orders at the factory often seem to take forever, especially if the car or truck is in demand. If you can afford to wait six months, fine. But if you need something in a month or two – or sooner – spell that out in the contract. If you're not sure how to specify what you want in writing, get advice from a knowledgeable third party who has no financial interest in the sale.

Offers and Contracts

Remember that until an authorized member of the dealership staff signs the contract, all you've done by inking the dotted line is tendered an offer. Salespeople usually aren't authorized to sign and bind the dealership to an agreement. Only a manager or the owner can do that. Make sure a manager signs the copy of the contact you have in your possession and that each additional contract is signed by a manager before you leave the dealership.

Failure to Disclose

Depending on your state's laws, you may or may not be entitled to learn of a used vehicle's crash history. In all fairness, the dealer may not know about it either, and most minor crash damage, if repaired properly, is not significant. Nonetheless, you have the right to know if the car has a branded title. In many states, a branded title means that the car has been salvaged or rebuilt, in a flood or in some other way rendered less valuable. You should specify in the contract that the vehicle has a non-branded title. Or you can run the car's VIN through aaa.com to get a vehicle history report.

In addition, have any used vehicle you're considering checked thoroughly by an automotive technician before you sign any contract or hand over any money. Significant damage that has been repaired doesn't always trigger a branded title, but it can make the car less desirable and far less valuable. Not even new, never-registered cars are above suspicion. Some states only require disclosure of significant previous damage. Unfortunately, the definition of "significant" often depends on whether you're buying or selling.

Liquidated Damages

The contract may call for any down payment you make to be considered liquidated damages if you back out of the agreement. In other words, the dealer gets to keep your deposit to cover the expenses associated with selling you a car that you won't accept. Don't leave more money on deposit than you are willing to lose if you change your mind. No dealer should require a deposit of more than $250. If one does, shop around. You'll probably find another who does not.

There's another reason not to be too generous with a down payment. If a dealership goes under after you place your order but before you pick up your vehicle, your deposit could get tied up in bankruptcy proceedings or disappear completely. Leave as little money on the table as possible until the sale goes through and you take possession of your car.

Warranty Questions

One of the joys of buying a new car is the factory warranty that comes with it. Since almost all manufacturers now offer at least three-year/36,000-mile bumper-to-bumper coverage, with some exceptions, few repair bills will come your way during the warranty period. Only normal-wear items – tires, brake pads, light bulbs, wiper blades and the like – are excluded under the terms of most warranties.

Every year, however, some buyers discover that they don't have the protection they thought they had. Dealers sometimes start the warranty clock running before the car is sold to a retail customer. This is normal when the vehicle is used as a demonstrator. The clock on the "three years" part of the warranty coverage may start when the vehicle begins its demo duties. That's why, when you buy a demonstrator, you should insist on a written explanation of the remaining warranty coverage to which you are entitled. You may even want to take the 17-character VIN and confirm the coverage with the vehicle's manufacturer. You should request confirmation in writing, just to avoid troubles down the road.

Dealers also have been known to claim that a vehicle was sold – even if it wasn't – to qualify for special manufacturer's incentives. Two months later, you come along and buy the car or truck. You now have a two-year, 10-month/36,000-mile warranty, not the three-year coverage you thought you had.

A few cars and trucks offer long extended warranties on their drivetrains. These are the expensive-to-repair engine, transmission and drive systems. The protection is often assigned only to the first registered buyer, however.

Make sure you don't buy a vehicle with this kind of warranty if it has been sold to another buyer first. You could be left without the protection you thought you had. Verification with the manufacturer can be a good idea if you have any doubts.

Used-car warranties also require careful attention. Make sure that you conform to any requirements necessary to get the remainder of the factory warranty on a late-model, low-mileage used car. If the car or truck is no longer under the manufacturer's warranty, but rather is guaranteed by the dealer, understand that the plan is only as good as the dealer standing behind it. Many dealers live up to their promises and willingly shoulder expensive repairs for used cars that they sell and cover under their own warranty. A few do not.

Any used-car warranty should cover 100 percent of the cost of both the parts and labor needed to make repairs. Some warranties are known as 50-50 warranties. These call for the service department to make repairs, draw up a bill and then cut it in half. You pay half while, in theory, the shop takes care of the other half. Unfortunately, shops have many ways to inflate the repair bill, which effectively shifts a larger percentage of the cost to you.

Some dealers will go out on a limb and offer a warranty on their used cars for 12 months or 12,000 miles. They are rare. Most choose a shorter time period – six months, two months or even one month – with as few as 1,000 miles of coverage. Just remember that a longer warranty from a dealer with a poor track record probably isn't nearly as much protection as a shorter warranty from a dealership that stands solidly behind its cars and trucks.

With repair costs escalating all the time, you may want to consider buying an extended service plan or extended warranty. You can get them from a variety of sources, including some AAA offices. Shop around. Prices vary and some plans come with very high profit margins for the seller. You don't have to take the plan offered by the dealer or the manufacturer.

Also Consider the Swap

Once you've driven a car you like, record the VIN. If it's a used car, make sure that you take the same car to your independent technician for its checkup. If you decide to buy the vehicle, make sure that the same VIN is on the sales contract and confirm the VIN of the car you're going to take home before you hand over any money and leave the dealership. With so many nearly identical cars coming off lease and out of fleets, dealers sometimes make legitimate mistakes.

Title Problems

Nothing can spoil the joy of driving a recently acquired, new-to-you car faster than title problems. Ask to see the title, if possible. If the title is not available because it's held by a lender, get written confirmation in the contract that the car is being sold with a clear, non-branded title that will be coming from the lender. More than one buyer has been shocked when the title arrives with a brand denoting that the car is salvaged, rebuilt or a lemon-law buyback. Better yet, check the VIN through aaa.com for a vehicle history report.

Prolonged Negotiations

When you work with any seller – dealer or private party – to buy a car, success is not preordained. The road can be bumpy, but you can smooth things out in your mind if you look upon the exercise as a process, even a game, in which there will be ups and downs.

A strategy some dealers follow, once you think you're close to a deal, is to try to get just a little more money from you. This really shouldn't be surprising and it's not unethical. After all, you and/or your employer may try to do the same thing in your field.

You may, therefore, find yourself on the receiving end of a request for more money. Why? Dealers are in business to make a profit. They know you've shopped around and compared prices. So your dealer figures that if you're still in this showroom trying to buy this vehicle, some other dealer somewhere has already asked you for more money.

Look at the situation from the dealership's perspective for a moment. The dealer knows there are competitors out there making more money on sales. As a bottom-line businessperson, that's got to hurt at least a little.

The solution is simple. Once everyone has come close to agreeing on a price, the salesperson gets sent back to the customer. The message is simple. "You've done too good a job negotiating and the dealer needs just $50 or $100 more to keep everything on track."

Weary of the process, many customers cave. If a customer doesn't readily agree, dealerships have another option. The salesperson can leave to "see what can be done." After a suitable time, he or she returns with word that the manager has reluctantly accepted the price.

Conveyance Fees

Many contracts include a paperwork processing or conveyance fee. It's a bit like the "shipping and handling" charge that mail order houses often tack on. At the dealership, this fee covers the cost of doing all the paperwork associated with a sale. Without the paperwork, you couldn't register your new vehicle. The fee, however, doesn't cover the registration charges imposed by your state. Rather, it covers the cost of filling out the forms and contracts and, in some states, sending a dealership employee with the necessary paperwork to a motor vehicle department office to register the vehicle. In other states, many dealers can take care of the registration right in their offices and mail the paperwork to the motor vehicle department.

Either way, the fee is printed right on the form, not filled in by hand or computer as all the other numbers are. That suggests that this fee is non-negotiable. It is not. You can haggle over this with the dealer just as you can negotiate every other aspect of the deal. Consider the charge to be part of the price of the car and proceed accordingly.

Trade-In Evaluations

If there's a trade-in, dealers reserve the right to reappraise the vehicle when it comes time to complete the deal. The language giving the dealer that privilege is probably in the contract you signed.

> **Did You Know?**
>
> A good used-car appraiser can spot almost every problem in your current vehicle just by taking it for a short drive. You have the option of going with the appraiser so you can keep track of your car and get the keys back immediately afterward. When the salesperson asks for your keys, just say you'll be along and he/she doesn't need them.
>
> **Tip Provided by AAA Akron Auto Club**

A lot can happen between the initial appraisal and the completion of the transaction. Your vehicle could be hit and damaged or suffer a mechanical breakdown, which would reduce its value. You, the owner, might strip it of good parts and use substandard replacements. These things happen, as any dealer can tell you. Or circumstances could change in the market. A safety scare, the disclosure of a mechanical problem, an unexpected shift in public taste – all can affect value and all can happen between the time your car is first appraised and the day you sign its title over to the dealer.

The time between the first appraisal and the completion of the sale can be significant if a custom order is involved or if the car or truck you're buying is popular and there many people in front of you who want the same vehicle. Much can happen to your current car's value during that six-month wait for a hot new car or truck. Is it any wonder that dealers reserve the right to reappraise a vehicle?

Perhaps most difficult to deal with are customers who damage their vehicle's trade-in value themselves. A dealer might look at a car on Monday and see almost new tires in excellent condition. On Saturday when the sale is to be completed, the car comes in with four bald and clearly illegal tires. The owner obviously made a switch and the dealer will have to buy four new tires before the vehicle can be put up for sale. The result: an instant reduction in trade-in value.

In other cases, owners remove accessories – a custom audio system, for instance – and leave gaping holes in the interior. Again, the value of the vehicle is reduced.

Unscrupulous dealers, however, use this clause in the contract for their own purposes, dramatically downgrading your trade-in's value when it's time to complete your transaction. If there have been no material changes in your car or the market, you should have the right to back out of the deal under these circumstances. Check the language in the contract and be prepared to fight for the return of your deposit.

Price Hikes After You Take Delivery

Surprisingly, some sellers try to change the contract after you've signed it, paid for your vehicle and taken delivery. Sellers occasionally call customers about problems with the deal and ask them to come up with more money. In some cases, the trade-in may not have brought as much as expected. If you haven't engaged in any fraud or misrepresentations, you should not have to renegotiate at this point. If a dealer got less than expected for your used car, too bad. It's not your responsibility. After all, this is the dealer's line of business. If he or she misjudges the market and loses money, that's unfortunate – but not your problem. Would the dealer give you a refund if your used car fetched more money than expected? Absolutely not.

Problem Loans

Dealers sometimes let customers have cars before the financing is complete. Customers who have trouble getting approved for a loan generally have to return the car. Read the terms of the contract for all the details. Many people verify verbally that the loan is approved before taking a vehicle home. You may want to have written confirmation noted on the contract.

Problems with Service

Insiders say that the salesperson makes the first sale for a dealership. The service department makes or breaks the second and subsequent sales. Service is important. Fortunately, both for service departments and customers, today's cars need less service and fewer repairs than ever before — with some conspicuous exceptions.

 New vehicles in their first year of production are likely to experience some problems simply because they are new. To avoid these "teething problems," buy a car or truck that has been in production for at least two years. That way, you can review its repair and performance history.

Tip Provided by AAA Carolinas

What should you do if you have a problem? In most cases, dealers can remedy the occasional difficulty. One experienced service manager has noted that the quality of new cars and trucks has shown amazing improvement over the past three decades. Thirty years ago, it wasn't unusual for people to come in for their first service with a page-long list of minor — and sometimes major — problems. Rarely does a customer go in today with more than one or two glitches that need to be addressed. If it's been a while since you bought your last new vehicle, you'll be amazed by how much better they've become.

From time to time, however, every manufacturer produces a vehicle that requires more service than it should. Things break. The car is undependable. Intermittent problems prove to be elusive and impossible to fix. After a few months, owners realize that they don't have a car, they have a garage full of problems and a payment book. In short, they have a lemon.

Be reasonable about demanding good service. Yes, you deserve it – but you're far more likely to get it if you don't irritate everyone you contact. The trick is to be a wheel that's just squeaky enough to get the grease, but not so squeaky that you force everyone to wear earplugs.

Most states with lemon laws define a lemon as a vehicle that proves to be unfixable, usually after four tries for the same problem at a dealer for that brand, within a given length of time, typically one year. Others say it's a car or truck that's out of service for a given number of days, usually 30, within the first year. For details of your state's law, contact the attorney general's office, the department of consumer protection or the department of motor vehicles.

When you discover a problem, your first reaction – returning the car to the dealer for repairs – is the right one. Try to write down what happens and when. If the car stumbles and stalls, note the conditions. Is the engine hot or cold? Is the car stopped or does the problem happen while you're driving? Did you take your foot off the gas, as you might when descending a long hill, or were you accelerating? What were the weather conditions? Develop a concise profile of the circumstances surrounding the problem.

Did You Know?

Don't get emotional. Vowing never to return to a dealership because of an unsolved service problem gets you nothing. When the factory tells you to go back to that very dealership so the service department can give the problem one more try, you might feel a little reluctant.

Then make an appointment and let the dealer take a crack at it. Sometimes the shop will need more than one try, even if it normally makes repairs correctly the first time. If the vehicle isn't fixed after two tries, it's time to notify the manufacturer in writing. You may want to review technical service bulletins – also called TSBs – with the factory or the dealership's service department. These also can be found at some websites, such as alldata.com. Ask for a meeting with the factory's zone representative, which can sometimes encourage the factory's technical experts and the dealership's technicians to make an additional effort to solve the problem.

Keep careful records of all the details, including mileage. While most dealers work diligently to solve a problem, a few others try the "sunshine" treatment. Here's how it works: You drop off your car in the morning. The dealer lets it sit in one position – out in the sun, generally – for several hours, then moves it to another position. Then he calls you and tells you the car is ready. Servicing your car means moving it around. By pointing out the lack of mileage, you often can put a stop to this practice. However, it means you have to become a stickler for details.

Tip Provided by AAA Lancaster County

Some problems are difficult to diagnose and repair. The fact that your car still isn't fixed doesn't mean that the service department is lazy or the technicians are fools. In some cases, even factory engineers are left scratching their heads when they try to determine what's going on.

If a third attempt at repairs proves unsuccessful, write the factory again. This time, cite your state's lemon law provisions. Let the factory know that you expect the car to be fixed. If it's not, you want your money back or a new replacement vehicle.

If the car still isn't repaired or it's been disabled for the required number of days, you can proceed with arbitration or a lemon law hearing. If you go with arbitration, consumer advocates usually recommend that you try to use an independent arbitration panel.

In severe cases of an unresolved problem, you should try another dealer. Sometimes a fresh perspective and a new beginning does wonders in getting to the bottom of a difficult situation.

If you go the lemon law route, understand that you may not end up with a new car or a refund. Some lemon law boards have reviewed a problem and agreed that it wasn't repaired within the bounds of the law...and then done nothing, ruling that the problem doesn't materially affect the use or safety of the vehicle. In other words, not all claims are winners.

To follow this course of action, you'll have to keep careful records. Make sure that everything you do is in writing and that you keep copies of all your correspondence and all the times you requested repairs at the dealer's service department. Keep the dealer service slips, too. You should get a copy of every service invoice, even if the repair was covered by warranty, every time you go to the service department. If the dealer doesn't offer you a copy, ask for one and don't leave without written evidence of your vehicle's service session.

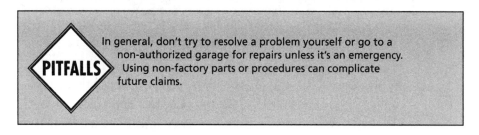

PITFALLS

In general, don't try to resolve a problem yourself or go to a non-authorized garage for repairs unless it's an emergency. Using non-factory parts or procedures can complicate future claims.

If you invoke the lemon law based on the number of days your car was out of service, understand that the clock starts when the car is supposed to be delivered and stops when the car is ready to be picked up – not when you decide to drop it off and pick it up.

If at all possible, don't let problems go beyond the warranty period. Be wary of a technician who tells you to "just keep driving it – once it gets a little worse, we should be able to find the problem quickly." This "advice" often pushes you over the warranty limits, especially with a used car. While there are precedents for pre-existing conditions – problems noted but not fixed during the warranty period – your life will be much easier if you don't let the problem go unresolved.

Tip Provided by AAA Merrimack Valley

When you phone the dealer, the factory zone office or the factory or import headquarters, keep a log of the number you called, the date, the time, the person you spoke to and the content of the conversation. If anyone promised you anything, follow up with a confirming letter, a copy of which you'll put in the file you're keeping on the vehicle.

Make sure that you pursue all the angles. Thanks to on-board diagnostics, it's often possible to install equipment in the car to monitor a variety of engine and transmission functions and record what was happening when the problem occurred. This can point technicians in the right direction when you take the car back to the service department for additional work.

If the problem continues, contact the Better Business Bureau, the state consumer protection department and local or national consumer advocates. If the problem presents a safety hazard, notify the National Highway Traffic Safety Administration, which is the federal agency that oversees vehicle safety and is part of the Department of Transportation. If enough similar complaints come in, the agency will open a file, conduct an assessment and perhaps even investigate and order a recall.

One pressure tactic that some frustrated consumers use is guaranteed to backfire. Stop making payments on the vehicle and neither the dealer nor the factory will care. They've already been paid in full. The bank that made the loan can't fix your car. The only one who'll be hurt is you, because you'll ruin your credit rating.

Service Schedules

For every vehicle, the factory develops what it thinks is an appropriate service schedule. Follow it and you'll keep the factory warranty in effect. Disregard it and you put that protection in jeopardy.

Unfortunately, a few dealers take the factory schedule – often contained in a book separate from the owner's manual – and substitute their own service recommendations for the factory's. These usually call for more service. Yet, inexplicably, they sometimes drop important procedures from the factory requirements.

While there are any number of reasons why you should do some maintenance procedures more frequently than the factory suggests, you should at least have the factory recommendations available to serve as a baseline. Tossing the factory-supplied schedule deprives you of this option.

When you receive your vehicle, make sure that all the owner's manuals are there. The service booklet, if it's separate, should be similar in appearance and feel to the other manuals. If it isn't, ask why. If the dealer's answers leave you suspicious, you might want to check with the manufacturer. Studies at one AAA club revealed that some dealers were substituting their own service schedules for those of the manufacturer and replacing some parts four times more often than recommended. Over 60,000 miles, the additional maintenance added up to $700. So be careful.

Of course, sometimes manufacturers change their minds on service schedules and issue service bulletins to alert dealers that some jobs should be done more frequently. One automaker, for example, recommended more frequent automatic transmission fluid changes after some transmissions began to fail prematurely. If a dealer's recommendations differ from those in the owner's manual, maybe it's a reflection of the latest knowledge of what should be done and when. You can verify this information with the manufacturer. Owner's manuals contain toll-free numbers and e-mail addresses.

When a Problem Turns Really Ugly

When a problem turns ugly, you may want to consider hiring an attorney. Some people feel that a lawsuit, according to an Italian proverb, is your fruit tree planted in your lawyer's yard. In some cases the contract you signed when you bought the vehicle may actually preclude your suing, specifying that disputes go to arbitration instead. Nonetheless, each year a few new-vehicle buyers have problems so severe that they hire attorneys. In our litigious society, legal action may come to mind first, but it should be used as a last resort.

If you're part of this extremely unfortunate group for whom litigation makes sense, all the records that you've kept – from the handwritten contract to the service department receipts and the notes on all your conversations – will be important. Even if you never have a problem, keeping a complete set of records makes it much easier to sell the vehicle to a private party years from now. Second buyers always like the complete documentation. So do attorneys.

That the vast majority of new vehicle customers have no serious problems is little consolation for those who do. Just remember that nearly any problem should be resolvable, one way or another, given the proper application of resources.

CHAPTER

15

Handling
Financing
and
Insurance

In This Chapter

• • • • • • • • • • • •

- Why the sales process isn't over when you think it's over
- What to expect when you finish the paperwork with the business manager
- How to determine whether a product or service is a good value

As competition erodes the retail profit margins for new cars and trucks, dealers are looking elsewhere for revenue. One solution is to start, or rely more heavily on, the dealership's finance and insurance department – or F&I department, as it's known in the trade.

When you look at it logically, an in-house F&I department makes sense for both customers and dealers. Customers get convenience – not just the vehicle itself, but financing, additional services and extended warranties right there at the dealership. For dealers, F&I is a profit center.

Some customers may be caught unaware by the F&I department's function. Having signed the contract and put down a deposit to hold the vehicle, they relax, thinking the deal is done. For the dealer, the second phase is just beginning. Maybe it starts when the contract is signed, maybe when you pick up the vehicle. Either way, you're ushered into the F&I manager's office where the critical paperwork – which has to be absolutely accurate – is completed.

But you'll do more than sign documents here. The seller will offer you a chance to change the whole deal. The F&I manager will talk to you about leasing. If you arranged financing elsewhere, the manager will ask if you'd be interested in letting the dealer try to secure a more attractive rate. "After all, it could save you money," the F&I manager will say. And it could.

You'll hear about extended service plans; fabric and paint protection packages; life and disability insurance that makes loan payments under certain circumstances, including death or inability to work due to sickness; and any number of additional services. Depending on your needs, one or more of these products and services could be valuable to you. They're also profitable for the dealership. In fact, some dealerships make more money in F&I than on the sales floor. According to N.A.D.A., the average dealership lost $228 per vehicle in the new-car department in 2000 when F&I income is excluded. With F&I income, the average dealership made a profit of $137 per new vehicle. Many dealerships would not be profitable without the income from F&I. Often, the best and most personable salespeople work in F&I.

You've probably done a lot of research to get to this point, but there are still more opportunities to use information to get the best value available by increasing your knowledge and taking time to review the following products in the F&I department.

Financing

Can the dealer really find a better rate and terms than you did? Maybe. If you let the dealership give it a shot, keep in mind all the details you checked before arranging the financing package you already have. Compare interest rates and determine how an early payoff would be computed. Are the interest calculations based on simple interest or the Rule of 78s? Some people take a dealer-arranged loan because the monthly payment works out to be significantly less. When they get home and read the paperwork, they realize that the payment period is several months longer than for the loan they originally arranged. There's no harm in comparing loans – just be sure to compare all aspects of the financing package.

Most dealers have relationships with dozens of different lenders including banks, credit unions and independent finance companies, as well as the financing arms of major manufacturers. This arrangement gives the dealer the flexibility to match the customer to the lender offering the best deal – lowest rate and/or highest F&I commission – on that particular day.

By controlling the financing, the dealers are able to generate additional profit from the sale of warranties, credit insurance and security systems. Therefore, if necessary, dealers will quote their "buy rate" and collect a flat fee from the lender with the hopes of upselling one or more of the add-ons.

If you decide to finance with the dealership, make sure that you can take the check back to the first lender. Usually you can, but some banks and finance companies charge you for failing to go through with the loan or for paying it back too soon. You already know that, of course, because you followed our advice and read and understood the financing contract before you signed it.

Since leasing is another form of financing, you suddenly may find yourself in a position of defending your decision to buy. Dealers sell lots of leases by emphasizing their smaller monthly payments. With new cars and trucks more expensive than ever, regular installment purchase payments can be high.

At this late date, be sure to go through all of the lease numbers thoroughly before changing your mind. Pay particular attention to the capitalized cost and residual value. You may need some time to crunch the numbers and review Chapter 4 of this book.

Dealer Packages

It is often up to the F&I manager to offer you everything from rust proofing to paint sealant. These services generally are unnecessary and some might even be harmful. For example, many automakers recommend against additional rust proofing, especially if it involves drilling holes in the body structure to apply the rust-inhibiting compounds.

Most modern cars and trucks are effectively rust-proofed at the factory and come with relatively long rust-through warranties. Rust on late-model vehicles may be the result of deep parking lot chips. (Be sure to buy a tube of touch-up paint along with the car and fill in minor chips quickly to keep your vehicle from suffering the same fate.) Improperly done collision repairs also can allow rust to start.

Climate can contribute to rust as well. If it snows a lot where you live and the local highway department uses generous quantities of road salt, or if your home is near the salty breezes of the shore, additional rust proofing may be of some value.

Other dealer packages include paint sealant and fabric-protection processes. They're often high profit-margin services of little use to car buyers. Paint does face an increasingly hostile environment, thanks to acid rain and contributions from the local pigeon population. A careful reading of paint protection warranties can reveal some interesting gaps in coverage. Also remember that the warranty is only as good as the company that backs it up. Such companies have been known to go out of business, leaving buyers with no protection whatsoever. If this happens to you, your local dealer isn't obligated to step in and fill the void.

Then there's fabric protection, floor mats – even mud flaps. If you're interested in these products, you already know you can buy them somewhere else. Factory floor mats, though, are often of noticeably better quality than what you find at the local discount store. Their shape and color also should be a perfect match for your interior.

Many buyers are concerned about security. While you're in F&I, the dealer will offer you alarm systems, vehicle recovery devices such as LoJack, window etching with the VIN or other devices.

Dollar for dollar, alarm systems installed at the factory usually work better than aftermarket versions. However, there are highly sophisticated alarm systems that work very well if installed by a skilled technician. Many have functions not included in the factory-installed systems.

Recovery devices such as LoJack aren't really alarms. Instead, they send out a beacon that police can follow to find the vehicle. Ask your insurance company if having one installed would earn you a lower rate. Some factory-installed and accessory telematics systems duplicate this function and provide additional services as well.

Insurance Products

Depending on state regulations on the sale of insurance, the F&I manager may offer you everything from liability, collision and comprehensive coverage to extended service protection plans. Compare what the dealer offers with products available elsewhere. New-car dealers often offer high-quality products at a fair price, but the only way to know for sure is to comparison shop.

Extended Service Contracts

One item that the F&I manager may be particularly eager to promote is an extended service contract. At one time, consumer advocates held these extended service plans in relatively low regard. Purchase prices were high, profit margins were generous and the potential for payback was low, they maintained.

That picture may be changing. As cars have become more complex, the cost of repairs has grown rapidly. Today's cars and trucks are less likely to need repairs – but when they do, the prices can be quite high. Where once an automatic transmission rebuild cost $800 to $1,200, today it can easily be $2,500 to $3,000. Engine and air conditioning repairs have become frighteningly expensive, too. Finally, add in the complex electronics and computer circuitry that every car now contains and even a common repair on a minor system can be economically debilitating. For many of us, an extended warranty or service plan could make sense.

Before buying one, consider what you get. Some plans cover specific parts; others claim to provide bumper-to-bumper protection. Without a doubt, bumper-to-bumper coverage is better, simply because contracts that list hundreds of parts may exclude the very ones that are critical and expensive.

Also, read how the company that issues the contract treats consequential damages. Here's what that means: In many contracts, if a part that's not covered causes damage to a part that is covered, the policy won't pay for the necessary repairs. Say the radiator, which isn't covered, overheats and damages something else under the hood. You're stuck with the bill. Read the terms carefully.

Before you buy any plan, consider the amount of protection it offers and how it meshes with the way you plan to use your car. A five-year, 50,000-mile extended service contract may sound impressive, but remember that it takes effect only after the manufacturer's warranty expires. If the car comes with a three-year, 36,000-mile warranty, your dollars are buying only 14,000 more miles and two more years of protection. If you drive 15,000 miles a year, the plan will cover you for just 14,000 miles or 11 months. Let's do the math: at 15,000 miles a year, your 36,000-mile factory warranty will run out in two years and five months. Then the extended service plan kicks in for the next 14,000 miles. You should reach the 50,000-mile mark at around three years and four months. Then you're on your own.

A five-year, 50,000-mile policy probably isn't your best bet. You might prefer a five-year, 75,000-mile plan. Or, if you plan to keep your car longer than that, you can look for a plan that takes you right up to the 100,000-mile mark, usually over a seven-year period.

Once you determine the coverage that gives you adequate protection, go shopping for it. In addition to new car dealerships and insurance companies, some AAA offices offer extended service plans. Compare prices, coverage and deductibles and research the issuing company's credit rating. Also check your responsibilities for maintenance and documentation. Compare deductibles, as few plans cover the entire repair expense, and determine what the repair shop needs to do to receive payment from the issuer.

Even if you don't keep the car or truck for the entire period of the extended warranty, you still may benefit when you sell your vehicle. Some plans can be transferred to the next owner, which can add value to your vehicle at trade-in time.

If you don't want any of these additional products, just say so. The F&I manager should move on. Most managers are pretty good at sensing which customers will buy more and which won't. Some F&I operations, however, are decidedly high pressure. Dealers figure there's little to lose at this point. They have your signed contract and your down payment, which means you're unlikely to get up and walk out.

You, on the other hand, retain your right to say no and ask that the dealership move on with the paperwork. Exercise this right whenever – and as often – as you wish.

CHAPTER 16

Taking Delivery

In This Chapter
• • • • • • • • • • •

- What to do before you take delivery
- The visual inspection
- Comparing the vehicle to the contract
- A brief drive

The big moment is finally here. You're about to take delivery of your new car or truck. Congratulations!

Don't let your enthusiasm cloud your vigilance, however. Sometimes, taking a level-headed friend with you to ensure you don't get swept up in the excitement of the moment is a good idea. Try to forget all those other friends and neighbors eagerly waiting to see your new wheels. Keep your mind on the business at hand for just a few more minutes.

Before you leave for the dealership, be sure you have everything you need to complete the transaction: the title and registration for your old vehicle, if you are trading it in; proof of insurance, if required; and a check, assuming you're not financing through the dealership. Most dealers will give you a list of what you need. They don't want anything to go wrong any more than you do. If your dealer hasn't given you a list, ask for one.

There are two possibilities at this point in the transaction. The first is that you are buying a vehicle from stock and that you have seen it, driven it and thoroughly checked it out already. If so, you still should give the vehicle a thorough visual inspection and take it for a brief drive, just to make sure everything is in order. If, on one of your previous inspections, you detected a problem that the salesperson assured you would be fixed, make sure the repair was done.

The other possibility is that this is a vehicle you ordered, sight unseen. This may be your first chance to look at it, so you'll want to do a thorough examination. Start with the contract. Is the VIN correct? Is the vehicle equipped with all the options listed on the contract? It's hard to believe, but customers have bought vehicles they were told had a six-cylinder engine, only to discover – in some cases months or years later – that they had a four-cylinder vehicle.

Check everything. Make sure the engine is correct and that the transmission is the one you wanted. Some manufacturers still give buyers the choice of a three-speed or four-speed automatic. It's easy to overlook a missing gear during a quick check. Then look for the options listed on the contract. Check the wheel and tire size against the factory price sticker, assuming the vehicle is new. Do they match? Sometimes dealers swap wheels and tires from one vehicle to another to make a sale. Factories also have been known to make mistakes. Did your vehicle end up with a less costly combination? Be thorough and take your time. With any luck, you'll be driving this vehicle for a long time. A few more minutes now won't make that much difference.

Once you're satisfied that the car is equipped the way it should be, take a careful look at the body. Be sure that the car is out in the open so you can see every panel. Try to do this in daylight, although fluorescent lighting will sometimes show defects not revealed by the sun. Don't do this in the rain, if at all possible.

Look for any body damage, including minor dings, dents or scrapes. Check every panel, including the roof and the undercarriage. Occasionally, cars are damaged in transit or while sitting on the dealer's lot. Make sure that you aren't buying a vehicle that's been dinged – or worse – and either poorly fixed or not repaired at all.

That done, you should take the car for a brief drive, using the dealer's license plate. The salesperson probably won't appreciate the time it takes to do this, but your money is on the line here. Make sure all those lovely options work properly and that the car functions as it should.

If you run into any problems, don't continue with the transaction. Say you discover a minor dent in a rocker panel. The dealer assures you it's not significant and says you should take the car today and allow the shop to fix it next week. The salesperson will even give you a loaner for the two or three days that the repairs will take.

Unless you are desperate for a new car, decline the offer. Have the repairs done before you take possession of the vehicle. Shops can do excellent bodywork these days. Paint matching can be particularly good. Properly done repairs, more often than not, are impossible to spot. That is the level of work you want and deserve. It is easier to make the case for repairs if the sale hangs in the balance.

A little visible body damage should alert you to the possibility of additional damage that you can't see. Cars are occasionally damaged in transit. A thorough under-chassis inspection may be in order before you accept delivery.

If you detect any problems on this drive – a rattle or a slight pull in one direction – make sure they're fixed before you complete the transaction and accept the vehicle. If repairs cannot be made quickly while you wait, delay the purchase until they are completed. If the dealer is uncooperative now, with the sale in the balance, how easy do you think it's going to be to get repairs done once you buy the car?

So the car passes your inspection. Now look at all the paperwork. You'll be given several forms to sign. Read each one thoroughly and be sure that you understand it. If a replacement contract is required, make sure that it matches every detail of the first contract, with the exception of mutually agreed upon changes. Make sure that there are no blank spaces. If there are, put the words "not applicable" in them.

This is when you might learn that you didn't qualify for that wonderful interest rate that was so heavily promoted. In some cases, the salesperson and business manager might even have a little skit prepared. "Oh no, you didn't call the customer? I thought you let them know that we got them a rate almost as good."

If something like this happens, stop everything right where you are and take another day to think through the ramifications. Surprisingly, some customers – eager to complete the deal and enjoy that new-car smell and feel – accept much higher interest rates without thinking about what the higher monthly payments will do to their budget. If the interest rate is not as you agreed, or if something else of major importance is wrong, you have the right to withdraw. Few people do, however. Others learn the hard way that a momentary disappointment would have been easier to live with than years of higher payments.

If you see substantial modifications to the original contract, you need time to think about whether you can live with the changes. It's unfair to ask you to make a snap decision.

Fortunately, most checks of the vehicle and the contract go smoothly and are problem-free. Now you can enjoy this vehicle for many miles and years to come – just be sure to read the owner's manual and pay attention to the service schedule.

In Conclusion

In theory, you should now be a car buying expert. There's a difference between reading about what's involved, however, and putting the advice into practice. When it comes to car buying, as with many other endeavors, first-time practitioners can feel a little nervous and in need of some hand-holding.

For AAA members, there's good news. Many AAA offices either have, or can put you in touch with, a knowledgeable person who can answer questions, give you advice and offer encouragement. Services vary from office to office, sometimes because of variations in state laws. Nonetheless, when you call your local AAA office, you should find people who can help. This is just one of the many benefits of a AAA membership.

A new vehicle can be a source of great pleasure. There's nothing quite like sliding behind the wheel of a new car or truck that will be yours to drive and enjoy for many miles and years to come. A new vehicle can give you a new sense of freedom and, thanks to its reliability, confidence.

New cars also are quite comfortable. Seating and seat belt designs have improved. New vehicles are generally quieter, too, and they ride and handle better than the cars and trucks of just a few years ago. The improvements you notice will depend on what you buy this time around and what you used to drive, of course.

Your new vehicle also is probably better built than your last car or truck and likely will require less service to keep it running smoothly. In addition, it probably has several safety enhancements your old car didn't have. Be sure to read your owner's manual carefully to get the most from all these new features.

There are many things that a new car will not do for you, however. It won't remake your personality. It won't give you higher status in life. It won't, by itself, bring you happiness.

So pick a car or truck that meets your needs. Don't be swayed by the conventions of the moment. You will, in the long run, be much happier with your purchase. You also may discover that buying the vehicle you need rather than one that's momentarily in fashion saves you a lot of money over the long haul.

Good luck.

Index

A

AAA Approved Auto Repair, 165

AAA Auto Guide: New Cars and Trucks, 19, 51, 52

AAA Financial Services, 160

aaa.com, 138

aaafts.org, 138

ABS, 52

Acceleration, 53

Accessories, 185

Active anti-whiplash systems, 64

Aero-packages, 186

Air bags, 22, 47, 48, 50, 53, 56, 57, 61, 64, 67, 88, 120, 122, 181

Air conditioning, 184

alldata.com, 138

Alloy wheels, 186

Antilock brakes, 62

Antilock braking. See ABS

Association surcharges, 202

Auctions, 93

Auto brokers, 208

Auto shows, 22

auto.com, 138

autoguide.net, 138

Automakers, 67

Automatic transmission fluid, 98

Automotive News, 191

autonews.com, 138

autosite.com, 138

B

Battery electrolyte, 98

Beginning driver, 119

Belts and hoses, 98

Bird dog, 211

Blind spot, 49

Brake assist, 63, 181

Braking, 52

Brush guards, 186

Buyers' guides, 90

Buyer's market, 193

Buyout amount, 105

C

Capitalized cost, 71

carfax.com, 139

Cargo compartment net, 63

Cargo nets, 182

cars.com, 139

Cash advances from a credit card, 155

Cash back, 154

Casual sales, 92

Center of gravity, 58

Certification programs, 103

Checklist for leasing a new car, 79

Child safety seat, 60

Children in the car, 60

Closed-end leases, 31, 67, 76

Compact pickup trucks, 58

Conditional contracts, 222

Consumer advocates, 231

Convertible, 122

Conveyance fees, 226

Cost-benefit, 28
Costs of ownership, 33
Crash rates for drivers 16 or 17, 124
Crash tests, 55
Credibility, 178
Credit agency report, 39
Cruise control, 185
Curbsider, 218
Customer complaints, 37
Customer service, 37

D

Dealer cost, 201
Dealers, 20, 23, 25, 26, 36, 37, 41,
    42, 44, 45, 67, 70, 73, 74, 77, 91,
    93, 97, 99, 104, 129, 130, 131,
    132, 133, 134, 135, 136, 137, 138,
    157, 160, 161, 162, 163, 164, 165,
    167, 170, 176, 177, 190, 191, 192,
    193, 195, 196, 197, 198, 199, 200,
    201, 202, 205, 208, 209, 210,
    211, 218, 219, 224, 225, 226, 227,
    229, 233, 235, 236, 237, 239,
    244
Dealer's website, 132
Debt repayment, 143
Depreciation, 29, 30, 31, 32, 45, 46,
    68, 71, 72, 75, 83, 86, 190, 203
digital-librarian.com, 139
Down payment, 71, 75, 77,
    144, 223
Drinking and driving, 124
Dual stage air bags, 61

E

Electric defrosters, 64

Electric rear-window defroster, 182
Electronic tire pressure
    monitors, 63
Electronically dimming
    mirrors, 64
Engine coolant, 97
Engine oil, 97
Engines, 187
Environmental disposal fees, 34
Equifax, 148
Equifax credit information, 151
Evaluations, 94
Experian, 148, 151
Extended service
    contracts, 103, 239
Extended warranties, 32, 93, 103

F

F&I department, 236
Face down, 145
Factory-to-dealer incentives, 201
Failure to disclose, 223
Fair, Isaac & Co., 149
FICO, 149
Finance contract, 40
Finance your vehicle purchase, 38
Financial advisers, 142
Financial institutions, 144
Financing, 38, 39, 68, 70, 81, 138,
    144, 147, 150, 153, 154, 155, 156,
    157, 160, 171, 199, 216, 220, 222,
    229, 236, 237, 244
    a used car, 156
First-tier vehicles, 88

G

Gasoline, 35
Gross vehicle weight ratings, 59
Group referral programs, 211

H

Handling, 51
Head restraints, 49
Heated seats, 184
Height-adjustable shoulder
   belts, 120
Highway driving, 101
highwaysafety.org, 139
Holdbacks, 200
Home equity loan, 155

I

IIHS crash tests, 56
In-car navigation systems, 183
Incentives, 136, 200
Inspections, 33
Insurance, 17, 31, 32, 34, 35, 57, 73,
   74, 75, 78, 80, 100, 103, 125, 126,
   138, 143, 155, 159, 160, 178, 180,
   182, 201, 236, 237, 238, 239,
   240, 244
   collision and comprehensive
   coverage, 34
   mechanical breakdown, 32
   products, 239
Interest rate, 40, 81, 143, 144, 145,
   146, 147, 151, 152, 153, 154, 155,
   156, 158, 159, 160, 216, 220,
   222, 246

Internet, 41, 91, 129, 130, 131, 132,
   133, 134, 135, 136, 138, 150, 193,
   195, 209, 213
ISOFIX, 60

J

J.D. Power and Associates, 33

K

kbb.com, 139
Kelley Blue Book, 41, 139, 157

L

Lap belt and shoulder harness, 54
LATCH, 60
Leasing, 66
Leasing checklist, 78
Leasing transactions, 73
Leather upholstery, 184
Lemon laws, 230
Lending institutions, 143
Lien holder, 104
Limited slip differential, 182
Liquidated damages, 223
Loan pre-approval, 159
Loan agreement, 159
Loan from 401k plan, 155
Low-ball offer, 194

M

Maintenance, 33
Maneuverability, 51
Manufacturers, 67

Manufacturer's suggested retail price, 73
Manufacturers' websites, 130, 137
Maximum payloads, 59
Mileage limits, 69
Misleading advertising, 217
Model to consider, 18
Monthly prices, 177
MSRP, 197, 201

N

N.A.D.A., 31, 42, 43, 157, 236
N.A.D.A. Official Used Car Guide, 31, 41, 157
National Highway Traffic Safety Administration, 58
Navigation systems, 64
Negotiating the purchase price, 36
New-car dealers, 91
NHTSA, 55, 56, 57, 65, 120, 121
nhtsa.dot.gov, 139
Non-factory roof and grille treatments, 186

O

Offers and contracts, 222
Official Used Car Guide, 42
Offset barrier crashes, 56
Oil changes, 33
One-stop shopping, 39
Open-end lease, 76
Optional. *See options*
Optional equipment, 31, 32, 42, 160, 188

P

Passenger-side air bag on/off switch, 62
Passive safety characteristics, 53
Passive-restraint, 123
Paying cash, 146
Personal information, 171
Personal unsecured loans, 155
Power steering fluid, 97
Pricing process, 40
Private party, 92
Private sellers, 100
Proper seating, 48
Purchase contract, 34

R

Rear spoilers, 186
Rear wiper and washer, 63
Rebates, 153, 200
Reduced incentives, 77
Refinancing, 159
Registration fees, 30, 86, 157, 160
Remote controls on steering wheel, 186
Rent charge, 71
Rental agreement, 66
Repair, 29, 32, 33, 61, 67, 89, 90, 95, 96, 102, 103, 134, 150, 165, 167, 184, 185, 186, 187, 190, 224, 225, 231, 239, 240, 244
  cost of, 33
Repair agreement, 32
Research, 90
Residual value, 71
Rude or abrasive treatment, 37

Rules, 123
Rules to remember, 35
Runzheimer International, 28, 190

S

Safe vehicle, 119
Safety, 23, 24, 25, 47, 48, 50, 51,
52, 53, 54, 56, 57, 60, 61, 62,
64, 67, 88, 94, 103, 119, 120,
122, 125, 127, 130, 138, 139,
177, 178, 180, 181, 182, 183,
184, 185, 186, 219, 227,
231, 233
belts, 60
options, 180
suggestions, 123
Salesperson, 16, 25, 35, 37, 38,
39, 40, 46, 132, 133, 134, 165,
167, 170, 171, 172, 173, 174,
175, 176, 177, 178, 187, 193,
194, 196, 199, 201, 202, 204,
211, 212, 218, 220, 221, 226,
229, 234, 244, 245, 246
Second-tier vehicles, 88
Service department, 33, 34, 163,
164, 165, 166, 167, 177, 195,
224, 229, 230, 231, 234
Service schedules, 233
Side-impact air bags, 61, 181
Side-impact testing, 57
Spare tire, 99
Sport suspension upgrades, 63
Stability control, 181
Stability enhancement
systems, 62
Sticker price, 198
Sticker prices, 135

Stopping distance, 52
Subsidized leases, 67
Subsidized loans, 154
Subvented, 67
Sunroof, 185
Suspensions, 187
SUVs, 58, 59

T

Taking a loan, 151
Taxes, 30, 71, 73, 79, 83, 86, 89,
93, 143, 146, 155, 157, 160
Remote entry and central
locking, 64
Technical service bulletins, 230
Technician, 85, 93, 94, 97, 98,
100, 102, 103, 164, 166, 188,
219, 223, 235, 238
Technician's evaluation, 94
Technology, 88
Teenage drivers, 122
Teens, 118
Telematics, 183
Test drive, 25, 26, 63, 93, 100,
101, 171, 177, 178,
191, 213
The 'Money' Factor, 73
The National Highway Traffic
Safety Administration, 55
The Wall Street Journal, 191
thecarconnection.com, 139
Third-party sites, 132
Title, 104
Title and registration, 244

Traction control, 62, 181
Trade-in, 31, 39, 41, 42, 43, 44, 45, 67, 71, 73, 75, 76, 77, 80, 81, 152, 154, 157, 175, 177, 178, 188, 198, 199, 220, 227, 228, 240
Trade-in evaluations, 227
Transaction Components, 38
Transmissions, 187
Transportation costs, 32
TransUnion, 148, 151
Trip computers, 186
TSBs, 230
Twins, 20, 22, 26

U

Under-the-hood inspection, 102
Upgraded seating packages, 184
Upgraded sound and video entertainment systems, 185
Used vehicle checklist, 106
Used vehicles, 87
Used-car dealers, 91

V

Vehicle use and operation agreement, 126
VIN, 42, 95, 138, 223, 224, 225, 238, 244

W

Warning lights, 99, 109
Warranty, 34, 163
Warranty questions, 224
Wear and tear, 69
Wheels and tires, 188
World wide web, 131
www.aaa.com, 90, 130, 132

X

Xenon headlights, 63

Y

Your budget, 89
Your credit rating, 147
Your driving costs, 28

The AAA Auto Guide series is designed to help you with all aspects of vehicle ownership and use, including car buying and car care. These comprehensive how-to guides give you a road map to navigate potentially frustrating experiences while helping you save time and money. Each book in the Auto Guide series feature practical tools like worksheets, checklists, charts and illustrations to show you how to get the most out of your car.

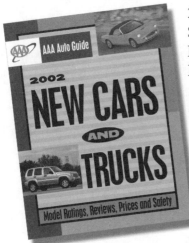

2002 New Cars and Trucks
$14.95 US $22.95 CDN
ISBN: 1-56251-615-9
Reviews and ratings, safety features, reliability, prices and specs. Updated annually.

Making Sense of Car Care
$16.95 US $25.95 CDN
ISBN: 1-56251-578-0
Learn how to save money, talk to a repair technician, and handle mechanical emergencies. Includes free *Emergency Car Care and Maintenance Log.*

The One That Does It All

For years, people have turned to AAA for their emergency road service needs. But AAA is more than just towing. Access to AAA's travel services can give you the world. Its financial services can help you pay for it. And AAA insurance can give you the peace of mind to enjoy the ride. Plus AAA gives you exclusive Show Your Card & Save® offers, bail bond benefits and much more.

Discover the ways AAA can simplify your life. Call 800-JOINAAA, visit aaa.com or stop by your nearest AAA office today to find out about the specific products and services AAA offer.

Notes

Notes

Notes

Lounge—a nightlife venue that is top rated on Tripadvisor and one of "Chicago's Best" according to *Chicago Magazine*.

Clark authored a cover story in the *Christian Century*, law journal articles, and countless legal briefs. He debated First Amendment issues at the Vail Symposium and lectured at the American Academy of Religion. He has delivered numerous speeches and commencement addresses.

Summary Judgment is his first book.

Visit Donald Cameron Clark, Jr.'s website by scanning the QR code above with your mobile device.

ABOUT THE AUTHOR

Donald Cameron Clark, Jr. is a renaissance man who believes in the power of storytelling, whether to a jury, to a theater audience, or to his grandchildren. His legal practice focuses on high-stakes trials and religious liberty jurisprudence. He established the constitutional right of clergy to solemnize same-sex marriages in North Carolina and reversed the conviction of an Alabama death row inmate.

Clark began his professional career as a trial attorney at some of Chicago's most venerable law firms. He became the general counsel for the United Church of Christ, a Protestant religious denomination with five thousand churches headquartered in Cleveland, and received a Lifetime Achievement Award from *Crain's Cleveland Business.*

A graduate of Rutgers Law School, Clark received its Distinguished Alumni Award and was recognized among "Rutgers–Camden's Finest." He received an honorary doctor of letters degree from the Chicago Theological Seminary, where he served as chair of its board of trustees and acting president and remains a life trustee.

Clark is executive producer of the award-winning feature film *Guest Artist,* written by and starring Jeff Daniels. He produces plays on Broadway and in regional theaters. Clark co-owns the Chicago Magic